Eco-House

Manual

First edition published in 2007
This second edition published in September 2012

British Library Cataloguing in Publication Data:
A catalogue record for this book is available from the British Library.

ISBN 978 0 85733 121 2

Published by Haynes Publishing, Sparkford, Yeovil, Somerset BA22 7JJ, UK
Tel: 01963 442030 Fax: 01963 440001
Int. tel: +44 1963 442030 Int. fax: +44 1963 440001
E-mail: sales@haynes.co.uk
Website: www.haynes.co.uk

Haynes North America Inc.
861 Lawrence Drive, Newbury Park, California 91320, USA

Printed in the USA by Odcombe Press LP,
1299 Bridgestone Parkway, La Vergne, TN 37086

This book is printed on Reincarnation Matte paper with 100% recycled fiber and bleached without the use of chlorine compounds..

Acknowledgements

This book would not have been possible without help and co-operation from many people and organisations.

For technical review of the first edition I am grateful to the Energy Saving Trust, the Water Demand Management Team at the Environment Agency, the National Energy Foundation, Natural England, and the Association of Environment Conscious Builders.

I am also grateful to: Bradfords Building Supplies, British Hydropower Association, City Electrical Factors, Kensa Engineering, South West Water, Lime Technology, Solalighting, Plumbase, Dr Kirk Semple, Dr Robin Curtis, David Moore, Garden Organic, Dr Rebecca Wade, Bryan Roe at The Green Shop, Imagination Solar, The Green Building Store, Plantlife International, Trada, EDF Energy, Powergen, The Heat Project, The Concrete Centre, Ian Constantinides, Ian Rock, Neil May, Geoff Stow, David Holloway, Mark Johnston, Julian Brooks, Matt Hill, Caroline Barry, Liz Clark, Jan Metcalf, Martyn Sawyer, Desmond Kerr, Martyn Gittins, Jim Carfrae, Gary & Cy Lane, Dan Dix, Patrick Stow, Rebekah Watson, Chris Yeo, Haldor Bjornson, Elisabeth de Veer, Alison Henry, Sue Lilleman, Bob & Dorothy Griffiths, Joyce Westwood, Tom Worthington, Jan Metcalf, Martyn Gittins, Desmond Kerr, Corina Reay, Martyn Sawyer, Ted Gange, Katie Bond, Darren & Phoebe Gray, Laura Roper, Mike & Sally Gange, John Tuer; and special thanks of course to Jo & Bryony.

Unless credited otherwise, most photographs are by John Peters. Thanks John

Eco-House
Manual

Nigel Griffiths

CONTENTS

INTRODUCTION

This manual is designed to help homeowners decide how to alter or renovate their properties in ways that will reduce their impact on the environment and, ultimately, benefit themselves.

Eco-renovation gives us an opportunity to put right some of the mistakes of the past. The consumption of energy, water and raw materials by our existing housing stock can be reduced through making appropriate changes to the building fabric, to the services systems and to our lifestyles. By using non-toxic materials, we have the opportunity to make a difference to our future wellbeing. Houses which are refurbished with healthy materials and which achieve low running costs will also command a higher price in due course.

Some of the strategies outlined in this book will cost money, some will save money and others are cost-neutral. It is certainly not necessary to be wealthy in order to be green and, in general terms, spending money means consuming resources.

If there is one shorthand way of summarising the approach to eco-renovation, it would be to think carefully and in the broadest possible terms before starting work. However, we all do things in ways that are familiar to us, without bothering to challenge convention and the consumer has unwittingly participated in wholesale damage to the environment, much of it occurring since the Second World War. Ultimately, I'm not trying to suggest to anyone what they should be doing or how they should live – the manual merely attempts to provide the necessary information so that the reader can make a more informed judgement.

Unlike most Haynes manuals this is not a 'how to' guide. The subject matter is very wide and covers many disciplines. Most of the potential alterations described require professional input in the design or implementation and for some technologies the use of accredited installers is required by law or necessary in order to claim a subsidy. This reflects an increasingly risk-averse society and a desire on the part of legislators to regulate building work.

Lastly, this manual reflects where we stand at the time of writing. The subject is constantly evolving as we come to understand the impact of our actions upon the health of the environment and each other. Older buildings and techniques have stood the test of time, whereas the long-term effects of many modern substances are not yet fully known. It is therefore necessary to keep up to date and to research the materials and technologies that may be useful or relevant to your own property. Not all subjects covered in this book are appropriate for all properties or lifestyles, but doing a little is more beneficial than doing nothing at all and even small gestures can have surprisingly positive consequences.

1 PRINCIPLES OF ECO-RENOVATION

This chapter begins by introducing some of the key environmental issues that are relevant to construction work, thus explaining why eco-renovation is becoming increasingly important. Some general principles are suggested to guide readers who may be planning projects, be they large or small, interior or exterior. Old buildings present particular challenges as conservation of their fabric and appearance is essential while at the same time they are poorly insulated, so this chapter finishes by presenting some key information to bear in mind when considering upgrading an old building.

The threat to the environment

GLOBAL WARMING

The greatest source of concern at present is the potential effects of global warming. Mean UK temperatures rose during the last century by two thirds of a degree and this rise is reflected by global temperature records. The period from 1993–2002 was the warmest decade in the UK since records began over 300 years ago although average temperatures do not appear to have risen since then. If this does indeed constitute an upward trend in global temperatures, there is a risk that sea levels will rise as a consequence of thermal expansion and of a net reduction in ice cover in the polar regions. This rise could, in turn, render large areas of the planet uninhabitable, particularly low-lying areas, which are some of the most densely populated.

In addition to causing sea levels to rise, global warming is also contributing to climate change. Extreme weather events such as floods, droughts, hurricanes and heat waves are thought to be more common now in the UK and snow is already less frequent. We may be experiencing a change in the intensity of rainfall, with more frequent spells of heavy rain and a shift in the distribution pattern, which means that dry places will become drier and wet places will become wetter. Wildlife ranges are already altering and it is feared that diseases once confined to warmer climates will spread further north.

Climate is a notoriously complex subject and there are many factors which influence climate from one decade to the next. Some scientists argue that observed climate change is a result of natural fluctuations which have occurred many times in the earth's history and that human impact on these cycles is negligible. It appears that the majority of climate scientists are of the opinion that human activity is contributing to climate change, largely through our emissions of 'greenhouse gases'.

The earth is kept at a steady temperature by the delicate balance between the incoming heat of the sun and by the radiation of heat back out into space. The radiation of heat is slowed down by gases in the atmosphere (including water vapour) which form a necessary warm blanket around the planet. These gases admit short wavelength energy from

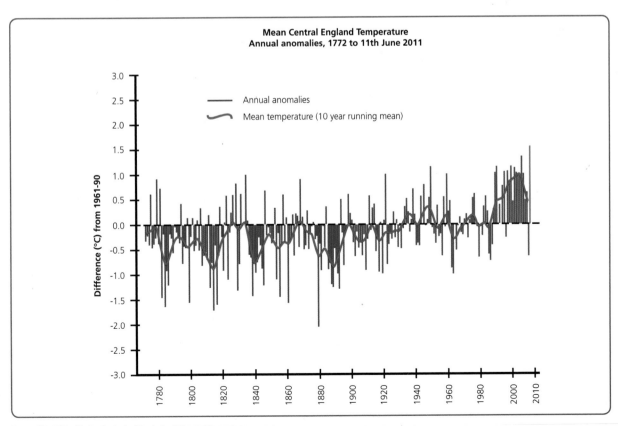

Source: Met Office. Hadley Centre for Climate Prediction and Research

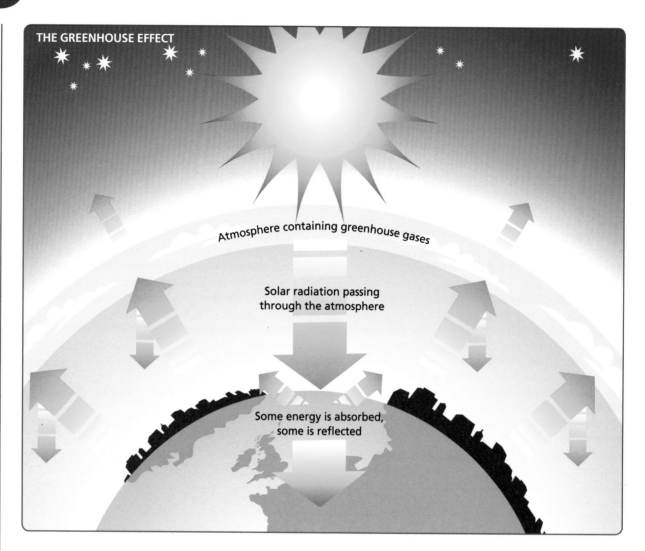

THE GREENHOUSE EFFECT

Atmosphere containing greenhouse gases

Solar radiation passing through the atmosphere

Some energy is absorbed, some is reflected

the sun but some of the longer wavelength energy reflected back from the surface of the earth is prevented from escaping. This is known as the 'greenhouse effect'.

Carbon dioxide, in particular, has increased in concentration in the atmosphere from 280 parts per million (ppm) in 1750 to 394ppm in 2011. The rise in CO_2 levels mirrors the pace of industrial development over the same period, which has led scientists to conclude that this rise is caused primarily by burning fossil fuels and deforestation. Carbon dioxide is thought to contribute approximately 2/3 of the greenhouse effect caused by greenhouse gases (i.e. excluding water vapour). The available ice core data does not suggest that CO_2 is a primary driver of climate change but it is possible that once global warming has begun, excessive CO_2 in the atmosphere could amplify the rate of temperature increase and therefore contribute to climate change.

CO_2 is an essential part of life on earth and it is only an excess of CO_2 which might be problematic. Other gases contribute to the greenhouse effect – methane is thought to

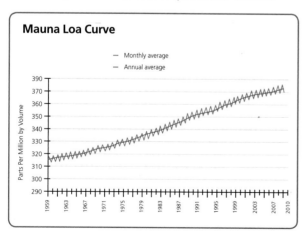

Mauna Loa Curve

— Monthly average
— Annual average

(y-axis: Parts Per Million by Volume, from 290 to 390; x-axis: years 1959 to 2010)

Kyoto gas	Global Warming Potential
Carbon dioxide (CO_2)	1
Methane (CH_4)	23
Nitrous oxide (N_2O)	296
Sulphur hexafluoride (SF_6)	22,200
Perfluorocarbons (PFCs)	4,800–9,200
Hydrofluorocarbons (HFCs)	12–12,000

contribute significantly – it is many times more potent than CO_2 as a greenhouse gas but currently it occurs in much lower concentrations in the atmosphere. The 1997 Kyoto Protocol identified 6 greenhouse gases which signatory nations are now committed to reducing.

The science underpinning the concept of man-made global warming is steadily gaining acceptance, although it is not without its detractors. What is undeniable is that by burning fossil fuels at an unprecedented rate we are adding many millions of tonnes of CO_2 per annum to the earth's natural cycle. By simultaneously reducing the vegetation cover on the planet we have reduced its ability to soak up this additional carbon dioxide, compounding the problem.

The UK Government has set targets for the reduction of CO_2 emissions in line wth the recommendations of the Kyoto summit (1997). The short-term target is to reduce emissions by 20% by 2020, from a 1990 baseline. The original longer-term target was to reduce emissions by 60% by 2050 but the UK Government is now committed to achieving a reduction of 80% by 2050. This is particularly challenging for the existing housing stock as there are limits to the cost-effective improvements that can be made to older buildings in particular.

DEFORESTATION

Forests are the green lungs of the planet. If we continue to reduce lung capacity at the present rate we will suffocate, but forests have a much wider function in the eco-system than simply the absorption of carbon dioxide. Tropical rainforests contain over two-thirds of the earth's living species and their store of plants and other organisms may yet hold the key to treating a wide variety of diseases for which there is currently

Photo: istockphoto.com

no cure in conventional medicine. Continued logging in many parts of the world reduces the habitat available to species for whom the rainforest is their only home and threatens the very existence of indigenous peoples.

RESOURCE EXHAUSTION

Recent concerns about global warming have overshadowed the dominant ecological issues of the 1960s and 1970s, which included the inevitability of exhausting supplies of fossil fuels and other materials. Conservation was focussed upon prolonging the life of these resources while alternative

sources of power were developed. However, the fact remains that the supply of fossil fuels is finite so our present rate of consumption cannot continue indefinitely.

There is also an ultimate limit to the amount of metals and aggregates at our disposal. Substitution with alternative and preferably renewable materials is essential if our enjoyment of a wide variety of goods and building products is to be sustained. A reduction in consumption and an increase in recycling will both be required as supplies of virgin aggregates and metal ores are steadily depleted. Quarrying for some materials has a substantial environmental impact in certain areas and ultimately this is also unsustainable.

WATER RESOURCES

Despite the increasing incidence of heavy rainfall, we may start to face water shortages more often as this is the 'wrong kind of rain'. If it continues, climate change will also redistribute existing rainfall and on a global scale this may require massive population movements, as human settlement only exists where there is adequate

Photo: istockphoto.com

water supply. Even within the UK, the South and East will receive progressively less useful rainfall, so we will have to reduce our water consumption or adjust our housebuilding programmes accordingly.

HEALTH AND WELLBEING

The environment in which we live can have a profound impact upon personal health. Materials with which houses are constructed, decorated and furnished contain a variety of toxic chemicals, not to mention those that are contained in sprays and disinfectants in everyday use. This chemical soup weakens the immune system; some substances merely cause allergic reactions or headaches, whereas others are now known to cause cancer. Many modern houses are hermetically sealed and lack sufficient ventilation, leading to air quality which can be far worse than that on the average urban street.

Houses constructed and refurbished with natural materials greatly reduce this 'sick building syndrome', while adequate levels of daylight and ventilation contribute towards a more comfortable internal environment and have significant health benefits. Gardens also have an important role to play in improving quality of life, and can do much to reduce the impact of modern housing upon the eco-system.

Photo: istockphoto.com

POLLUTION

Construction is not the only culprit when it comes to polluting the environment as transport, mass food production and many other forms of commerce have caused enormous pollution. However, the production of materials for construction is directly responsible for damage where mines pollute rivers or factories release chemicals into the air and soil. Some synthetic materials present in buildings are now regarded as pollutants – asbestos is a good example, as it has now been spread widely throughout the UK. Construction also contributes to transport pollution, so careful choice of materials can reduce this problem. On the positive side, new construction provides an opportunity to clean up brownfield sites after centuries of contamination as a result of industrial processes. When building or refurbishing a house, many opportunities arise to embrace a lifestyle that generates less pollution.

Principles of eco-renovation

These suggested principles fall into basic categories. The first few, not surprisingly, are to do with energy. The second major category is materials, then the remainder concern water, drainage, outside space and the local community.

ENERGY

1. Reduce heat losses and make use of natural light and heat gain.
2. Use energy-efficient heating systems.
3. Reduce electricity demand.
4. Assess the potential for alternative sources of energy.

MATERIALS

5. Conserve existing building fabric. Repair, rather than replace.
6. Reuse materials. Specify reclaimed and recycled building materials. Minimise waste.
7. Use sustainable and, where possible, locally-sourced materials.
8. Avoid unhealthy building materials.

OTHER

9. Reduce water consumption.
10. Minimise demand on drainage systems.
11. Maximise the environmental benefit of external space.
12. Aim to have a positive effect on the local community.

None of this amounts to anything more than common sense. If we are running out of something quickly, we have to reduce our consumption of that resource, by finding a renewable alternative or by reducing consumption overall. On the other hand, if we have a problem with waste, we need to find ways to reduce the amount that we discard and then learn to treat the waste stream as a resource rather than as a problem to be buried.

However, the environmental consequences of certain building materials are not always obvious. The damage is frequently done far from the place of eventual sale and use of the product, and the consumer is not encouraged to find out how, or even where, the raw materials were produced. The effects of habitat destruction, or chemical spillage, or the long-term difficulties of disposing of certain materials, are all invisible to the consumer. However, these effects are already being experienced acutely in many other countries and may affect later generations in the UK.

From time to time, situations will occur when these principles conflict with each other. For example, when substituting a naturally produced material for a synthetic and non-renewable material, it may be found that the natural item is produced thousands of miles away and there is a significant energy cost in transporting it to the UK. This partly reflects a market in transition and more local alternatives are likely to become available as demand increases and producers take advantage of the opportunity. The UK manufacturing capacity for a wide range of recycled and renewable materials is already expanding every year in response to consumer demand.

In the rush to combat climate change by altering our housing stock to reduce CO_2 emissions, we are in danger of losing sight of all the other issues that are important if we are to live and build sustainably. Eco-building recognises that human quality of life depends upon the health of the whole environment, and that wildlife, ecology and aesthetics must all be considered when making choices about how to refurbish property.

Sustainability is about more than just energy use.

CODE FOR SUSTAINABLE REFURBISHMENT

The refurbishment of the UK's housing stock is both a challenge and an opportunity. The challenge of delivering the CO_2 reductions to which the UK Government has committed us is vast, yet there is also an opportunity to deliver wider goals of sustainability from reducing the impacts of materials and water use through to community regeneration.

The BREEAM Domestic Refurbishment assessment scheme (to be released 2012) builds on the family of

BREEAM schemes already widely used in new construction – including the Code for Sustainable Homes. BREEAM Domestic Refurbishment will assess specifications for housing refurbishment and produce a rating based on the predicted reductions in CO_2 emissions, water, waste and material impacts. The scheme also takes account of flood risk reduction and project management then produces an overall rating from pass to excellent. It is intended to support and be consistent with the Green Deal (see Chapter 3).

Approach to old buildings

Photo: National Trust Picture Library

"These old buildings do not belong to us only…they have belonged to our forefathers and they will belong to our descendants unless we play them false. They are not… our property to do as we like with. We are only trustees for those that come after us."

William Morris 1889

Great damage has already been caused to the fabric of many old buildings by misguided attempts to modernise and improve them. Speculative restoration, repair with inappropriate materials, subdivision, unsympathetic extension, the introduction of services, and even

Photo: Patrick Stow

Heating pipes and cables chopped into floor joists in Grade I listed building.

regulatory intervention have all contributed to this process. It is crucial to ensure that any attempt to make ancient buildings more 'efficient' in energy performance terms does not add to this list of miscreants. An understanding of how traditional materials perform is essential before making any alterations to a historic building.

Even buildings which are not listed or considered significant or ancient can be a vital part of the visual fabric of our society, so considerable thought is needed before deciding to alter the appearance of our Edwardian, Victorian and Georgian housing stock in the name of eco-renovation. Much can be done to improve these buildings without ripping out irreplaceable historic fabric and adding materials which may not last as well or which cause damage to the original building.

uPVC replacement windows and timber originals.

Technology is constantly evolving and some advances are actively helpful. For example, the advent of wireless communication systems may reduce the number of cables that need to be threaded through the fabric of houses and thus reduce the damage often inflicted during installation.

Service cables on Grade I listed building.

Lime repointing in progress.

Lime repointing complete.

Regular maintenance and conservative repair with original materials are the first principles of conservation. Although the knowledge and skills necessary for the repair of old buildings were once commonplace, nowadays this is a specialist area and professional advice should always be sought from a builder genuinely experienced in historic building repair, or possibly an architect or surveyor.

In terms of sustainability, old buildings have already performed well simply by being there for so long. Their embodied energy is extremely low because they were generally constructed with locally sourced labour and unprocessed materials. However, old buildings are not as easy to keep warm as modern insulated dwellings. It is usually

Insulation of primary truss roof in progress.

Slate

2" x 1" batten

Breather membrane

Rafter

Insulated roof leaving primary trusses and purlins partly exposed.

Primary truss

Insulation

Plasterboard

Purlin

Bearer for plasterboard

possible to super-insulate at least the ceiling or roof without hiding historically interesting features, in order to compensate for the lack of insulation in walls or solid ground floors.

Most historic buildings that survive today have done so because they are well-ventilated. It is important to understand water vapour movement through a building before considering any alterations or reducing the existing ventilation in any way. The potential effects of adding any impervious insulation material to walls, floors or roofs in all older buildings (not just historic buildings) should also be researched and assessed.

Well-detailed modern roof windows are watertight, unlike their earlier prototypes. They admit good quantities of daylight and conservation roof windows blend in well with the appearance of many old buildings. Solar water heaters designed to look like conservation roof lights have now become available, so it may become possible to take selected steps towards energy efficiency without adversely affecting the character of a building.

Energy is, in some senses, renewable. Historic fabric is not.

The eco-renovation of old buildings represents a trade-off between the need to conserve energy and the need to conserve historic fabric. It is thus always necessary to err on the side of caution when considering thermal upgrades. Ironically, many of the techniques employed in eco-building and described in this book are similar to those used during the 19th century and earlier. It was only in the 20th century that many common-sense principles of construction were abandoned.

English Heritage has published useful and detailed guidance on thermally upgrading old buildings entitled

'Energy Efficiency and Historic Buildings – Application of Part L of the Building Regulations to historic and traditionally constructed buildings'. Part L is explained further in Section 3 of this manual but it is worth noting here that listed and historic buildings and those in conservation areas are exempted from the energy efficiency requirements of the Regulations where 'compliance would unacceptably alter their character and appearance'.

There are of course methods of space heating (such as biomass) which do not involve burning fossil fuels and it may be that this is the answer to the particular needs of older buildings, rather than making wholesale alterations to the structure as a response to climate change. Perhaps we should not expect old buildings to be able to perform to the thermal standards required of new construction. Living in an old building has been compared to the experience of driving an old open-top car – it may require a different kind of lifestyle and possibly a different kind of occupant:

"If you really want to live in an old building then you have to come from the kind of culture whereby you are prepared to make a mad dash from an open fire to a hot water bottle with no prospect of any succour in between."
Ian Constantinides 2006

For further information see:
English Heritage http://www.helm.org.uk
www.climatechangeandyourhome.org.uk/live/climate_change_publications.aspx.
Society for the Protection of Ancient Buildings (SPAB)
www.spab.org.uk

2 CONSTRUCTION MATERIALS

Construction is one of the world's largest industries so if we can make the process of construction sustainable then we will be a long way down the road to a healthier and greener world. **This chapter examines the impact of construction materials, by explaining the ways in which materials can affect the environment and how the impact can be assessed. Common construction materials are then reviewed and the issues to consider are identified in each case, together with any eco-friendly alternatives available. For the more adventurous there is a section on deep green construction.**

Selecting materials

EMBODIED ENERGY

Energy is used to extract raw materials, to process them and then to transport them. Once the materials have reached their destination, further energy is then required to fit or fix them. The sum of all this energy is known as the 'embodied energy' of a particular material.

This is a difficult subject as the economy and the environment are both so complex. It is possible to calculate the energy required to extract coal at the coal-face, but practically impossible to calculate the energy consumption of the communities whose main reason for being there is the work which the pit affords. The energy required to produce the mining machinery must then be added and it rapidly becomes apparent that the calculations are very open-ended and it is difficult to know where to draw the line.

However, it is necessary to make an estimate of the embodied energy of various materials, if only for comparative purposes. Having done so, it is then necessary to take into account the volumes in which differing materials are used. For example, concrete has a much lower embodied energy than aluminium, but aluminium is only used in small quantities in house construction (and renovation) while concrete is currently used in very large quantities.

This table is useful when faced with a choice between two materials which will do substantially the same job. For example, a suitably sized hardwood lintel will perform similarly to a steel lintel at a fraction of the embodied energy cost. In general, materials that are used in a form which is as near as possible to their natural state will have the lowest embodied energy, in contrast to materials that are highly processed.

LOCAL MATERIALS AND LABOUR

The energy required to transport goods and people constitutes a large percentage of the embodied energy of a building. Historically, most buildings were constructed from natural materials which could be obtained as close as possible to the site. Transport and communications systems were undeveloped and large or heavy materials could not be moved without considerable difficulty and significant cost.

Material	Embodied energy: MJ/kg	Embodied carbon: kgC/kg
Bricks	3.0	0.060
Cement – average	4.6	0.226
Mortar (1:3)	1.4	0.058
Concrete (1:2:4)	0.9	0.035
Blocks (average)	3.5	0.089
Glass (general)	15.0	0.232
Glass – toughened	23.5	0.346
Glass – wool	28.0	0.417
Steel – primary	35.3	0.749
Steel – secondary	9.5	0.117
Steel – Stainless	56.7	1.676
Sawn hardwood	7.8	0.128
Sawn softwood	7.4	0.123
MDF	11.0	0.161
Particle board	9.5	0.139
Plywood	15.0	0.221

This data is selected from Table 2: Embodied Energy and Carbon Coefficients Hammond, G. P. and Jones, C. I., 2008. Embodied energy and carbon in construction materials. Proceedings of the Institution of Civil Engineers - Energy, 161 (2), pp. 87–98.

Photo: Jackie Abey

The farmhouse in this picture, for example, was constructed almost entirely out of materials sourced within a few hundred yards of the site. The walls are built of cob dug from the adjacent field, the roof is thatched from locally grown reeds and the timber for joists, rafters, floorboards and joinery would have been harvested from the wood surrounding the farmhouse.

It is extremely difficult to assess the environmental impact of obtaining construction materials, even down to the number of trips made to the local suppliers to collect them at the end of their journey. Complex computer programmes are available to calculate CO_2 emissions costs but a simple rule for householders would be to buy locally wherever possible, to be prepared to ask where things come from, and to expect an answer.

In just the same way as materials used to be sourced locally, in the past it would have been unthinkable for small construction projects to utilise anything other than the most local labour. The craftsmen would have been familiar with the available materials and, just as importantly, would understand the local methods of building. There would have been little concern over guarantees when the builders still lived in the same village. Large construction projects are a rather different matter.

In addition to the benefits of the experience and implicit guarantees gained by using local labour, there is a benefit to the community as a whole. Money spent within the community can be recycled several times, increasing the prosperity of the whole area, which benefits everyone – if only indirectly. This is known as the local economic multiplier and it is most keenly felt in more isolated communities.

LIFE-CYCLE ANALYSIS

Assessment of embodied energy does not stop with the fitting of the material. An estimate needs to be made of the energy cost of any future maintenance which may be required and ultimately the costs of disposal once the building (or that element of the building) has reached the end of its life. Certain materials are difficult or impossible to recycle, especially when combined with other materials and bound together with adhesives.

Life-cycle analysis/assessment (LCA) looks at all the issues which arise during the life of a building material, through to the demolition of the building. This is often referred to as 'cradle to grave' analysis, but the term increasingly used is 'cradle to cradle'. This reflects the use of waste as a resource and the need to design materials so that they can be recycled at the end of their use. LCA also takes into account embodied pollution, resource depletion and the expected life of the material or product. LCA is not a precise science as it compares many different kinds of impacts so it is always necessary to interpret the results – in other words, a value judgement is still required.

SUPPLIERS

Where a number of suppliers sell apparently similar materials, it is sometimes worth checking on the environmental policies of the suppliers to discover whether there are any significant safeguards in place. Policies regarding transportation and embodied energy, pollution or resource degradation may help in deciding between potential sources of supply.

SOURCES OF FURTHER INFORMATION

Several internet-based resources have been developed to assist customers and builders to make informed choices about building materials. For example, Greenpro is an online database providing detailed descriptions and environmental data on over 1,000 green building materials available in the UK. A small one-off registration fee applies. **http://www.greenbuildingpress.co.uk/gp/greenpro/login.php**
The BRE publishes the 'Green Guide to Specifications', which has over 1,500 specifications for building products which are then ranked A to E depending on their performance against Life Cycle Assessments (LCA), using BRE's Environmental Profiles Methodology 2008.
http://www.bre.co.uk/greenguide/page.jsp?id=2069

Masonry

Masonry comprises bricks, blocks, stone, concrete and mortar. Masonry is employed everywhere in buildings, from foundations to floors and walls and even in some cases for roofing. Its stability and longevity make it ideal for use in construction; but there are some environmental issues to consider.

- The main drawback to masonry is that it is heavy. The embodied energy needed to transport products from a quarry or brickworks to a builders' merchant or direct to site is the primary environmental cost of masonry.
- Quarrying has a destructive effect at the quarry face and considerable environmental impact in the surrounding area. While some quarrying is obviously economically and practically necessary, measures to reduce its impact and to return spent quarries to areas of ecological diversity do go some way towards reversing the process of destruction.
- Local supplies of sand, gravel, clay and stone will run out eventually. These materials were laid down by geological activity thousands or millions of years ago and cannot be replaced.

The more slowly we consume the local resources, the less energy will be needed in the future to transport alternative supplies over longer distances. The dredging of marine aggregates also has a significant environmental impact and measures have already been introduced to control and reduce the effects of this kind of extraction.

Above: Active quarry. Below: Restored quarry.

RECYCLED AGGREGATES

Recycled aggregates are steadily gaining acceptance in the construction industry. Rather than digging up virgin aggregates, recycled hardcore is commonly used for road base material, blinding, granular fills, temporary working platforms for heavy plant, oversite concrete and a variety of precast concrete products.

STONE

Stone is a natural and extremely versatile building resource. The majority of stone buildings in the UK were built from the most locally available stone, as it would have been impossible to move stone over anything more than a short distance except where water-based transport was readily available. This accounts for the wide variation in colour, texture and style of stone-built property throughout the country.

Above left: Flint. Above right: Morte Slate. Below: Hamstone.

As transportation is such a high proportion of the cost of heavy materials, especially aggregates, it should make economic as well as environmental sense to use local materials wherever possible. It is not uncommon to find stone in DIY stores and builders' merchants which has been imported from the other side of the world. Although the UK has a great variety of natural stone, the internal supply chain at present is weak. However, if a more locally sourced product can be found which is affordable, equally attractive and performs just as well, the embodied energy of the stone will be far lower.

MORTAR

Mortar is simply sand (or other fine aggregate) mixed with a binder such as cement or lime. Cement is the most common binder now in use in the UK but there are considerable advantages to using lime in some situations. In like-for-like

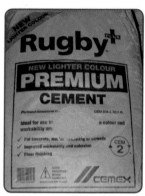

mortars, lime is responsible for slightly lower CO_2 emissions.[1]

Both lime and cement can cause burns to the skin but it is worth noting that the supply or use of cement (or cement products) which has a chromium VI concentration of more than two parts per million was prohibited after July 2005. Chromium VI was responsible for the contact dermatitis which many people report after touching wet cement. This is one example of how the construction industry is, very belatedly, cleaning up its act.

Lime is softer than cement and more permeable to both air and water. Many forms of green construction require the use of a weathering skin which can flex and breathe, so lime render is more effective than cement render in this kind of application.

Most houses constructed in the UK before 1920 were built with lime mortar so repair (or renovation work) is best achieved with similar materials. Repairing brickwork with lime mortar also prolongs the life of the brickwork, which makes it inherently much more sustainable than cement mortar.

Mortar needs to be of similar strength to (or slightly weaker than) the materials which it binds together. When water enters lime masonry as a result of driving rain, it will eventually find the easiest way back out, which is generally via the joints. With the added action of frost, over many years the joints will tend to weather back a little, which leads to the

Cement repointing leading to brick decay.

need for repointing. If repointing is carried out with cement mortar, it prevents the water from flowing out through joints. As cement mortar is so much harder than most stone or old bricks, the water then seeks the next easiest way out, which is via the edges of the bricks or stone. In exposed locations, such as chimney stacks, this in turn leads to weathering of the brick edges and to the eventual loss of the face. Once a brick has lost its hard face the softer core rapidly decays, leading to substantial and costly repairs.

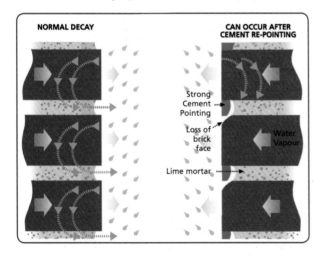

In terms of embodied energy, it is generally better to repair than to replace. This is particularly true of heavy items such as masonry, so good conservation techniques have an important role to play in reducing our consumption of materials and energy.

Lastly, since lime mortar does not adhere as firmly as cement mortar, materials which have been bound together with lime mortar are much easier to clean and reuse at the end of the life of the building.

CONCRETE

Concrete consists of aggregate, sand and a binder, usually cement. Due to the high energy cost of producing cement and the energy required to transport the aggregates, the production of concrete accounts for 5–10% of the world's man-made annual CO_2 emissions.

Although, by volume and weight, concrete has a relatively low embodied energy compared to steel and plastics, so much of it is produced – over 14 billion tonnes are poured every year – that there is great potential to reduce energy consumption by using concrete more efficiently. Most of this concrete is used in new construction but domestic renovators can still make a difference by avoiding the use of concrete or concrete products for external surfaces where other, less energy-intensive, materials would work just as well (see section on 'Hard landscaping' in Chapter 10).

When building an extension, the use of concrete can be reduced by pouring concrete pads to underpin post-and-

Reinforced concrete ground beam spans between piles, supporting walls

Reinforced concrete short bored piles support ground beam (often only reinforcement at top)

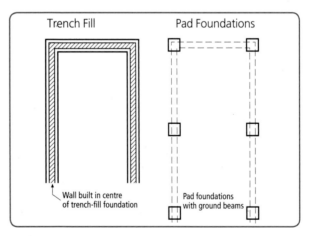

beam foundations rather than the 'trench fill' technique commonly used to create strip foundations.

'Oversite concrete' refers to the slab which is usually poured to form the ground floor of a dwelling. Oversite concrete is unnecessary where it is possible to build a highly insulated suspended floor rather than a solid floor resting on the ground. It is worth noting that most of the older housing stock in the UK was built without the use of oversite concrete. On the other hand, where insulation has been fitted underneath the concrete, the concrete acts as 'thermal mass' (see section on 'Passive solar design' in Chapter 4). Together with underfloor heating, this can form part of the thermal strategy for a building.

BRICKS AND BLOCKS

Bricks are made from clay which is fired in a kiln to bake it hard and give it a weatherproof outer surface. Although clay is a naturally occurring material, the firing is obviously an energy-intensive process. To reduce the transport cost of

the operation, brickworks were originally built near housing developments, taking advantage of the locally available clay. This accounts for the variety of colours of older bricks.

Most of these brickworks have now disappeared and bricks are now mass-produced in a much smaller number of factories, which means that the transportation (thus energy, CO_2 emissions, pollution) costs are now much higher.

Concrete blocks are made with cement. The energy required to produce the cement is greater than the energy required to fire the equivalent volume of bricks so, generally speaking, blocks have a higher embodied energy than bricks. Blocks vary from dense to lightweight, depending on their load-bearing characteristics and thermal performance. For some years, concrete blocks have been manufactured using recycled aggregates such as fuel ash and, more recently, glass. Some blocks may contain up to 80% recycled material (by volume). Recycled aggregates are also used in paving slabs and any cement-based product could in theory make use of recycled aggregate.

For further information on the recycled aggregate content of blocks see: **http://rcproducts.wrap.org.uk/** – part of WRAP – Waste and Resources Action Programme.

Thermalite blocks.

Photo: Oak.Apple Frames

Timber

Timber is the most versatile building material of all. It can be used for structures, cladding, joinery, flooring and decorative purposes.

In contrast to most other materials, timber absorbs CO_2 as it grows. Of course, some energy is required to log, mill and transport the timber, so the same principles of local sourcing and waste minimisation apply as with all other materials. However, there is a serious downside to timber production: illegal logging is responsible for the destruction of forests world-wide, together with the resultant loss of wildlife habitats, biodiversity and, in some cases, traditional lifestyles. Soil erosion and downstream river sedimentation add to the damaging effects of deforestation.

CERTIFICATION SCHEMES

Contributing to this type of environmental destruction can be avoided by insisting upon timber which is certified as having been produced from a sustainable source. This generally means that the impact of the logging has been minimised and that replanting is replacing the harvested timber – although not necessarily in the same place.

Forestry Stewardship Council (FSC)
The FSC standard is widely recognised as the most rigorous of these schemes and it is the only one which is entirely independent of the forestry industry.

Programme for the Endorsement of Forest Certification (PEFC)
The PEFC is an umbrella scheme that assesses and endorses national certification schemes. Codes covered under the scheme include:
Sustainable Forestry Initiative (SFI)
Canadian Standards Association scheme (CSA).

The Code for Sustainable Homes awards maximum credit for the quality marks described above, but it does also provide recognise timber certified by other schemes which comply with BES6001: 2008.

The UK Government has established the Central point of Procurement on Timber (CPET) to ensure that all timber used on public buildings is sustainably produced. Many builders' merchants and DIY stores now obtain some or all of their timber from certified sources but if the marks are not visible or the policy is not clear then it is wise to check.

In addition to these schemes, timber may be available which is harvested from local gardens or woodlands which are then replanted. Together with reclaimed timber, this is the most sustainable supply of all. Most timber used in the UK construction industry is imported, but the embodied energy cost of shipping timber from Sweden is far less than from the Far East, so not all imported timbers are comparable.

For further information see:
Forestry Stewardship Council **www.fsc-uk.org/**
The Central Point of Expertise for Timber Procurement **www.cpet.org.uk**

Many tropical hardwoods are non-renewable. Reducing or eliminating demand for tropical hardwoods may eventually reduce the speed at which the remaining forests are being destroyed. Remaining tropical rainforests cover approximately 2% of the land surface of the earth but 1.5 acres are lost every second.[2]

Rainforests play a vital role in absorbing CO_2, proving unique habitats for plants and animals, and many other resources besides. They also help to drive and maintain the world's climate, as much of the rain which falls there is later returned to the atmosphere via evapotranspiration and is then conveyed to other parts of the world.

For further information visit **www.savetherainforest.org**

EFFICIENT TIMBER PRODUCTS
Timber I-beams are the timber equivalent of the steel I-beam. Most of the strength in a steel beam is provided by its top and bottom sections, which the centre section mainly serves to separate – which is why an I-beam is the shape it is, discarding the parts that do less work. The strength of a beam increases in relation to the distance between the top and bottom flanges, so the deeper the beam the stronger it becomes.

The timber I-beam works in exactly the same way. By taking out the middle section of the joist and replacing it with a separating web, the I-beam can be engineered to accept the same loads but with a greatly reduced consumption of timber and a more reliable bearing capacity. Timber I-beams are also lighter to handle than equivalent solid joists, which makes construction easier. The separating web is usually constructed from oriented strand board (OSB) or structural board manufactured from wood waste – see the next section for more information on these products.

Photo: Jackson Moulding

Material-efficient timber frame

A similar concept is also used in modern timber frame construction for walls where an inner and an outer skin are joined together by a series of connecting plates. This is particularly useful where a building is designed to be superinsulated, as the separation of the inner and outer skins allows for an almost complete thermal break between the two and for thick walls to be constructed without having to use deep timber studs, which are prone to warping or twisting. This type of construction also allows for reclaimed timber of varying sizes to be used if available.

REPAIR RATHER THAN REPLACE
In old buildings, decayed beams can be cut back to sound wood and structural repairs carried out while minimising the loss of original timber. Certain types of repair can be achieved purely by well-designed carpentry joints, but other situations may require the addition of steel plates or splicing with steel rods and epoxy grouts.

Photo: Nick Spollin

Splice repairs.

Untreated softwood (above) and treated softwood (below).

The environmental impact of the materials used to carry out these repairs far outweighs the impact of replacing the entire section of timber, even if this is technically feasible. The added advantage is that the maximum amount of historic fabric is retained and the disruption to the building is reduced.

It is a poor use of resources to replace windows which can easily be repaired; the embodied energy of producing, transporting and fitting new windows is considerable, in addition to the costs of disposing of the old ones. Contractors are usually likely to recommend replacement as this maximises profit.

People frequently fall into the trap of having windows replaced when there is rot damage only to the lower sill. Rot in this area is understandable, since all the rainwater which falls on the window will have to pass over the sill while draining away and, with the accumulation of debris and poor maintenance, water is more likely to collect and do damage there than anywhere else.

New timber can be spliced in where the rot is severe. Rot is also commonly found in the first few inches of the upright frame members above the sill. This type of rot can also be repaired effectively with the use of modern resins which bond to and expand and contract like the timber, thus preventing the cracking which is common after hard fillers have been used. Once a repair job like the one pictured below has been carried out the windows are quite literally as good as new. For older properties there is the added benefit that the character of the building is not compromised. (Also see the sections on draughtproofing and upgrading windows in Chapter 3.)

TIMBER PRE-TREATMENT

During the last 50 years, the pre-treatment of structural timber has become commonplace. The long-term effects of these chemical treatments on human health cannot yet be fully known. The most commonly used preservative for many years was CCA – copper chromated arsenic. This was finally banned for domestic use in 2004, a good example of how the government is responding to public pressure for healthier buildings.

In many cases this type of treatment is unnecessary. A well-detailed timber building may have no need of treatment for the great majority of its structural members. The converse is also true – where the conditions exist for rot or other forms of timber decay to commence, as a result of poor detailing and lack of maintenance, timber treatment will only slow down rather than prevent the onset of decay.

Some species of timber can survive for centuries even when exposed to the elements, irrespective of timber treatment.

Any timber which may come into prolonged contact with damp will still need to be protected – for example, base-

Resin repairs.

Photos: Repair Care International

plates in some wooden buildings. In the garden, fence posts, decking bases and any garden buildings should be treated, although larch, cedar and local hardwoods may be used as cladding with no necessity for treatment at all. Oil-based treatments for decking surfaces work by nourishing the wood rather than trying to seal it and can be an effective and non-toxic alternative to chemical treatment.

Alternative timber treatments are available which are potentially less harmful to the environment. The relevant British standard for timber treatment is BS 8417. If the need for treatment has been established, builders' merchants should be able to supply timber which has been treated with chemicals such as Tanalith-e (based on copper triazole), CCB (copper, chrome and boron) or simply boron.

Boron is a naturally occurring mineral that already exists in the environment and has a toxicity to humans similar to that of common salt. Plant and aquatic toxicity is also relatively low. Inorganic borates are also water-soluble, which eliminates the need to use solvents and gives them a much better penetration into the wood than many conventional preservatives.

REMEDIAL TIMBER TREATMENT

When there has been an outbreak of dry rot or woodworm, it is common practice to treat the affected timbers and any surrounding timber with chemicals. There are potential risks to human health associated with chemical woodworm eradication treatment in domestic property. The most common chemical in use at the present time is Permethrin, which is a suspected endocrine disruptor and possible carcinogen.[3]

However, there should be no need to introduce toxic chemicals into the living environment. Wood-boring creatures only flourish in a damp, dark, unventilated environment, perhaps arising as a result of defective rainwater fittings or incorrect ground levels. Failure to maintain joinery and the seals around frames is another common cause of damp ingress and timber decay. Sometimes, woodworm damage is treated long after the woodworm have done their work and disappeared, so it is best to check for signs of fresh activity (clean wood dust) before taking remedial action.

Experts on old buildings recommend locating and eliminating the source of the moisture which has caused the problem before resorting to chemical remedies. However, the necessity to use chemical treatment against apparent or actual wood decay

Above left: Old woodworm damage.
Left: Dust produced by active woodworm.

frequently arises at the suggestion of surveyors and at the insistence of mortgage providers. Either party may still need convincing of the efficacy of alternative approaches to timber treatment. Furthermore, treatment with toxic chemicals will not necessarily prevent the recurrence of decay if the original source of moisture is not eliminated.

Most buildings, if properly maintained, function perfectly well indefinitely without the need for any chemical treatment but where it is unavoidable there is a range of products based on boron which are effective against dry rot, wet rot and woodworm, while having a greatly reduced environmental impact.

For further information see:
Explanatory leaflet from the Centre For Alternative technology (CAT) **http://www.cat.org.uk/information/pdf/TimberTreatment.pdf**
Pesticide Action Network **www.pan-uk.org**
Toxic residues from timber treatment – Tim Hutton Building Conservation Directory, 2008 **http://www.buildingconservation.com/articles/toxic/toxic.htm**
Society for the Protection of Ancient Buildings **www.spab.org.uk**

Composite/ particle boards

STRUCTURAL BOARDS

Several composite sheet materials are used for flooring, kitchen worktops and other structural purposes. They fall into three basic categories – particle boards such as chipboard, fibre boards such as MDF and laminated boards such as plywood.

Five issues arise when deciding which board to choose:

- ■ Where does the raw material come from?
- ■ What is used to bind it together?
- ■ How much energy is used in its manufacture and transportation?
- ■ Does it last well?
- ■ Can it be recycled at the end of its useful life?

Source of the raw material

The small size of particles and fibres in composite boards means that they can be manufactured from the waste generated in the processing of raw timber, although this is not always the case. Some manufacturers use raw material produced from non-sustainable sources so, as with unprocessed timber, it is necessary to look for the FSC or PEFC label on sheet materials. OSB was designed in part to use smaller logs which could not be processed into plywood. It thus represents a more efficient use of raw materials than some structural boards.

MDF.

Plywood.

Chipboard.

OSB.

Binders

The most common binders used in laminated boards, particle boards and fibre boards are urea-formaldehyde and phenol-formaldehyde. Even at relatively low levels, exposure to formaldehyde causes irritation to eyes and to the breathing system. 'Safe' levels of formaldehyde vary, as each country sets its own limits. Where particle boards (or other products containing formaldehyde) are to be found in homes, the formaldehyde present in the air is significantly higher than in the air outside but the levels are normally below the permitted UK maximum exposure. Coating MDF and chipboard with a non-toxic sealant can reduce the amount of gas which is released.

The International Agency for Research on Cancer (IARC) – part of the World Health Organisation – has evaluated the available evidence on the carcinogenicity of formaldehyde and concluded that it is carcinogenic to humans.[4]

The Wood Panel Industries Federation (WPIF) states that "The UK's Building Research Establishment has tested the air quality in typical British homes and found the average concentration of formaldehyde is less than one-quarter of the guideline limit from all formaldehyde emitting sources in the home."[5] However, it is acknowledged that off-gassing reduces over time and that these figures are averages, so it is easy to envisage a scenario where a newly refurbished house might have a range of products present leading to levels of formaldehyde which significantly exceed the permitted exposure levels.

OSB is commonly bound with phenol formaldehyde, considered to be more stable than urea-formaldehyde. Formaldehyde-free chipboards and MDF (European E1 grade) are now starting to become available in the UK.

Alternative structural sheet materials with much lower formaldehyde content could be Birch plywood, HDF (high density fibreboard) and OSB.[6]

For further information on the risks of exposure to dust arising from working with wood products see: *COSHH and the woodworking industries* – Woodworking Sheet No 6 (rev 2) – Health & Safety Executive (2007).

Embodied energy

Most man-made boards have a high embodied energy in comparison to natural timber due to the processing needed to create the board and the embodied energy of the binders which are added. It appears that hardboard, medium board and softboard have a somewhat lower embodied energy than MDF and chipboard, if no synthetic resin binders are used. Medium board is made by steaming wood into fires and adding water to form a slurry. When it is finally pressed, it is bound together by the natural lignin in the wood. Medium board should not be confused with MDF, where the fibres are allowed to dry before the binder is added, as with particle boards. The raw materials for OSB and plywood are less processed than those in particle board or chipboard.

Many plywood products are imported from Brazil or the Far East, giving them a high embodied energy and increasing the risk that illegally logged timber has been used as raw material. European-sourced plywoods are generally available as an alternative.

Durability

The durability of fibre boards and particle boards is their main downfall as most will swell up and lose their strength when in prolonged contact with water. Even moisture-resistant boards will fail in the long run but a laminated board such as plywood generally has a better strength and durability than the alternatives.

Disposal

Advice from County Councils is not to burn MDF or particle boards such as chipboard as they contain toxic glues; there is often a separate skip at the municipal site for processed wood.[7] This advice would presumably not apply to the wet process fibre boards described above.

PLASTERBOARD AND ALTERNATIVES

Plasterboard is composed of gypsum which is processed into a board and faced with paper. Natural gypsum is a mineral – calcium sulphate dihydrate ($CaSO_4 2H_2O$) – which is mined in Sussex, Lincolnshire and Yorkshire. A large source of gypsum for plasterboard is flue gas desulphurisation from power plants – a good use of a waste material.

Working with plasterboard inevitably generates offcuts. According to WRAP, up to 1m tonnes of plasterboard waste arises from refurbishment projects each year. These used to be added to general hardcore, but the sulphate content of gypsum breaks down if mixed with biodegradable waste and produces hydrogen sulphide. This causes odour issues and pollutes water run-off from landfill. From April 2009, all plasterboard must either be disposed of in separate skips or, if added to a mixed skip, it must be separated and identified. It can then be sent by the waste operator for recycling elsewhere. If plasterboard has to be landfilled it is now contained separately from biodegradable waste.

http://www.environment-agency.gov.uk/business/topics/waste/32148.aspx

Photo: Haldor Bjornson

Wall boards can be made from renewable material such as hemp or recycled newspaper, the latter containing some gypsum. Some are stronger than plasterboard but none are as cheap. For small renovation projects or extensions the additional cost will be relatively minor compared to other build elements.

Fermacell.

Photo: Xella Dry Lining

Clay board.

Photo: Construction Products

At present these boards have the slight disadvantage that the supply chain is weak and for small projects it is often useful to be able to pick up a couple of extra boards from the builders' merchant. It is also worth noting that the fire-resistant properties (plus sound attenuation, thermal mass, thermal conductivity and moisture conductivity) of gypsum plasterboard are well known, and that standard details for their use are familiar to the trades. Alternative products may perform equally well or better but it is important to seek expert advice when using alternative products in critical locations.

Straw boards.

Photo: www.stramit.co.uk

Insulation products

Environmental assessment and comparison of insulation products is a complex subject and includes the following considerations:

- Thermal performance (R-value) of any particular material
- Energy (per kg) required to manufacture the material
- Whether the material is produced from a recycled, sustainable or renewable source
- Where the material is manufactured (road miles)
- Potential to cause irritation
- Whether toxins are released during manufacture, use or disposal
- Whether the material can be recycled at the end of its use

Natural products score better in most of these categories but there are still some situations where a 'conventional' product may be preferred and in most cases it will be necessary to comply with the new part L of the Building Regulations. Fire resistance and sound insulation properties of the various products mentioned are not addressed here, although it is worth noting that in critical locations mineral wool is the most effective firestop.

There are three main types of insulation – loose, semi-rigid and boards. Loose insulation is designed to be injected into cavities or placed over flat ceilings. Semi-rigid insulation is also useful over ceilings but can also be fitted into walls as they are built. Rigid boards can be used within walls, under floors or fixed directly to the rafters in pitched roofs.

CELLULOSE

Recycled newspaper insulation – cellulose – is a loose-fill product which is ideal for use in lofts. UK-manufactured Warmcel 100 is designed for DIY use and is pre-treated with inorganic salts against fire and rodent attack. This is in stark contrast to the toxic fire retardants and pesticides found in many other insulation products. Cellulose uses very little energy to manufacture, it is non-toxic and non-irritant.

Warmcel 100 is supplied in bags which can be simply

Cellulose.

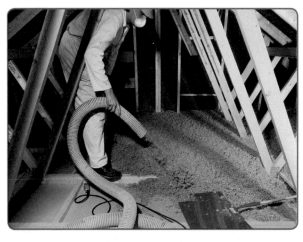

emptied out into the loft space. The current target U value for a loft ceiling is 0.16 w/m²k (see section on 'Insulation values' in Chapter 3), which can be achieved by adding 225mm of Warmcel to an uninsulated loft, or less where there is already some insulation present. Warmcel 500 is also used in new construction but must be blown into a closed structure by specialist contractors or sprayed while damp into an open structure.

SHEEPSWOOL

Sheepswool is a natural fibre from a renewable resource with low embodied energy as it requires very little processing. Natural wool can absorb and release water vapour rapidly, which increases its effectiveness as an insulant. It is simple to fit and does not irritate the skin in the way that mineral products do.

The majority of sheepswool insulation sold in the UK is supplied in batts which contain a very small amount of a recycled polyester binder to give them sufficient rigidity. Batts can be built into walls, placed over ceilings as a loft insulator, or used to insulate suspended timber floors. They are available in a range of thicknesses which can be used to build up to the required amount, and in a range of widths to suit most joist or rafter spacings. Wool is naturally fire resistant, melting away from an ignition source rather than igniting. It is essential to ensure that any sheepswool is correctly treated to guard against insect attack. Inorganic salts such as borax, are currently used for this purpose.

Photo: Black Mountain Insulation

Photo: Natural Building Technologies Ltd

Isonat (hemp-based insulation)

Photo: Natural Building Technologies Ltd

Above: Finished house after external insulation.

HEMP

Hemp-based insulation is treated with inorganic salts to provide fire and pest resistance. It is easy to handle, simple to install and does not irritate the skin. Hemp insulation is normally supplied in batts and used in lofts or within timber stud walls, as with sheepswool.

Photo: Natural Building Technologies Ltd

Photo: Black Mountain Insulation

Hemp Insulation

are made almost entirely from waste softwood which effectively 'locks up' CO_2 in its production. They can be used for external insulation (see 'Improving wall insulation' in Chapter 3) and either clad with a timber rainscreen or rendered directly.

The flexible version of this insulation, known as Pavaflex, can be installed between timber studs, as shown here.

For further information visit **www.greenspec. co.uk/html/ materials/ insulation.html**

Photos: Natural Building Technologies Ltd

OTHER RENEWABLE INSULATION PRODUCTS

Several other natural and non-toxic insulation materials are available, such as Strawboard, Flax, Cork and a batt form of cellulose, but at present all of these are imported into the UK, thus increasing their embodied energy in comparison to locally-produced alternatives. A UK-manufactured insulation batt made primarily from recycled carpet wool is now available.

One product for which there is no locally-produced alternative is extremely useful and versatile. Pavatex boards, manufactured in Switzerland,

Below: Pavatex boards for external insulation.

Photo: Natural Building Technologies Ltd

MINERAL WOOL

Mineral wool is a generic term which covers rockwool, glasswool and slagwool. Rockwool is spun from volcanic rock, which is a plentiful resource. Fibreglass, like other glass products, is derived from silica, which is also abundant; some manufacturers use recycled glass. Many people report that they suffer from skin irritation and rashes after coming into contact with glass wool. Slagwool is made from one of the waste products (slag) of the steel industry and so constitutes a good use of a waste product. Mineral wool is also available loose, normally for cavity wall insulation.

Mineral wool has a higher embodied energy than natural and renewable materials such as those described above. Given that the aim of insulation is to reduce energy use, it may be more sustainable to use materials which need minimal processing, and to provide a market for recycled materials.

POLYSTYRENE

Polystyrene is a closed-cell product derived from oil. It is expanded or extruded by the use of pentane, a gas that does not contribute to global warming or to ozone depletion. Polystyrene does not degrade when in contact with moisture so it is particularly useful in those parts of a dwelling where this is a risk. It can also bear spread loads so it may be used on the ground floor under screeds or under timber floating floors in some instances.

Expanded polystyrene-backed plasterboard allows builders to insulate and provide a finished surface at the same time.

However, as the amount of insulation required by Building Regulations has increased in recent years, it should be noted that this product alone may not be sufficient to bring a structure up to modern thermal standards, depending on the thickness of the polystyrene.

Expanded polystyrene beads are used as an alternative to loose mineral wool in cavity wall insulation. They are blown

in by specialist contractors, together with a bonding agent to provide long-term stability.

Both expanded and extruded polystyrene are toxic when burned and they do not biodegrade in landfill, although they can be reclaimed and recycled. Polystyrene reacts with the plasticisers used in some electrical cables, causing degradation in the cables. It may therefore be necessary to prevent the two coming into contact with each other.

POLYISOCYANURATE/POLYISOCYANURATE-MODIFIED POLYURETHANE FOAM

Polyisocyanurate boards are also closed-cell plastic-based products, ultimately derived from oil and they are widely used in the construction industry. For many years the blowing agents used in their manufacture were CFCs or HCFCs but these have now been banned in the UK due to their damaging effect on the ozone layer. Hydrofluorocarbons (HFCs) are now used instead. Although they do not have the same ozone depleting potential as CFCs, HFCs are potent greenhouse gases which have significant global warming potential. Care must be taken when disposing of old stock which may have been expanded with CFCs or HCFCs.

Facings are aluminium foil or fibreglass-based. In addition to their use in wall and roof construction, specific products exist for use under compression in floor slabs. Polyisocyanurate has a relatively high thermal resistance

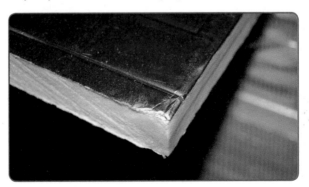

compared to most other products so it is particularly useful where space is at a premium. Polyisocyanurate boards emit fine particles when cut, are toxic when burned and do not biodegrade.[8] [9]

A plasterboard with 65mm of insulation has been developed specifically to meet the requirements for upgrading previously uninsulated solid walls under Part L of the Building Regulations (2010) for refurbishment work.

MULTI-LAYERED FOIL INSULATION

Multi-layered foil insulation consists of several thin layers of reflective and insulative material bonded or sewn together. It is generally supplied in wide rolls, the joins being lapped and taped together when it is installed. It has a number of advantages, principally that it is very thin – often not more than 25mm – so is extremely useful

Photo: Actis Insulation Ltd

Photo: Actis Insulation Ltd

in refurbishment projects where space is at a premium, although it does require an air gap to achieve its optimal thermal performance. Foil insulation also acts as an effective reflector of solar energy in hot weather and as an impermeable membrane. It is easy to handle, simple and safe to cut and attracts no dust.

Test results differ as to the exact thermal properties of this insulation so it is wise to check with the local building inspector if a specific thermal performance must be achieved. Multi-foil insulation does not breathe so it should not be used in old buildings where it is critical that breathability is maintained.

INSULATION SUMMARY

Material	Green Guide Rating
Cavity blown glass wool insulation - density 17 kg/m³	A+
Cavity blown stone wool insulation density 30 kg/m³	A+
Cellular glass insulation - density 100 kg/m³	A+
Cellular glass insulation - density 110 kg/m³	A
Cellular glass insulation - density 115 kg/m³	A
Cellular glass insulation - density 120 kg/m³	A
Cellular glass insulation - density 130 kg/m³	A
Cellular glass insulation - density 155 kg/m³	B
Cellular glass insulation - density 165 kg/m³	B
Cellular glass insulation - density 200 kg/m³	C
Corkboard insulation - density 120kg/m³	A
Dry blown recycled cellulose insulation - density 24kg/m³	A+
Expanded polystyrene (EPS) - density 15 kg/m³	A+
Expanded polystyrene (EPS) - density 20 kg/m³	A+
Expanded polystyrene (EPS) - density 25 kg/m³	A+
Expanded polystyrene (EPS) - density 30 kg/m³	A+
Extruded polystyrene (XPS) (HFC blown) density 35 kg/m³	E
Glass wool insulation - density 10 kg/m³	A+
Glass wool insulation - density 12 kg/m³	A+
Glass wool insulation - density 24 kg/m³	A+
Glass wool insulation - density 32 kg/m³	A+
Glass wool insulation - density 48 kg/m³	A+
Glass wool insulation - density 80 kg/m³	A
Rigid urethane (pentane blown) - density 32 kg/m³	A
Sheepswool insulation - density 25 kg/m3	A+
Stone wool insulation - density 100 kg/m³	A
Stone wool insulation - density 128 kg/m³	B
Stone wool insulation - density 140 kg/m³	B
Stone wool insulation - density 160 kg/m³	C
Stone wool insulation - density 33 kg/m³	A+
Stone wool insulation - density 45 kg/m³	A+
Stone wool insulation - density 60 kg/m³	A+
Stone wool insulation - density 80 kg/m³	A
Straw bale used as insulation	A
Strawboard thermal insulation (420kg/m³)	C
Wet blown recycled cellulose insulation - density 45 kg/m³	A+

Source: Energy Saving Trust

Roofing

The key environmental questions to address when choosing roofing products are durability, embodied energy and recycled content. It may also be necessary to check with the local planning department if considering a roof with a different material from the original.

NATURAL SLATE

Natural slate is a very durable and attractive roof covering. When renovating a roof, the most energy-efficient approach is usually to repair. Slate roofs tend to be replaced when the bearings or fixings have rotted but it is normally possible to reuse most of the slates once the battens and nails have been replaced. A breather membrane is normally added during the process.

This requires sourcing reclaimed slates of the correct size and colour to match the existing slates. The chances

of achieving this are greatly increased if there is a local reclamation yard, but it may be worth knocking on doors locally to see if anyone has held on to original slates when their roof was replaced with composite slates, as has so often happened. There is an active second-hand market for

significant quantities of natural slates in good condition. The majority of new slate available today is shipped in from Spain, Portugal, China and Canada but it is still possible to source new UK slate – for example from Wales – although it is rather expensive. The decision therefore rests on a compromise between cost and embodied energy.

RECONSTITUTED SLATE

Much of the material quarried for natural slate is waste. This waste can be crushed and reprocessed to make a reconstituted slate. The proportion of recycled material

Britlock slates.

varies between different manufacturers but can be as high as 80%. The riven pattern is similar to a natural slate.

RECYCLED PLASTIC

'Slates' are also available in the UK made from recycled plastics. These slates are

lightweight and durable, and have passed all the relevant tests in terms of uplift, driving rain and fire spread. The most valuable aspect of this type of product is that it provides a market for recycled plastics, many of which cause long-term pollution in land and sea.

COMPOSITE 'SLATE'

Composite slate consists of fibre held together with a binder such as cement. Composite slates are not as durable as natural slates, although the worst offending brands which failed after ten years have now been withdrawn from the market. Early slates also contained asbestos and these have also been withdrawn. Composite slates generally do not have the 'riven' appearance of reconstituted or recycled slates and they also have a relatively high embodied energy due to their cement content.

The main advantage of composite slate is that it is somewhat lighter than natural slate, although the same is true of recycled plastic slate. Sometimes in Victorian or Edwardian housing the purlins were slightly undersized and will have sagged under the weight of the slate, so replacing natural slate with composite slate is one way of reducing the load. This can be important if considering adding insulation and a finished surface while undertaking a loft conversion. Building Regulations apply to loft conversions and no significant weight should be added to a roof structure without consulting a structural engineer.

CLAY TILES

Clay is a plentiful and natural resource. Clay tiles have a high embodied energy due to the firing process. However, like natural slate they are very durable as millions of roofs throughout the country still have their original tiles, manufactured well over 100 years ago. Although tiles can lose their outer surface and then decay rapidly, deterioration is usually due to failure of the support structure, especially the battens, rather than the tiles themselves.

New clay tiled roof.

Old clay tiled roof.

METAL ROOFING

Zinc, copper, lead, stainless steel and especially aluminium all have a high embodied energy. There are numerous ecological issues concerning the extraction and processing of metals but they are durable and recyclable and have a high 'material efficiency', so they cover a large area of roof in relation to their weight, which offsets their high embodied energy.

Above: Zinc roof.

Above: Copper roof. Below: Stainless steel roof.

Photo: JTC Roofing

TIMBER SHINGLES

Common in the USA and elsewhere, timber shingles are a very environmentally friendly roofing material as they are lightweight and sustainable, if harvested from certified forests. Usually of oak, sweet chestnut or western red cedar, the natural oils present in the wood serve to protect them from the weather and make them durable. Western red cedar is normally imported from the USA or Canada so the embodied energy rises due to the transportation cost. Timber absorbs CO_2 as it grows, so timber shingles have a neutral environmental impact if the timber can be sourced closer to home.

The main downside to timber shingles is that, in areas prone to wildfires, fire has been known to 'jump' from roof to roof but this is unlikely to be a concern for one-off projects in the UK.

THATCH

Thatch has perhaps the lowest environmental impact of all roofing materials. Reed lasts longer than straw – say 60 years as opposed to 30, although ridges need attention more regularly than this. If the raw material is harvested locally, the embodied energy is negligible. There are no toxic chemicals, no treatment is needed, and of course thatch is an excellent insulator.

FLAT ROOFING MATERIALS

Most flat roofing products contain PVC and some contain plasticisers. As an alternative, there are several synthetic rubber (EPDM) products now available in the UK, some of which are bitumen compatible – so they can be laid over existing bitumen-based membranes.

For current information on available products visit:
www.greenspec.co.uk/html/design/materials/flatroofs.html

GREEN ROOFS

A green roof is simply a vegetative covering over a sealed weatherproof layer similar to flat roofing, although green coverings can be installed on pitched roofs up to a certain angle. There are several reasons for planting a green roof:

- To provide a habitat for plants and wildlife
- To improve the appearance of roofs at low levels
- To reduce rainwater run-off as part of a SUDS strategy
- To absorb CO_2

Photos: Blackdown Horticultural Consultants

Above: Sedum roof. Below: Turf roof.

The two most common types of green roof are grass and sedum – sedum is often used because it requires very little maintenance as the plants are low-growing and form a thick matt in a short time. Alternatively, a 'blanket' of ready-grown sedum can be laid to provide an instant green roof.

The additional insulation provided by a green roof is unlikely to have any significant effect in a well-insulated building. Grass roofs are heavier than sedum roofs but either will add significant weight, so not all roofs will be suitable without strengthening the underlying structure.

Green roofs do require maintenance – to remove unwanted seedlings, keep rainwater fittings clear and fertilise where required. The frequency depends on the type of green roof installed but there are specialist companies that provide this service. It is important to note that maintenance adds to the cost and overall environmental impact of the system over its lifetime.

RAINWATER FITTINGS

The most commonly used rainwater fittings in the UK are made from PVC. They are quick to fit and standardisation means that sections can usually be replaced without having to discard the whole system. However, after a few years many PVC gutters tend to become brittle as a result of exposure to ultraviolet light. Cracking can sometimes occur when roofers are obliged to lean ladders against the building to gain access to carry out repairs.

The fact that some cast iron rainwater fittings may still be seen on old buildings shows that it is possible to specify rainwater fittings which last far longer than PVC. Cast iron is expensive, difficult to work with and heavy to fit, but alternatives do exist. Galvanised steel guttering is steadily gaining popularity in the UK.

In addition to lasting much longer than plastic, galvanised steel can withstand impact from ladders and looks much better than plastic. Appearance is important, as rainwater fittings constitute such a strong feature of many buildings. It can be ordered

Lindab galvanised steel guttering.

through some builders' merchants and its longevity outweighs the additional cost of the system in comparison to PVC. Copper rainwater goods do the same job and look and last even better but they are prohibitively expensive for most project budgets.

For homeowners who prefer to stick to PVC, there is a guttering system available made from over 80% post consumer recycled PVC, reducing its embodied energy and providing a valuable market for recycled plastics.

Swish guttering.

Reclaimed and recycled materials

RECLAIMED MATERIALS

Reclaimed building materials are in a sense the most eco-friendly materials available. For years we have been dumping millions of perfectly serviceable Victorian bricks into landfill rather than storing and reusing them, although attitudes are at last beginning to change.

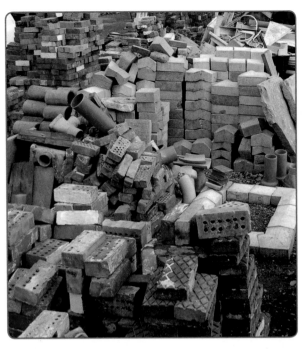

Unlike recycled materials, reclaimed materials require no energy for reprocessing and only minimal energy for transportation as they tend to be reused near their original location. Of course, this does not apply so much to high value decorative architectural salvage, which is even traded internationally.

In some cases the quality of reclaimed products is considerably higher than that of newer products. For example, timber used a century or more ago was harvested from trees which had been allowed to grow more slowly and to a greater age, so the grain is tighter, the appearance is better and the wood is more rich in resin. Consequently, the strength and durability are higher than modern fast-grown timber.

Original pine floor (top) and new repair.

Salvage works two ways. In restoring or renovating a property the householder can become a supplier as well as a consumer of reclaimed goods. Most products can be reused but bricks, doors, tiles, slates and timber are the most actively traded.

In older houses, materials which cannot be reused in situ can often be recycled. Problems occur mainly when dissimilar materials have been combined together – windows are a good example, containing putty, paint, glass, timber and ironmongery as a minimum. Working with reclaimed materials demands particular skills and almost always takes longer. Timber which contains nails or other fixings is time-consuming to prepare and considerable care must be taken to avoid damage to cutting tools in case they encounter hidden metal. Hardwoods can also be very difficult to work once they have aged. On the other hand, reclaimed timber has the great advantage of being much less prone to deformation than new timber as it will have already done all

its warping and twisting unless it is substantially re-milled, as this can release tensions within the wood.

For further information visit your local reclaim yard or see **www.salvo.co.uk**

RECYCLED MATERIALS

Specifying products which have a high recycled materials content not only reduces the demand for raw materials but also helps to create a market for materials which are already recycled. WRAP – the Waste and Resources Action Programme – provides an online guide to available construction products that are wholly or partially made from recycled material. Detailed specifications and lists of suppliers are provided for all the products mentioned under these headings, together with the percentage of recycled materials used in each product. The guide covers a wide range of materials used in domestic refurbishment:

- Bricks & Blocks
- Boards
- Cement & Concrete
- Decking and fencing
- Doors
- Drainage products
- Floor coverings
- Insulation
- Kitchen carcassing
- Mats and membranes
- Paving and other landscaping products
- Plasterboard
- Roof coverings
- Soundproofing
- Trunking
- Wall cladding

For example, there is a damp-proof membrane available which is made entirely from post-use polyethylene waste, while meeting all relevant British Standards requirements.

Photo: Visqueen Building Products

Some underground drainage pipe is now produced using 50% recycled plastics – the point is that it is not possible to tell from inspection if recycled product has been used. It takes a little research and careful specification – or just a word to your builder to use recycled materials wherever possible – and bear in mind that clients can sometimes be better informed than builders if they've had time to do the research.

For further information visit **http://rcproducts.wrap.org.uk/**

Photo: Wavin Ltd

Deep green construction

No book on eco-building would be complete without at least mentioning some of the alternative construction methods that are available. Even though the primary subject of this manual is refurbishment, an extension or garden building sometimes affords the opportunity to experiment with different forms of construction.

TIMBER FRAME

There are two basic types of timber frame construction – primary frame and stud frame. Primary framing is based upon ancient techniques of post-and-beam construction and uses hardwoods such as oak or softwoods such as Douglas Fir. The primary frame accepts all the building loads and panels are usually infilled with insulated stud framing. The method gives a very fast build time and of course has the added attraction that the frame can be left visible on the interior.

Stud frames are more common and have even been used by some of the volume housebuilders – normally clad with brickwork on the outside although wooden cladding works just as well. Vertical studs are placed at regular intervals to form the basic frame and accept all the structural loads of the building including the upper floors and roof. The resultant void can then be filled with insulating material. As a finishing board is used on the inside face, it is not easy to tell from the inside that a timber frame construction has been used rather than a conventional masonry construction but there is the satisfaction of building with natural materials which have a low embodied energy.

Photo: Oak-Apple Frames

STRAW BALES

Straw is a waste product. It is inert, hard to ignite when compressed and of little interest to vermin as it contains negligible amounts of food. Foundations need to be raised to a sufficient level to avoid the bales becoming damp but as long as straw is kept relatively dry it has a life expectancy similar to conventional building materials. Rammed earth within old car tyres has been used as a low-impact foundation design for straw-bale buildings.

There are two principal types of straw-bale construction

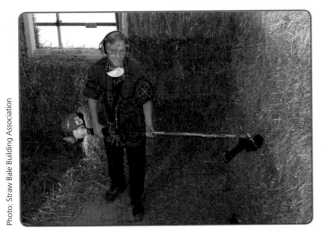

Photo: Straw Bale Building Association

– load-bearing and non-load-bearing. In load-bearing straw-bale buildings the bales take the place of whatever normally holds up the upper floors and the roof. Essentially this is Lego on a giant scale, the bales being placed on top of each other in a stretcher bond pattern. Hazel pins are driven down through the bales to provide a positive connection between the layers.

The other way to use straw bales is to build a primary frame out of timber which accepts all the structural loads. The bales are then used to infill the panel walls. This avoids the risk of compression of the bales but still takes advantage of the excellent insulating properties of straw.

In both cases the bales are then coated with lime render. The use of lime is important here as it is much more flexible than cement and can accommodate

Photo: ARCO2

minor movements. Lime render will sometimes self-heal when cracks occur. It also breathes, which is essential as vapour must be allowed to pass through the bales.

For further information visit

www.strawbalebuildingassociation.org.uk

HEMP

The fibres extracted from the hemp plant have a wide variety of uses including rope, paper and clothing. The residual material, including pith and sap, is known as hurds. The hurds can be processed and then combined with lime to make a type of lightweight concrete which is a highly effective building product.

Photo: Suffolk Housing Society

Photo: Suffolk Housing Society

Many houses have now been built of this material in France and there are a handful in England and Canada. A lightweight timber stud frame is built and shuttering panels are fixed temporarily to both sides. The resulting void is then infilled with a hurd/lime mix and compressed. The mix sets to give rigidity and strength and the panels are then removed. Hemp is an excellent insulator,

Photo: Suffolk Housing Society

is water resistant, and can be trowelled to a finish for the internal walls. One single building element can therefore replace the five or six elements that commonly make up walls in newly constructed houses in the UK, offering savings in time and material costs. Hemp is also much lighter than other aggregates, so it is possible that foundation widths can also be reduced.

The experimental hemp buildings at Haverhill in Suffolk were part of a larger development where 'conventional' buildings were constructed alongside similarly designed hemp buildings to compare their performance. In summary, the hemp houses have proved very comfortable to live in and, once builders become familiar with the construction

Photo: Suffolk Housing Society

Hemp homes.

method, the costs should be equivalent to (or less than) the costs of 'conventional' construction. For further information and results of the tests visit **www.suffolkhousing.org**

Blocks made from hemp and lime are now available and may soon offer a realistic alternative to conventional cementitious blocks.

Photo: Lime Technology Limited

Hemp block.

COB

Cob is an ancient building material and there are many cob houses still standing in the UK, mainly in the South-West. It generally consists of wet clay subsoil mixed with straw and laid in layers to form walls approximately 2ft thick, gaining strength as it dries. Cob is regaining popularity among eco-builders as it is a natural material

which provides very good insulation and thermal mass. It also has negligible embodied energy as it is generally used at the site where the mud is dug. Cob is permeable to air and moisture so it needs protection from driving rain but

Cob in construction.

Photo: Genesis Project

any coatings must allow the walls to breathe. It can also be pressed into blocks which are then laid with an earth or earth/lime mortar.

CLAY BLOCKS

Clay-block construction is common in Europe but as yet few projects have made use of this technology in the UK. As with hemp construction, one building element can replace the complex series of materials used to make up the average wall. Some fired clay systems are designed so that the large blocks interlock and no mortar is required; others only require a thin joint. Either system will deliver reduced build times and the structure of the blocks gives a superior thermal performance in comparison to conventional blocks. Unfired clay blocks are more commonly used for internal partitioning and to add thermal mass.

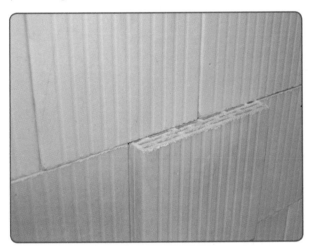

Clay block.

Rammed earth wall finished with beeswax.

RAMMED EARTH

Rammed earth is similar to cob in that the principal component is subsoil. Subsoils vary widely so a small amount of cement is often added as a binder. A vertical channel 300–450mm wide is constructed, into which the earth mixture is poured. The earth is then compacted approximately every 300mm in depth before the formwork is removed. The resultant wall is extremely strong and decorative materials can be added to the mix or designs can be carved in the formwork to improve the appearance. Due to its density, rammed earth provides good thermal mass and excellent sound insulation.

EARTH/CLAY PLASTERS

Earth and clay plasters have essentially the same ingredients as cob and rammed earth, with the addition of more sand, water or cow dung to increase workability and achieve a smooth finish. Lime can be added to increase strength, depending on the nature of the available soil. Earthen plasters can be applied over cob walls or over wooden lath structures – otherwise known as wattle and daub. In many parts of the world these are still the most common plastering materials.

For further information see: *The Natural Plaster Book* by Cedar Rose Guelberth and Dan Chiras, New Society Publishers (2003).

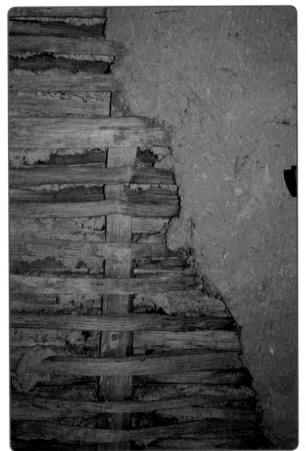

3 REDUCING HEAT LOSS

Photo: www.aranservices.co.uk

This chapter explains the importance of insulation and then takes a detailed look at the potential for improving various ages of property. Focussing on the main elements of a building, we look at what can be done to reduce heat loss from common roof structures, wall and floor types and windows. We also cover the importance of draught-proofing and maintaining the balance between air tightness and the need for fresh air.

Why insulate?

OWNERS AND OCCUPIERS

The domestic sector accounts for approximately 30% of the UK's total energy use.

Over 60% of domestic energy use is for space heating. When most of our housing stock was built there was little understanding of how buildings perform thermally. Poorly-insulated older houses leak energy which is then dissipated and lost. Reducing energy consumption for space heating by the effective use of insulation will make a significant difference to CO_2 emissions and will certainly save money.

When renovating property it is more effective to spend effort and money retaining heat before considering any investment in renewable sources of heat generation. In crude financial terms, the cost of heating an uninsulated house is nearly three times that of heating a modern well-insulated property of the same living area.

The chart below illustrates the cost-effectiveness of insulation in comparison to most other forms of investment designed to save CO_2 (or energy).

Insulation therefore not only reduces the environmental impact of housing, but also saves money in the medium term. Increasingly, houses are rated through Energy Performance Certificates (EPCs), so it is likely that a well-insulated house which is in theory cheaper to run will

Above: Thermally uninsulated and insulated properties.
Below: Thermal image of city from above.

command a higher price in the resale market. *It could therefore be a false economy not to insulate on the grounds that the payback period appears to be longer than the time you plan to stay in the property.*

It's worth pointing out that the full savings from improved insulation will only be realised if heating controls are sufficiently responsive to adjust and turn down the heating where necessary. In some cases this may require upgrading controls – as explained in Chapter 4 – Heating. Where houses are previously underheated, improved insulation may result in higher living temperatures rather than reduced heat demand. This is known as the 'comfort factor' – and needs to be taken into account in any calculations of expected savings.

Old buildings present particular challenges and it may not be possible or desirable to apply insulation in the same way as can be achieved in modern buildings. A recommended approach to old buildings is set out in Chapter 1 and it would be wise to check the guidance published by English Heritage if you are contemplating improvements to any building constructed before 1920.

RENTED PROPERTY

Private rented property is a much more difficult subject, as the person responsible for the structure of the building is not the person responsible for paying the heating bills. The 2011

Graph: Property Tectonics (Carbon in Homes Assessment)

Return on investment (kg CO_2 saved per £1 spent)

0.001   0.01   0.1   1   10

- Upgrade incandescent lightbulbs to CFLs (to all rooms)
- Insulate cavity walls (As built)
- Upgrade old boiler to combi boiler and remove hot water cylinder
- Install internal solid wall insulation to solid walls
- Insulation loft to current building regs stands (<=50mm)
- Upgrade controls to include TRV's
- Add hot water cylinder thermostat
- Upgrade old boiler to new efficient boiler (condensing)
- Insulate flat roof externally
- Insulate ground floor
- Install solar hot water panel
- Upgrade single glazed windows to double glazed windows
- Install air source heat pump in place of boiler
- Install 4m^2 solar PV panels

Energy Bill seeks to address this question and make it easier for tenants to get their landlords to improve the energy efficiency of the building. It is proposed that:

- from April 2016, domestic landlords should not be able to unreasonably refuse requests from their tenants for consent to energy efficiency improvements, where financial support is available, such as the Green Deal and/or the Energy Company Obligation (see below).
- from April 2018, all private rented properties (domestic and non-domestic) should be brought up to a minimum energy efficiency standard rating, likely to be set at EPC rating 'E'. This requirement would be subject to there being no upfront financial cost to landlords. Where there are costs on landlords (such as time or hassle costs), we are committed to ensuring the benefits meet or exceed these. The intention is that landlords would have fulfilled this requirement if they had either reached 'E' or carried out the maximum package of measures funded under the Green Deal and/or ECO (even if this does not take them above an 'F' rating).

In the meantime, landlords can claim a tax allowance on energy saving improvements. The Landlord's Energy Saving Allowance (LESA) can be claimed by private or corporate landlords, with the exception of properties covered under the Rent-a-Room scheme, and those let for furnished holiday accommodation. The LESA is set at a maximum of £1,500 per annum and is due to be available until 1 April 2015. The allowance covers investments in:

- Cavity wall insulation
- Solid wall insulation
- Draught proofing
- Hot water system insulation
- Floor insulation [1]

The Green Deal

At the time of writing, the Green Deal has been announced but not yet finalised. The basic idea is that homeowners should be able to borrow money from private lenders to finance energy-saving home improvements, and to repay the loans through a charge on electricity bills. Loans of up to £10,000 are expected to be made available through Green Deal 'Providers' who are likely to be recognised institutions such as energy suppliers and financial services companies.

Loans would attach to the property rather than to a person, so that when a property changes hands, the new owners take on both the costs and the benefits of the improvements. The maximum Green Deal loan is expected to twenty five years.

The 'Golden Rule' of the Green Deal is that the expected financial savings from any measure (or combination of measures) must be greater than the costs attached to the energy bill. The measures installed must have been recommended for that property by an accredited, objective adviser who has carried out an assessment, although details of the both the assessment and the accreditation have yet to be published. The measures must also be installed by an

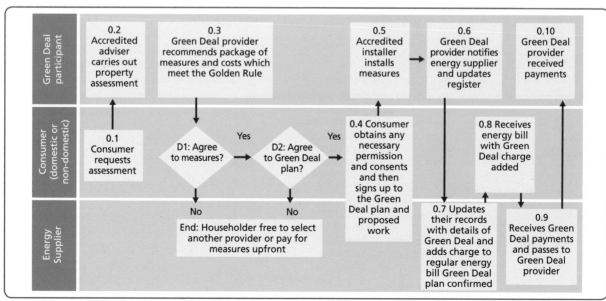

Source: DECC: Green Deal - Summary of the Government's Proposals 2010.

accredited installer, which prevents DIY enthusiasts (including readers of this manual) from taking advantage of the lower costs that this can deliver – and generating 'sweat equity'.

For updated information see **www.decc.gov.uk**

The Green Deal covers England, Scotland and Wales. In Northern Ireland the "Green New Deal" is expected to provide a similar stimulus to retrofitting the housing sector, along with other energy-related initiatives.

SUPPORT FOR LOW INCOME AND VULNERABLE HOUSEHOLDS AND HARD TO TREAT HOMES

A new Energy Company Obligation (ECO) will come into force at the same time as the Green Deal. Under this obligation, "energy companies will be required to focus their assistance on low income and vulnerable households as well as those in hard to treat properties which cannot achieve financial savings without a measure of support, helping them manage their bills for the long term and heat their homes more affordably."

The ECO replaces the subsidy schemes CERT and CESP when the Green Deal is introduced in 2012.

PAYBACK PERIODS

A payback period is the amount of time that it will take for an investment in an energy saving measure to repay the homeowner by means of reduced fuel bills. While payback periods for insulation of specific structural elements are quoted in some publications, insulation tends to be applied as part of a package of energy efficiency measures, including draughtproofing, which is one of the most important.

For example: if you are confident that you will save £200 per year from a measure costing £1,000, the simple payback period would be 5 years. There are often other factors to be taken into account such as increased or reduced maintenance.

In practice the precise amount of money that can be saved by the application of insulation in specific cases is extremely difficult to quantify, so payback periods have not been included here. Energy use in homes is a complex function of building structure and services, patterns of occupation and lifestyle, so the effects of improvement measures in practice will vary widely. At the time of publication, the methodology for estimating reductions under the Green Deal has not yet been published but this will be important – as it will determine whether a measure meets the 'Golden Rule' and thus qualify for Green Deal finance (see above).

The minimum amount of insulation which is required for upgrading any thermal element will, in any case, usually be determined by the Building Regulations.

HOW TO READ AN EPC

If you live in a house that has changed hands or been rented out since October 2008 then an Energy Performance Certificate should have been produced for that dwelling. EPCs are valid for 10 years.

The rating tells you how efficient your house currently is, and gives an idea of the potential for improvement. Older houses constructed without insulation will tend to be in the E-G categories whereas newer houses will normally be in the B-C categories. The national average is D. EPCs are calculated by looking at the *theoretical* energy use of the property, based on information collected about size of rooms, type of heating system, lighting, glazing and building fabric. Actual energy use may of course vary widely, as people use buildings differently.

The EPC should be accompanied by an advisory report which suggests measures that would improve the energy performance of the property. It is important to realise that these measures are produced generically and there may be reasons why certain measures are not appropriate for your property – i.e. it is no substitute for a bespoke assessment by a surveyor or builder experienced in the practical challenges of efficiency retrofit measures. In theory, by following these measures, it should be possible to improve the energy performance to achieve the rating indicated in the right hand column of the EPC certificate.

ADVICE LINE

For further information on energy efficiency and the Green Deal call 0300 123 1234 (England, Wales and Northern Ireland) or 0800 512 012 (Scotland).

Insulation values

It is possible to design and insulate a new house in such a way that no space heating is required at all. The heat generated from passive solar gains and from occupation – that is from lights, from cooking, from the occupants themselves – can be sufficient to maintain a comfortable internal temperature in all but the most extreme climates. This requires that the heat generated by occupation is retained within the building and that ventilation systems recover heat which would otherwise be lost with the exhausted air.

Older housing presents much more of a challenge when it comes to insulation as the structure already exists and floor heights are largely determined by staircases or by door and window lintels. In addition, the doors and windows themselves may be an essential part of the character of the building. Insulating an existing building therefore requires a series of compromises and the measures necessary or possible will vary widely according to house type and date of construction.

Working out how much insulation to add to a house can be a complicated process because:

- The effectiveness of different types of insulation varies widely
- Certain types of insulation are not appropriate in some locations
- Some houses already have some insulation present
- Different elements of a house require varying levels of insulation
- An integrated package of measures also needs to include allowances for ventilation and heating
- Building Regulations specify certain minimum requirements and these have changed recently.

THICKNESS OF INSULATION

The amount of insulation required will vary according to which element is to be insulated, which will then determine the target U-value to be achieved (see the 'Elemental U-values' table on pages 48–49). Insulation materials also vary in their effectiveness, otherwise known as resistivity. A greater thickness of a material with a low resistivity will be needed in order to give the same resistance as that from a material with a high resistivity.

Resistance = Resistivity x Thickness.

TECHIE CORNER: U-VALUES

Definition

A U-value is a measure of how much heat is conducted through a particular section of construction. The lower the U-value, the better insulated the structure is. For example, a wall with a U-value of 1.0 will lose heat twice as fast as a wall with a U-value of 0.5.

How to work out a u-value

All materials, however thin, have some thermal resistance. The higher the resistances, the less heat gets let through. The resistances of all the separate elements in a construction, together with their thicknesses, need to be considered. Added together, these give the total resistance or R. U-values are calculated by working out the reciprocal of the total resistance ($U = 1/R$). If R is large, U will be small. In other words, the greater the resistance, the lower the U-value.

In practice, the resistance of individual materials tends to be quoted whereas U-values are used to refer to the conductivity of a whole structure. For example, working from outside to inside, a typical 1970s cavity wall construction in the UK might consist of an outer layer of brickwork, a cavity, and inner skin of non-insulating blockwork, plaster and paint.

The total resistance for this type of wall construction is therefore 0.67. The U-value of this type of wall construction is therefore:

$$U = 1/0.68 = 1.47 \text{ W/m}^2\text{K}.[2]$$

Such a construction would conduct heat at a rate of 1.50 watts (W) per square metre (m^2) for every degree of temperature difference (K) between the inner and the outer surfaces of the wall.

Typical 1970s wall construction

Brick outer skin

50mm Cavity

Dense concrete blocks

Plaster

Element	Thickness	R-value
External Resistance (Rse)		0.04
Brick	100mm	0.14
Unventilated Cavity	50mm	0.18
Blockwork	100mm	0.16
Gypsum Plaster	15mm	0.03
Internal Resistance (Rsi)		0.13
Total		0.68

Source: Building Research Establishment

Manufacturers often quote conductivity values (λ) rather than resistivity.

Conductivity = 1/Resistivity

A low conductivity value indicates an efficient insulant.

In practice, the calculation of required thicknesses to meet specific U-values is carried out by manufacturers. The calculations take into account the U-value of the existing wall and the thermal bridging through any stud fixing system used.

REGULATION CORNER
Building Regulations on insulation

In 2006 (now revised 2010), the Building Regulations for England and Wales introduced a requirement that any replacement of a thermal element (for example a roof, wall or floor) must, by law, be carried out to the thermal standards set out in Approved Document L1B. The element in question must be insulated to specified U-values which are set out in the next section. However, the stipulation goes further than this. Wherever a new *finished surface* is created the regulations apply, so replacement of a floor deck or screed, re-roofing, or even dry-lining or rendering a wall, could all trigger the Building Regulations, depending on what proportion of the relevant area is being refurbished. If in doubt, consult your local authority 'Building Control' department. If the regulations are triggered, an application or notice to the local office must be made, along with the associated fees.[3]

There are certain exceptions to the values laid down in Approved Document L1B and Building Control may be prepared to accept higher U-values where a calculation shows that the insulation will not pay back financially within 15 years, or that it is impractical to fit the required levels of insulation in certain locations, or that the floor area of a room would be decreased by more than 5%. Where it is impractical to meet the target values it is possible to 'trade off' reduced insulation for one element of a structure for enhanced insulation in another. This is subject to certain limits for individual elements.

Under self-certification schemes, work can be carried out by a 'competent person' who may issue a certificate to the local authority to demonstrate that the works have been carried out in accordance with the regulations, rather than requiring a visit from Building Control. The replacement of doors and windows, for example, is covered by several self-certification schemes. It is worth noting that there are substantial fines for non-compliance and that the responsibility for compliance rests with the person who orders the work – in many cases this will be the householder.

It is also worth noting that while Building Regulations are stringent on levels of insulation and there are increasingly powerful means of enforcement, the regulations are silent on questions of embodied energy, resource depletion and the potential toxicity of some of the materials (or their manufacturing and disposal processes) which may be required to achieve compliance with the current standards.

For information on regulations in Scotland see: 'The Domestic Technical Handbook (2011)' and the Building (Scotland) Amendment Regulations 2011.
Visit **www.sbsa.gov.uk**

For information on the application of regulations in Northern Ireland see: Building Regulations Northern Ireland (2000), 'DFP Technical Booklet F1: 2006 – Conservation of fuel and power in dwellings'.
Visit **www.dfpni.gov.uk/building-regulations**

2010 Building Regulations require the following U-values when elements of a property are upgraded or replaced (or cavities infilled):

Element	Typical original U-value	Required U-value
Uninsulated floors	1.00	0.25
Solid 9in external brick walls	2.10	0.30
Cavity Walls	1.50	0.55
Pitched roof (with insulation at ceiling level) (100mm already)	0.44	0.16
Pitched roof (with insulation at rafters) (none already)	1.90	0.18
Flat roof	1.00	0.18

Source EST and Approved Document L1B (2010)

Notify Building Control when:

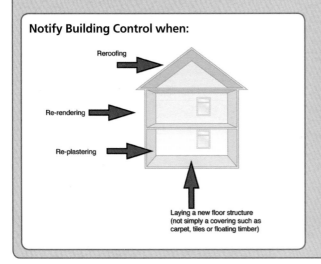

Reroofing

Re-rendering

Re-plastering

Laying a new floor structure (not simply a covering such as carpet, tiles or floating timber)

WHAT TO USE WHERE

The table shows which products are commonly used for particular applications.

The domestic insulation market has recently seen the development of innovative high performance aerogel and vacuum panel insulants, as well as multifoil products[1].

Note that the coloured cells indicate only the most common uses – the fact a cell is blank does not necessarily mean that the type of insulation is not used for the application.

Key:

1 Multifoil products work by reflecting radiated heat back into the internal space, and unlike other insulants are not assessed via a hot box test. For this reason their thermal conductivity is less crucial as a performance characteristic. Total wall thickness to achieve U=0.25 W/m²K is 380mm and include 85mm supplementary PU (pentane) insulation.

2 U-values calculated based on 9" solid brick wall, internally applied insulation (with battens and/or air gap where appropriate) and 125mm plasterboard. Fixings and air movement accounted for in calculated figures. All thicknesses rounded to nearest 5mm.

3 The thermal conductivity ranges are the minimum and maximum obtained by UK manufacturers (or suppliers) and those given in the European Thermal Values publication [Final report to the Thermal Values Group (March 1999) submitted to DG XII of the European Commission].

4 The effect of low emissivity surfaces has been included in U-value calculations.

5 Monolithic insulant thicknesses quoted exclude external render and internal plastered finish.

6 Flexible thermal linings are thin layers designed to be applied directly to a solid wall, prior to finishes. A solid wall with 10mm flexible thermal lining will achieve a U-value of approximately 1.5W/m²K.

Insulation materials chart

Highest performance	Vacuum Insulated Panels
	Aerogel
Polyurethane (PU)	Polyurethane with pentane up to 32kg/m³
	Polyurethane soy-based
	Foil-faced polyurethane with pentane up to 32kg/m³
	Polyurethane with CO_2
	In-situ applied Polyurethane (sprayed or injected)
Polyisocyanurate (PIR)	Polyisocyanurate up to 32kg/m³
	Foil-faced polyisocyanurate up to 32kg/m³
	In-situ applied polyisocyanurate (sprayed)
Phenolic foam (PF)	Phenolic foam
	Foil-faced phenolic foam
Expanded Polystyrene (EPS)	Expanded Polystyrene up to 30kg/m³
	Expanded Polystyrene with graphite (grey)
Extruded Polystyrene (XPS)	Extruded Polystyrene with CO_2
	Extruded Polystyrene with HFC 35kg/m³
Wool and fibre	Glass wool [up to 48kg/m³]
	Glass wool [equal/greater than 48kg/m³]
	Stone wool [less than 160kg/m³]
	Stone wool [160kg/m³]
	Sheep's wool [25kg/m³]
	Cellulose fibre [dry blown 24kg/m³]
	Hemp fibre
	Polyester fibre
	Wood fibre (WF)
Alternative	Hemp line (monolithic)
	Cotton
	Cork [120kg/m³]
	Vermiculite
	Perlite (expanded) board
	Cellular glass (CG)
	Flexible thermal linings
	Strawboard [420g/m³]
	Straw bale

Source: Energy Saving Trust, Insulation Materials Chart (CE71)

Insulant thickness (mm) to achieve U-value = 0.25W.m²/k²	Range of Thermal Conductivities[3] (W/mK) Lower numbers indicate better thermal performance								
	00.0	0.01	0.02	0.03	0.04	0.05	0.06	0.07	0.08
30	0.008								
50–55		0.013 / 0.014							
105–115			0.027	0.03					
100–145			0.026	0.038					
75[4]			0.02						
130				0.035					
80–100			0.023 / 0.028						
95–105			0.025 / 0.028						
80–85[4]			0.022 / 0.023						
80–100			0.023 / 0.028						
80–95			0.020 / 0.025						
75–85[4]			0.020 / 0.023						
115–165				0.03	0.045				
115–120				0.03 / 0.032					
95–140			0.025	0.037					
110–120			0.029	0.031					
135–180				0.03	0.044				
155				0.036					
150–160				0.034 / 0.038					
160–170				0.037	0.040				
150–215				0.034		0.054			
150–190				0.035	0.046				
165				0.039					
150–180				0.035	0.044				
145–225				0.039			0.061		
260[5]							0.067			Monolithic
165–170				0.039	0.04				
155–200					0.041	0.055			
235				0.039			0.06		
190						0.051			
140–185				0.038		0.05			
n/a[6]					0.04		0.063		
295									0.081
175–235[5]					0.047		0.063			Monolithic

Typical applications

Roofs: Insulation on pitch | Ceiling insulation | Flat roof

Walls: Internal insulation | External insulation | Cavity (full fill) | Cavity (partial fill) | Timber frame | Steel frame | Panel

Floors: Solid concrete | Suspended beam & block | Suspended timber

Roof insulation

The greatest heat loss from domestic property is generally through the roof because the roof is the part of the house most exposed to the elements and because warm air rises

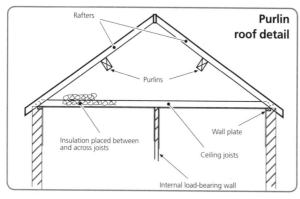

Purlin
roof detail

Rafters

Purlins

Wall plate

Insulation placed between and across joists

Ceiling joists

Internal load-bearing wall

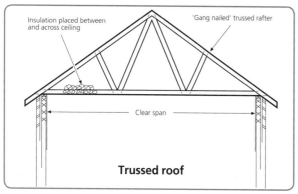

Insulation placed between and across ceiling

'Gang nailed' trussed rafter

Clear span

Trussed roof

so heat tends to be concentrated on the top floor. Building Regulations therefore require a lower U-value for the roof structure than for any other element of a house. In summer months, attic rooms can easily overheat as a result of direct solar gains passing through the roof structure so the addition of insulation will also help to combat this problem.

When considering how best to insulate a roof, it is first necessary to work out how it is constructed and to ensure that ventilation is maintained, if the structure was originally designed to be ventilated. Failure to do this can lead to condensation or the trapping of leaked water, which can lead to outbreaks of dry rot, which can in turn cause structural failure. It's therefore important to get the detailing right.

PITCHED ROOFS WITHOUT A ROOM IN THE ATTIC

It is normally straightforward to install roof insulation to these types of buildings as insulation can be placed over the flat ceiling of the rooms on the top floor. Care must be taken to avoid damaging any electric cables which run over this ceiling structure and cables should not be covered by the insulation as they can overheat. Similarly, any recessed lights should have a sealed air space around them to prevent overheating. The ceiling structure itself will normally be capable of supporting the small additional load, but if there is any doubt the opinion of a suitably qualified professional should be sought.

Where insulation is already present and more is required to bring it up to the latest recommended level, current advice is to leave the existing insulation where it is and place the new insulation over the top, but laid at right angles to the existing. For example, 100mm of mineral wool has

Warmcel loose insulation.

Photo: Excel Industries Ltd

been already installed in many properties. To achieve the current recommended U-value of 0.16W/m^{2}K using mineral wool, 250mm would be required. Subtracting the 100mm already present, this would require an additional 150mm to be laid, or slightly less if using a renewable product such as sheepswool, hemp or cellulose.

A boarded passage will be needed to access tanks and other essential services, as the thicker insulation will obscure the ceiling joists. When loft insulation is increased, the temperature in the attic will be reduced in cold weather, so water tanks located above the insulation will themselves need to be insulated. Omitting the insulation directly beneath the tank but returning it up the side and over the top of the tank will help to prevent freezing while maintaining the continuity of the loft insulation.

This kind of attic is normally ventilated at the eaves. If insulation is pushed into the eaves without making provision for ventilation the airflow through the roof will be

interrupted and any water which finds its way in will be trapped and will not be able to evaporate easily. Eaves ventilators can be used to ensure that this does not occur.

Lastly, don't forget to insulate and draughtproof the loft hatch!

PITCHED ROOFS WITH A ROOM IN THE ATTIC

The insulation of houses with attic rooms is more complex because they do not have space available above the living accommodation, so the insulation must follow the line of the rafters.

While re-roofing a property, insulation can be fitted on top of the rafters. This is known as a warm roof because the structure (rafters and ridge beam) is then encapsulated within the insulated envelope of the building. However, this is inappropriate for terraced streets – as the roofline will not be able to follow the rest of the terrace or any other location where ridge or eave height is a sensitive issue. Economically and environmentally, insulating above the rafters is only worth considering at the same time as re-roofing a property.

In all other cases the choice comes down to fitting insulation between the rafters, under the rafters, or a combination of both. The decision must take into account the following factors:

■ Insulation placed under rafters reduces headroom, which may be an important consideration in an attic
■ Rafters act as a thermal bridge – heat can pass through the timber, albeit at a reduced rate, even if there is insulation between the rafters
■ Where insulation is being placed between the rafters it is important to leave a gap above the insulation to preserve the crossflow ventilation in the roof
■ The risk of interstitial condensation

For example, where there are 100mm (4in) rafters, 50mm of phenolic foam insulation could be placed between the rafters, allowing 50mm for ventilation above the insulation. Next, the ceiling could be under-lined with 80mm of phenolic foam insulation.

Left: Insulation on flat ceilings.
Right: Rafters before addition of insulation.

Insulation added internally to pitched roof

(diagram labels: Batten, Slate, Roofing felt, 100mm Rafter, 50mm Phenolic foam insulation, Vapour control layer, 80mm Phenolic foam insulation, Plasterboard)

Finally a vapour control layer and plasterboard are normally added. This would reduce the U-value of the roof to 0.18, which would conform with the new regulations.[4]

Substitution by less efficient materials may have other environmental benefits but a greater depth of material would be required. Similarly, reducing the thickness of under-lined insulation to preserve headroom would also reduce the insulative value and therefore would not comply with the Building Regulations, although it may be possible to argue successfully for reductions in some circumstances.

Where rafters are only 75mm deep, effective rafter depth can be increased by fixing battens to the undersides of the rafters. In some cases it may be possible to reduce the ventilation gap above the insulation to 25mm. The additional load of the insulation plus finished surface on the rafters should in any case be checked by a suitably qualified professional.

Where the finished surface follows the rafters all the way to the apex of the roof, care must be taken to ensure that the ventilation is not compromised at the apex. This can easily happen if insulated plasterboard is placed hard up against the ridge beam.

This can be avoided either by installing ridge vents, which requires access to the roof and can be a significant expense, or by flattening the ceiling at the top to preserve the crossflow ventilation.

INTERSTITIAL CONDENSATION

When installing insulation to the underside of rafters, the possibility of interstitial condensation must be addressed (see the technical note at the end of the next section). Manufacturers of insulation will normally carry out calculations and assess whether the addition of insulation to a pitched roof will give rise to any risk of interstitial condensation and may recommend the incorporation of a vapour control layer on the warm side of the insulation prior to applying the finished surface.

FLAT ROOFS

Flat roofs are normally designed to be walked on, so in general there will be no structural issues relating to added insulation. Insulation can be added above, below or between the roof members (joists/rafters) to achieve the U-value of 0.18 W/m²K required by the 2010 regulations.

(diagram labels: Weatherproof membrane, Rigid insulation with R-value greater than 3.7m²K/W, Weatherproof membrane, Timber or concrete deck)

As with pitched roofs, if the insulation is added over the top of the structure this is known as a 'warm roof'. In some cases, as long as the structure and decking is sound, insulation can be added without having to remove the existing covering. Either a new weatherproof layer can be added over the top or ballast can be laid to hold down the insulation, which means that the weatherproof layer underneath must still be watertight to keep out any water which seeps through the joints in the insulation. Details are best agreed with the manufacturer of the insulation chosen, and with the installer. If ballast is used, the roof must be capable of supporting the additional load.

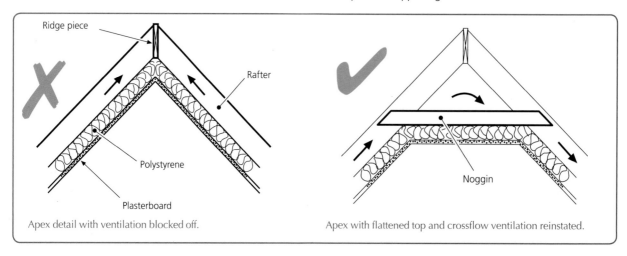

Apex detail with ventilation blocked off.

(left diagram labels: Ridge piece, Rafter, Polystyrene, Plasterboard)

Apex with flattened top and crossflow ventilation reinstated.

(right diagram label: Noggin)

DECISION TREE FOR INSULATION OF PITCHED ROOFS

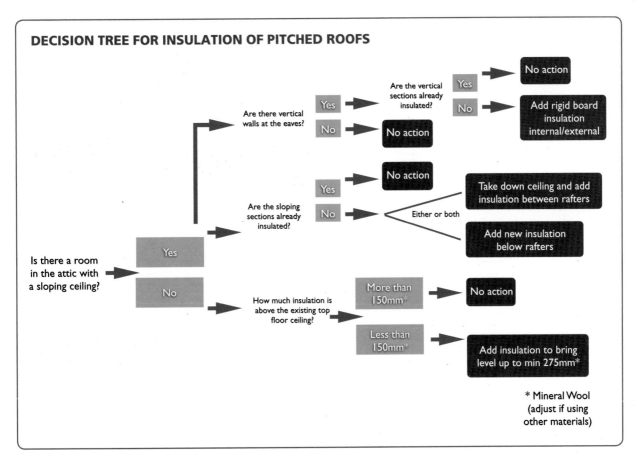

Is there a room in the attic with a sloping ceiling?

Yes → Are the sloping sections already insulated?
- **Yes** → No action
- **No** → Either or both → Take down ceiling and add insulation between rafters / Add new insulation below rafters

Are there vertical walls at the eaves?
- **Yes** → Are the vertical sections already insulated?
  - **Yes** → No action
  - **No** → Add rigid board insulation internal/external
- **No** → No action

No → How much insulation is above the existing top floor ceiling?
- **More than 150mm*** → No action
- **Less than 150mm*** → Add insulation to bring level up to min 275mm*

* Mineral Wool (adjust if using other materials)

Wall insulation

TYPES OF WALL CONSTRUCTION

Before considering insulation to walls it is first necessary to work out how the walls of your house are constructed, in order to work out the U-value of the existing structure. Wall construction evolved considerably during the 20th century so it is helpful to know when your house was built. Note that these dates are only general guides and in all cases the exact nature of the construction should be ascertained by careful investigation on site.

Up to 1930s
- 9" Solid brick
- Plaster

1930s–1960s
- Brick
- 2" Cavity
- Wall ties
- Concrete block
- Plaster

1970s
- Brick
- 2" Cavity
- Insulating block
- Plaster

1995 onwards
- Brick
- 100mm Cavity partially or fully filled
- Insulating block
- Plasterboard on dabs

Summary and U-values of existing masonry walls

Construction	U-value (W/m²k)
1. Solid masonry 225mm (9in)	2.10
2. Brick, 50mm cavity, block	1.60
3. Brick, 50mm cavity, insulated block	1.00
4. Brick, 50mm cavity, 50mm insulation, insulated block	0.40
4. Brick, 50mm cavity, 65mm insulation, insulated block	0.35
6. Brick, 90mm insulation, insulated block	0.30

SOLID WALLS

This wall has some bricks at right angles to the face of the wall, known as 'headers', which act to tie the two skins of brickwork together. This is almost certainly a solid brick wall with no cavity, typical of Georgian, Victorian and Edwardian property.

Solid wall, no cavity, header bricks arrowed.

Where there is no cavity in the structure, insulation can be added either on the inside or on the outside. Also refer to the note on interstitial condensation at the end of this section.

EXTERNAL SOLID WALL INSULATION

External wall insulation is the addition of insulation on the exterior side of the walls, and covering it with a new weathertight layer. Insulating the outside of a property has the advantage that the original masonry within the insulation acts as 'thermal mass'. Heat which is generated inside the property is stored within the masonry walls, which then act as a reservoir or storage heater. The heat is retained by the new insulated outer skin. There is no loss of living space within the property.

There are a number of methods of covering or 'cladding' the insulation once installed, including timber rain screens, cement or lime renders and other bespoke systems including boards manufactured from wood fibre, which have the lowest environmental impact of all.

The roofline has to be extended to take account of the increased thickness of the walls, windows may need to be reinstalled and wider cills will be required. Drainage pipes have to be adjusted and external pathways may need to be widened, so the process can be very expensive.

External wall insulation is inappropriate for older buildings (especially our Victorian and Edwardian housing stock) where

Above: External wall pre-insulation.

Right and below: External wall during installation.

External wall after insulation.

Photos: archipelago architects

External insulation (plan view)

- Render finish to insulation
- Original masonry wall
- Vertical battens

External insulation: Roof line adjustment

- Tiles on battens
- Breather 'membrane'
- Extend rafter as necessary
- Rafter birdsmouthed onto wall plate
- Loose fill insulation restrained with ventilation tray
- New gutter on ventilated boxed eaves
- External insulation with render finish on vertical battens
- Insulation between and across ceiling joists
- Original masonry wall

the appearance of brickwork or stonework needs to be maintained. On the other hand, where the walls have already been rendered, the addition of external insulation makes little difference to the appearance of the building if a similar rendered finish is applied afterwards, although the eaves details will often be changed.

INTERNAL SOLID WALL INSULATION

Where external insulation is not possible, or where the external appearance of the building is important, insulation can be added to the internal surface of the walls. It will be necessary to refer to the note on interstitial condensation at the end of this section. The main disadvantage to internal insulation of solid masonry walls is that space will be lost on the inner face of the external walls. There will be no thermal mass in the wall within the insulated shell of the building so the building will heat up more quickly but also cool down more quickly than an externally insulated dwelling.

After any electrical or plumbing services have been disconnected, and skirting boards and other projections have been removed and made good, rigid insulation boards faced with plasterboard can be glued directly to the internal face of the wall.

Alternatively, vertical treated timber battens can be plugged and screwed to the wall, spaced to suit the insulation and the plasterboard. Rigid or semi-rigid insulation material can then be friction-fitted between the vertical studs. A vapour control layer may be required over the entire

Internal insulation

- Mechanical fixings if required
- Adhesive
- Batten for fixing skirting

Direct glued method

- Vertical timber studs at 600mm centres to suit typical 1200mm plasterboard
- Vapour control layer
- Plasterboard
- Insulation inserted between studwork

Stud method

wall before a finishing board is fixed to the studs. The use of studs slightly reduces the effectiveness of the insulation, so boards glued directly to the wall will minimise the amount of space lost within the room. However, it is necessary to check carefully the environmental issues relating not only to the insulation boards but also the glue, as some products may emit toxic fumes over a long period.

The addition of 100mm of mineral wool insulation fitted between studs on the inside of a 220mm solid brick wall would reduce the U-value from 2.10 to 0.35, which meets the current regulations.[5] In this case the loss of area within a room, including the plasterboard and skim, amounts to 115mm along the external walls.

When adding internal insulation, light switches, power outlets and wall lights will all need refitting in their new positions. This is relatively straightforward if there is excess cable which can be pulled through but is otherwise a more demanding task. Electricity cables heat up when carrying current, so hiding cables within insulation can lead to overheating or an increase in disconnection time. If in any doubt, seek advice from a qualified electrician. If there is a window in the wall to be insulated, the windowsill will need to be replaced with a deeper one.

Some insulating dry-lining manufacturers have bespoke metal framing systems that may reduce the thickness of insulation required. An air gap may be required between the insulation and the masonry wall.

THERMAL BRIDGING

Thermal bridging occurs in an otherwise insulated structure where insulation has been missed out. Sometimes this occurs for technical reasons when refurbishing old buildings, as it can be impossible to 'break' the path from inside to outside where the structure is solid and there is no room to add insulation. Moist air will tend to condense on the coldest spots, so condensation or mould growth may form on internal walls for no apparent reason. In addition to ensuring that thermal bridges are avoided, good ventilation will help to prevent condensation from forming.

It is recommended that internal insulation should be returned at window and door reveals (i.e. fitted around the corner up to the frame) to avoid the risk of thermal bridging, where practicable. Where an internal partition wall interrupts an external wall, the insulation cannot be continuous unless the internal wall is partially rebuilt. The current prescription is to return the insulation 300mm along the internal wall to reduce the risk of condensation at that point.

Wall junction post insulation

300mm

TECHIE CORNER: INTERSTITIAL CONDENSATION

Water vapour passes through walls in properties which are not built with integral vapour control layers. Many people assume that the main risk is that rainwater will penetrate from the outside but the problem is often the converse. Water vapour generated by normal occupation of property passes from the inside to the outside of the wall and then evaporates. The temperature is normally higher inside than outside in the UK, so the temperature within an external wall will fall, moving from inside to out.

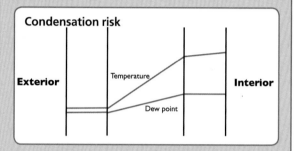

Condensation risk

Exterior

Temperature

Dew point

Interior

Given the relative humidity, if the temperature falls below a critical level the 'dew point temperature' is reached and condensation will occur. If condensation occurs in a cavity, moisture can collect and cause problems. To avoid the risk of interstitial condensation, a vapour control layer should be installed on the warm side of the internal insulation. The sheet must be carefully sealed at any penetrations and any joints lapped and taped.

A vapour control layer may not always be required. Once the insulation material has been selected, the manufacturers are normally prepared to carry out the calculations and advise accordingly. Some green builders are opposed to vapour control layers as they prevent walls from breathing.

There is at present only limited data available on how the addition of internal or external insulation will affect the movement of moisture within walls or within buildings generally, particularly in solid-walled old buildings which have hitherto always been able to breathe. It is also true that different elevations (north/south/east/west) perform differently in terms of their thermal characteristics and rates of absorbing and evaporating moisture, so considerable research is needed before arriving at definitive conclusions on this subject. The Building Regulations do not distinguish between elevations and currently determine the minimum levels of insulation that must be applied but in many cases this will be inappropriate and possibly damaging for solid brick or stone buildings.

CAVITY WALLS

Cavity wall construction was introduced into the UK in the 1930s. If your house was constructed after 1930 it is likely that there is a cavity between the two layers of masonry which make up the external walls. A useful guide as to whether there is a cavity is to look at the pattern of bricks on the outside:

The bricks in this picture, on the other hand, are all running along the face of the wall. The bricks are called stretchers and the expanse of brickwork is referred to as stretcher bond.

Cavity wall, no 'headers'.

The absence of headers indicates that there is probably a cavity between the inner and outer skins of the wall.

Another useful way to find out whether there is a cavity is to measure the thickness of the walls by any entrance door or window. Cavity walls are normally at least 250mm (10in) thick, comprising two skins of 100mm masonry and a 50mm cavity (later cavity walls which include built-in insulation are even thicker). However, solid walls are sometimes as thick as 250mm, as internal plaster, careless bricklaying and external rendering will all have added to the thickness. Sometimes the ground floor of a larger solid wall construction is 1.5 bricks (13.5in) thick up to first floor level and reduces to 9in for the upper floors. Stone walls are much thicker, although if the inside of the construction is also stone it's fairly safe to say that there is no cavity present (as opposed to stone-faced buildings which have a cavity and internal blockwork).

Above: Insulating block. Below: Dense block.

The requirement to insulate houses was only introduced in 1985. The insulation strategy used at that time was to introduce an insulated block in place of the inner skin of dense blockwork.

It is difficult to tell whether an insulated block has been used as it will be covered with plaster on the inside. A good tip is to take the cover off a penetration in the structure to check – for example where a vent or a cat flap has been inserted through a wall. Another way to tell is that insulated blocks are much easier to drill into than dense blocks or brickwork, as they are lightweight and contain plenty of voids/air.

If you are unsure about the construction of your house and you have neighbours who live in similar houses, it is likely that one of them will already know the answer.

CAVITY WALL INSULATION

Where there is already an insulated cavity (4, 5 and 6 in the summary table on page 54) between the two skins of masonry, the potential for savings from adding further insulation to the wall is greatly reduced. The precise calculation is difficult to carry out, but it is important to be aware that, in certain cases, the energy saved over the lifetime of the building may not even exceed the energy required to manufacture, transport and install any additional insulation, given the materials currently available. In some recent house designs the structural cavity is fully filled, so there is no possibility of adding further insulation.

If you live in a house with uninsulated cavity walls, the injection of insulation into the cavity will significantly improve the performance of the building without having to make any disruptive structural alterations. There are two main types of insulation used for injection into cavity walls: loose mineral wool or glass wool, and polystyrene beads.

The installation of cavity wall insulation requires specialist tools it must be carried out by professionals. The environmental impact of insulation products is discussed in more detail in the section on 'Insulation products' in Chapter 2. Normally holes are drilled in the outer skin of masonry and the insulation is blown in under pressure.

Photo: www.aranservices.co.uk

Left: Cavity wall insulation built-in.

Above: Polystyrene beads being injected into cavity.

The holes are then made good with mortar – so there is no significant impact on the occupants.

After loft insulation, this is considered to be the most cost-effective long-term measure to reduce energy losses through building fabric and approximately half the potential homes in the UK have now received cavity wall insulation.

TIMBER-FRAME

Most people are aware if they live in a timber-frame house but it is impossible to tell whether there is a timber frame present simply by looking at the property, as it is common in the UK to clad the outside of timber-frame structures with a skin of brickwork.

Typical UK timber frame construction

- Ply sheathing
- Brick outer layer
- Vapour control layer
- Water resistant membrane
- Metal ties
- Timber studs
- Ventilated cavity
- Plasterboard

Timber-frame buildings are often already insulated, as the void which is created during the construction of the frame will have been filled with insulation when the house was built. If you are unsure as to whether there is insulation in the walls, check any penetrations in the structure such as power points, making sure to turn off the relevant fuse first. Alternatively, remove the plasterboard and open up a small section of wall, taking care to avoid pipes and cables which may be running through the void.

Sometimes a small amount of insulation is present, for example 25mm may have been included when the frame was constructed. Frames are normally a minimum of 90mm deep so in this case a considerable amount of insulation can be added without having to increase the thickness of the wall. However, the requirements of the Building Regulations as explained at the beginning of this chapter should be noted.

If there is no insulation within the frame there are two methods by which it can be added. Either remove the inner skin of plasterboard and fit rigid or semi-rigid insulation between the studs, or drill holes in the plasterboard and blow loose fill insulation into the void. Blowing insulation requires specialist equipment but is less disruptive to the fabric of the building. It is possible that a vapour control layer will have to be added, which would necessitate the removal of the plasterboard in any case – see the note on page 56 on interstitial condensation. If there is a ventilated cavity between the timber frame and a masonry outer skin, this should not be filled with insulation.

DECISION TREE FOR WALL INSULATION

Does your house have solid walls or cavity walls?

Solid Walls → Is the building listed?
- Yes → No action
- No → Is your house in a conservation area?
  - Yes → Consider INTERNAL wall insulation
  - No → Consider INTERNAL or EXTERNAL solid wall insulation

Not sure? → Pre 1920?
- Yes → Is the building listed?
- Unsure → Look for headers (bricks at right angles to wall). If headers present then you probably have solid walls
- No → Cavity Walls

Cavity Walls → Have the cavity walls already been insulated?
- Yes → No action
- No → Install cavity wall insulation
- Unsure → Look for marks on outside of building where insulation may have been injected

Timber/steel frame → Has insulation already been built in?
- Yes → No action
- No → Insulate void in timber frame but not the cavity between frame and cladding

Ground floor insulation

Firstly it is necessary to work out how the ground floor has been constructed. There are four common forms:

- Cellar/Victorian   Pre-1930
- Sleeper/1930s   1930–63
- Concrete slab   1963–90
- Insulated slab   1990–present

Many older properties have a combination of suspended and solid floor types, especially if they were built on a slope. Solid uninsulated concrete ground floors conduct heat directly away into the ground upon which they are laid. The primary heat loss through suspended wooden floors is caused by draughts as the cold air which intentionally circulates below the floor is drawn up into the living areas through gaps in butt-jointed floor timbers. Later timber floors were constructed with tongued-and-grooved boards that reduce or eliminate the draughts from below.

Butt-jointed floor.

T&G floor.

SUSPENDED TIMBER FLOOR WITH CELLAR

Insulating this type of floor is relatively straightforward as access to the underside of the floor is clear. Batt (semi-rigid) insulation can be friction-fitted between the joists and they can be under-lined with netting, hardboard, plasterboard or recycled timber to retain the insulation in position.

Photo: Patrick Stevenson

50 x 175mm Clear span joist

CELLAR

Cellar/Victorian – pre-1930

Sleeper/1930s – 1930–63

50 x 100mm Joist

Honeycombed sleeper wall

Concrete slab – 1963–90

100mm Concrete

D.P.M.

150mm Compacted hardcore

Earth

Insulated slab – 1990–present

65mm Min screed

Building paper

100mm Insulation

100mm Concrete

D.P.M.

150mm Compacted hardcore with soft sand binding

Earth

Insulated slab – 1990–present

50mm Min screed

100mm Concrete

Building paper

100mm Insulation

D.P.M.

150mm Compacted hardcore with soft sand binding

Earth

Evolution of 20th Century floor construction.

Photo: Patrick Stevenson

Above: Sub-floor vent obstructed.
Below: Sub-floor vents protected.

SUSPENDED TIMBER FLOOR CRAWLSPACE/ SLEEPER WALL CONSTRUCTION

Where access to the sub-floor space is restricted it is more difficult to retro-fit insulation, and there are basically two methods by which it can be achieved. Either open up a small section of the floor and persuade a small agile person with no fear of spiders or vermin to crawl in and friction-fit insulation while lying on his/her back, or else completely remove the floor and install the insulation from above.

Where the floor surface is completely removed, netting can be laid over the joists to retain the insulation and avoid having to fix anything to the underside of the joists. The original floor surface can then be fitted back down. It would be a waste of resources to replace good-quality timber floorboards with a sheet material at this point, as the draughts will have been eliminated by the insulation. There are also health concerns about the chemical binders used in some panel products (see section on 'Composite/particle boards' in Chapter 2). If a small number of boards are damaged, cut out the bad sections and replace with new. Most builders' yards carry planed timber which can easily be machined down to the correct width and, after some staining down, it will make a good match.

Alternatively, where the original floor surface is of poor quality and there is no prospect of ever reusing it, draughts can be reduced by fixing hardboard to the surface of the floor. If there is movement in the underlying floor, screwing the hardboard down rather than nailing will prevent the problem of nails lifting after repeated use. Glues are best avoided as some emit a variety of toxic fumes and combining materials with glue makes them difficult to recycle. Draughts also arise from gaps under the skirting boards and from penetrations through the floor to allow for radiator pipes so it is important to seal these gaps at the same time as laying sheet material. Technically this might trigger the requirements of Part L1B but in practice Building Control are unlikely to object to this kind of measure.

Note: The undersides of floors in these types of houses are designed to be ventilated. While insulation is being installed, check to make sure that vents are open and unobstructed – they often get covered by 'improvements'

to front or rear gardens and it is only the gaps in the floorboards that draw through adequate ventilation to prevent rot and mould growth.

UNINSULATED CONCRETE SLAB

This is the most difficult type of floor to insulate, and concrete slabs are very cold surfaces. It is sometimes the case in this type of construction that the load-bearing walls have been built on top of the concrete slab (it will have been thickened under the walls), so even if a homeowner is brave enough to want to break out the floor and insulate

Concrete block
Cavity
Brick
Raft foundation with reinforced concrete

underneath it before relaying concrete, it may not be technically possible to accomplish. Also see the section on radon in Chapter 9 if considering breaking out a solid floor.

Instead, the only practical way to address this problem is to insulate above the floor.

Building Regulations require upgrading insulation to modern standards whenever a new permanent finished surface is added. The maximum U-value is 0.25W/m²K for floors. The U-values achieved in practice will vary according to the size and shape of the room and the build-up of the existing solid floor slab.

Insulation over existing slab

- 65mm Floating screed
- Building paper
- Insulation
- New D.P.M.
- Existing concrete

OR

- Boarding fixed to battens
- Insulation
- D.P.M.
- Existing concrete

Head-height then becomes the critical issue, particularly at door openings. It is worth remembering that a little insulation is better than no insulation at all and that insulation generally has a graph of diminishing returns – adding more and more insulation will keep improving the thermal performance of a building, but by progressively smaller amounts. As a guide:

- 25mm of polystyrene
  will improve the U-value to 0.45W/m²K
- 40mm of polyisocyanurate foam
  will improve the U-value to 0.31W/m²K
- 50mm of polyisocyanurate foam
  will improve the U-value to 0.25W/m²K (Compliant)

A new floor surface must of course be laid over the insulation. This must be secured down, so bearers can be fixed to the concrete sub-floor and insulation placed between them. The finished surface can then be fixed to the bearers. Some floating floor installations may be sufficiently stable to be laid directly over this type of insulation without the use of bearers but specialist advice should be sought from the manufacturer.

Note: Care must also be taken at the junction of the floor and the wall, as there is a possibility that a thermal bridge at this point will cause condensation, damp and mould if not correctly detailed. It may also be necessary to install a damp-proof membrane whilst carrying out this type of insulation if this was not built into the floor when the slab was cast.

REGULATION CORNER

Where a staircase rises from an area which is to be insulated, the increase in ground floor level would effectively reduce the height of the first step.

Building Regulations require that risers (the amount each step goes up) are consistent throughout the staircase to avoid trip hazards. To address this problem, the first step needs to be extended and effectively become a landing. The landing must be at least as deep as the width of the staircase.

This alteration is not always possible, especially, for example, where the entrance to the staircase is restricted in a hallway. It is advisable in all cases to check with the local Building Control officer before making alterations to a staircase. Door handles and door heights may also become an issue if floor levels are raised. Where it is impossible to fit any insulation to a solid concrete ground floor, a great deal of heat can still be retained by fitting a carpet or even a wooden floor using a thermal underlay.

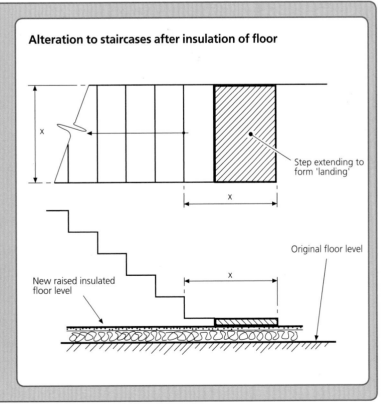

Alteration to staircases after insulation of floor

- Step extending to form 'landing'
- Original floor level
- New raised insulated floor level

Windows and doors

More heat is often lost through badly fitting doors and windows than is lost through the conduction of energy by thin glass. The first, and cheapest, place to start when looking at energy savings from doors and windows is therefore to draughtproof and seal wherever possible. (See the section on draughtproofing at the end of this chapter.)

The insulation of glazing has evolved considerably during the 20th century. To assess the improvement in U-values that may be achieved through replacement glazing, the table above shows U-values for glazing specifications in common use during the past 100 years.

SECONDARY GLAZING

Old glass has a look that cannot be replicated by modern production techniques. The imperfections and interesting reflections of old glass can be retained while the thermal performance is improved if secondary glazing is installed. It is important that sufficient sections of secondary glazing can be opened, both for the thermal comfort of occupants during hot weather and for reasons of fire safety. Metal windows cannot accept thicker glazed panels so secondary glazing is a realistic and cost-effective measure to reduce heat loss while leaving the building's fabric and appearance essentially unchanged.

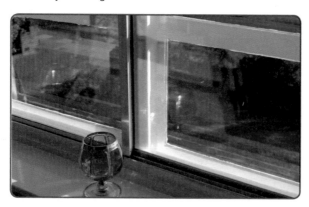

REPLACING GLAZING

Double glazing became – for a time at least in the UK – synonymous with uPVC replacement windows, although attitudes are again changing and estate agents are now beginning to mention original windows as a selling point, as inappropriate replacement windows can substantially reduce the value of a property. For substantially fixed glazing in timber structures such as bay windows it is normally possible to remove the original thin glass and to insert double-glazed panels without replacing the frame. Opening casements may require replacement but with minor adaptation the outer frames can often be retained.

Above: Original timber window with double glazing added.

Left: Steel-framed window with secondary glazing added.

Right: Detail of window above showing double glazed panel.

U-VALUES OF SINGLE GLAZING AND ADDED LAYERS (LABORATORY MEASURED) [6]

SINGLE-GLAZED	SINGLE-GLAZED + HEAVY CURTAINS	SINGLE-GLAZED + WELL FITTING SHUTTERS	SINGLE-GLAZED + ROLLER BLIND	SINGLE-GLAZED + HONEYCOMB BLIND	SINGLE-GLAZED + LOW-E SECONDARY GLAZING	SINGLE-GLAZED + LOW-E SECONDARY GLAZING + SHUTTERS
U - 4.3	U - 2.5	U - 1.7	U - 2.7	U - 2.1	U - 1.8	U - 1.6

Source: Energy Efficiency and Historic Buildings, English Heritage 2011.

DOOR AND WINDOW REPLACEMENT

In some circumstances, replacing doors and windows is unavoidable. Natural materials such as timber generally have a much lower embodied energy and environmental impact than synthetic materials.[7] Synthetic materials can also be impossible to repair. If softwood joinery is well designed and made it should last a lifetime with minimal maintenance – paint technology has improved markedly in recent years. It is important to ensure that the timber comes from sustainable sources (see the section on 'Timber Sourcing' in Chapter 2). By using timber, the existing windows and doors can be matched in order to avoid changing the appearance of the property.

Hardwoods are a scarce resource and the use of tropical hardwoods should be avoided. As window and door replacement is carried out very infrequently during the life of a building it would be worth specifying good-quality softwood joinery and well-insulated glazing.

If window or door replacement is carried out by someone registered under a competent person scheme, it is not necessary to submit a building control application.

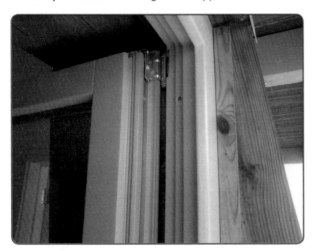

WINDOW EFFICIENCY RATING (WER)

As an alternative to the required U-values quoted above, the 2010 changes to the Building Regulations in England and Wales accept replacement windows with a window efficiency rating in band C or better. The WER takes into account the energy performance of the whole window. U-values can be difficult to compare, as the performance of the frame must be taken into account in addition to that of the glass; thermal bridging also occurs through the spacers between sheets of glass. The WER takes all these

REGULATION CORNER

In England and Wales, the Building Regulations (2010) refer to windows and doors as 'controlled fittings'. The regulations require replacement windows to have a U-value of 1.6W/m²K covering the performance of the whole window, including the frame. (Also see the section on WER ratings below.) Replacement doors must now have a maximum u-value of 1.8W/m²K.

factors into account and also allows for the calculation of heat gain through glass and arrives at a net figure over a year. Through good design and the use of low-energy glass, some windows can now result in annual thermal gains rather than losses. Some changes to glazing specification can increase the U-value (making it appear to lose heat more quickly) while improving the WER, which illustrates the contrast between the two systems.

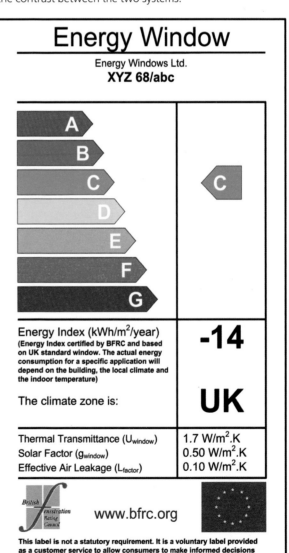

Draughtproofing

On average, just over 20% of the heat loss from domestic buildings arises from ventilation so this is one of the most important areas to focus on when trying to reduce heat losses.

Draughtproofing is relatively cheap compared to many improvements and as it is not regulated it is easier for the DIY enthusiast to save money by taking on the task. As it is cheap, it will produce the fastest paybacks of all energy-saving measures. Having said all that, it is necessary to maintain aqequate ventilation to ensure good air quality. Ventilation and Heat Recovery systems are explained in more detail at the end of this chapter.

AIR LEAKAGE

In older properties, it was understood that air leaks through windows and doors (and even through the main body

Source: Energy Saving Trust GPG268

Wind driven flow

Temperature driven flow

Common air leakage paths

Source: Energy Saving Trust

KEY
1 Underfloor ventilator grilles
2 Gaps in and around suspended timber floors
3 Leaky windows or doors
4 Pathways through floor/ceiling void into cavity walls and then to the outside
5 Gaps around windows
6 Gaps at the ceiling-to-wall joints at the eaves
7 Open chimneys
8 Gaps around loft hatches
9 Service penetrations through ceilings
10 Vents penetrating the ceiling/ roof
11 Bathroom wall vent or extract fan
12 Gaps around bathroom waste pipes
13 Kitchen wall vent or extractor fan
14 Gaps around kitchen waste pipes
15 Gaps around floor-to-wall joints (particularly with timber frames)
16 Gaps in and around electrical fittings in hollow walls

of the structure itself) would be sufficient to provide the necessary amount of background ventilation. As warm air tends to rise, fresh air will be drawn in through the lower parts of the house and ultimately exit through the upper floors. This is known as the 'stack' effect.

Uncontrolled ventilation results in substantial heat loss, which increases significantly on windy days.

DRAUGHTPROOFING DOORS AND WINDOWS

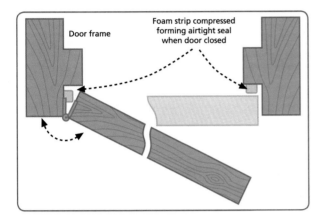

Door frame

Foam strip compressed forming airtight seal when door closed

The best time to check for draughts is during cold weather when there is some wind. Spiders can be helpful here as they will often build webs in air leakage paths where there is a better chance of catching tiny flies. If no draughts can be detected at the edges of a door or window then there is evidently a good insulating fit and no point adding further material to that particular edge. If the fit is already very tight, the addition of some types of draught excluder can even cause problems with the operation of the door/window.

Once a draught has been detected, check the door/window in the closed position and see whether there is a uniform gap between the door and the frame. If the gap is consistent then strips of compressible foam tape can be used.

These strips are self-adhesive and are fitted to the door/window frame rather than to the door or window itself. On the opening side and at the top the tape is fitted around the inside of the closure. On the hinge side the tape should be fitted to the frame face. Once these have been fitted, a door tends to close slightly further out than before so the receiving plate on the latch and lock may need slight adjustment.

If the gap between the door or window and the frame varies, or if adhesive tape strips have been applied and there is still a draught problem, it is likely that the door/window has warped. Brush-strip draught excluders can compensate for a slightly warped door as they do not have to align exactly with the door closure (part of the frame) when they are fitted – in other words they can follow the shape of the door. If fitted properly, they compress slightly in the closed position, forming a seal.

Several other draught strips are in common use. Rubber or silicone 'O' tubes are useful for draughtproofing windows and v-shaped seals are useful where a large or

Notch for corner joint.

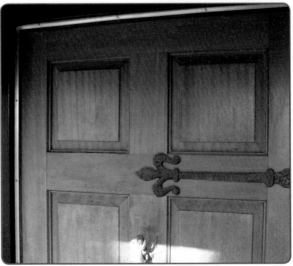

variable degree of compression is required. BS 7368 is the performance standard for draught strips fitted to doors and windows that are already installed.

If a warp in a wooden door or casement window is greater than can be overcome with such strips the services of a carpenter will be needed to adjust the shape of the frame to match the warp in the door or window. Draught excluding strips can then be fitted.

Metal windows do not warp like wooden windows but they are prone to small gaps on the hinge side. Specialist draught strips are available, similar to those used for wooden windows. uPVC windows and doors are often specialist proprietary systems so if they need maintenance to correct draughts it is usually necessary to contact the manufacturer or installer.

DRAUGHTPROOFING FRAMES

Cracks often occur in buildings where dissimilar materials meet, due to differing rates of thermal expansion. Doors and windows are also subject to considerable wear and tear, especially if they have been binding or sticking and have been slammed, so cracks such as this are not uncommon. Sometimes it is possible to feel air passing through these cracks, so a good-quality sealant should be used to fill any

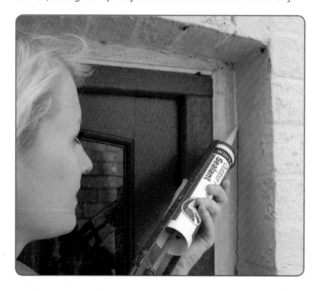

gaps. It is advisable to re-anchor the frame if it has worked loose and to correct any sticking doors or windows in order to reduce the likelihood of the problem recurring.

There are also companies that specialise in the upgrading and draughtproofing of sash windows. A strip can be inserted into the casement which allows it to glide easily as the window slides open but which prevents the draughts associated with these windows.

It is even possible to replace the sliding casements themselves with double-glazed versions, but this is a specialist job as the counterweights in the sash boxes will need to be enlarged and space within the boxing is usually limited.

Draughtproofing strip inserted into frame.

Ventrolla sash repair system.

Modern sealants and mastics not only contain a variety of synthetic chemicals but may also appear incongruous when applied to older buildings. There are several DIY recipes for alternative mastics, the main ingredients being sand and linseed oil. This type of filler takes much longer to set than 'conventional' mastics. Alternatively, VOC free mastics are now appearing on the market.

Ventilation and heat recovery systems

As insulation levels are increased, air leaks become a more significant source of heat loss. Improving air tightness to reduce this loss can, in turn, result in poor indoor air quality, so controlled ventilation becomes more important. The ventilation system itself then becomes a more significant source of heat loss, so it may be necessary to introduce a heat recovery system.

Ventilation can be organised on a single-room basis or by means of a whole-house system, with or without heat recovery. The flow of air can be mechanically driven or operate passively as a result of wind or temperature and pressure differential.

THE NEED FOR VENTILATION

In most modern houses, indoor air is substantially more polluted than the outside air, even in cities. As people spend up to 90% of their time indoors, indoor air quality is a serious health issue. A wide variety of airborne toxins are introduced into dwellings by carpets, furnishings, cleaning products and several modern building materials (see Chapters 2, 8 and 9).

Sources of indoor air pollution

VOC's from pesticides

Aerosols

Perfume

Wall insulation

Carpets

Cleaning agents

Chipboard flooring

Flame retardants

Tobacco smoke

Detergents /fabric conditioners

VOC's in paint

For further information see: Residential Ventilation Association (RVA), Indoor Air Quality Statement (July 06). **http://www.feta.co.uk/rva/index.htm**

Moisture generated by bathing and cooking needs to be expelled, as condensation and mould growth result from excessive humidity. Boilers are always ventilated to the outside but gas cookers release the products of combustion, including moisture, into the indoor environment unless an extractor has been fitted. Cooker extractors that simply filter rather than expel stale air to the outside do nothing to reduce condensation. Tobacco smoke is also a significant pollutant where there is no direct ventilation.

Fires and stoves require an adequate supply of oxygen and the amount of air required for this purpose is laid down in the relevant Building Regulations, although a higher level of ventilation will in any case be required in order to expel pollutants and humidity.

time overrun have also resulted in the operation of fans for up to 20 minutes when the bathroom light may only have been switched on for a minute or two; this is not only a waste of energy but can also be a nuisance to the occupants.

Mechanical extract ventilation simply combines the ducts from wet rooms and expels the air through a common vent. As the fan works continuously at low speed, the system can deliver a more consistent flow of air than intermittent extractor fans; the fan can be set to a higher speed manually or automatically when greater ventilation is required. A well designed and built installation can minimise the energy required to run the system.

Passive ventilation is based upon a combination of wind pressure and the stack effect. Warm (moist) air is drawn from the wet rooms and expelled at ridge height, as the vent design uses the available wind to pull the air through the system. Fresh air can be supplied from background ventilation or admitted at roof level through different channels in the same system and then ducted to the rooms below.

REGULATION CORNER

Poor indoor air quality and the associated condensation which is common in modern buildings have led to the requirement to provide specified levels of ventilation as set out the 2010 edition of the Building Regulations – Approved Document F – Means of ventilation.

MECHANICAL VENTILATION VS PASSIVE VENTILATION

In most houses air is expelled by means of fan vents in the 'wet' rooms – bathrooms and kitchens. Replacement air is admitted by means of trickle vents and air leakage. When fans are not operating in these rooms, in modern 'sealed' houses, the ventilation is unlikely to be sufficient, particularly in rooms which do not lie on the ventilation pathway unless there is a substantial gap under the door.[8] When fans are working, they consume energy, in addition to the energy which is lost with the warm expelled air.

These fans are likely to have been installed in accordance with earlier Building Regulations or during previous renovations and are unlikely to provide a balanced whole-house system of ventilation. Previous regulatory requirements on wiring fans to light switches in bathrooms with an added

Mechanical Extract Ventilation

Passive stack ventilation

Prevailing wind

Heat recovery

Heat recovery unit

Bedroom

Bathroom

Lounge

Kitchen

Passive stack ventilation has the advantage that it is silent and energy-free in operation, but the disadvantage that its operation is dependent upon available wind, so it may not deliver sufficient ventilation when most needed unless it is mechanically assisted. As with simple mechanical ventilation, the heat in the expelled air is lost.

HEAT RECOVERY

For much of the year in the UK, the temperature of outside air is below what most people regard as a comfortable internal temperature, so the arrival of fresh air is commonly perceived as an uncomfortable draught. However, ventilation does not necessarily mean the loss of warm air and the introduction of cold air. The heat which is present in the stale air can be partially recovered (up to 75%) and used to preheat the incoming fresh air by means of a simple heat exchanger. This is known as heat recovery.

Heat recovery ventilation systems in theory deliver the best of both worlds – plenty of fresh air and minimal heat loss. They are most effective when designed for a whole house, so that warm air can be drawn from rooms where the moisture level is high, such as kitchens and bathrooms, and used to heat the incoming air which is ducted and fed into other rooms. Compared to single-room heat recovery ventilators, whole-house systems also have the advantage that the source of the incoming air can be kept at a distance from the exit point for stale air to avoid used/moist air being drawn back in.

However, as with other system-based ventilation strategies, the required ductwork may be highly visible or otherwise difficult to fit to downstairs rooms in existing

properties. It is also worth noting that heat recovery systems only deliver an energy-saving benefit in properties which are airtight, so that all the warm air is forced to pass through the heat exchanger.

POSITIVE INPUT VENTILATION

In most ventilation strategies, the system is designed to expel stale air and to allow fresh air to filter in through trickle vents and leakage pathways. By reversing this principle, ventilation can be achieved by pushing fresh air into the building by means of a fan, which is normally located in the attic space if available. The air is supplied to a central communal space such as a landing and then finds its way out through the air leakage pathways described above. This type of system is not so effective at removing the moist air generated in kitchens and bathrooms but is particularly useful for areas where radon is a significant risk.

CLEANING INDOOR AIR

In addition to the ventilation strategies outlined in this section, it is worth noting that indoor plants can significantly enhance indoor air quality. Spider plants in particular are thought to be effective at reducing formaldehyde levels indoors.[9] Household plants, in varying degrees, can also reduce concentrations of carbon monoxide, benzene and trichlorethylene among other chemicals. There are increasingly inventive ways of introducing plants to the indoor environment

Ionisers are also thought to improve indoor air quality by attracting pollutants to the negatively charged ions which they produce and causing them to fall to the floor, where they are gathered in the normal cleaning process.

4 HEATING

This chapter considers all possible ways of providing space heating and hot water to a house, from conventional fossil fuel boilers through to renewable forms of heat. Methods of making central heating systems more efficient are explained in detail, followed by guidance on what to do with less common systems including air-based and electric distribution. Water-heating systems are complex and not everyone understands how their water is heated, so there is a lengthy section on common configurations as this determines the options available for improvement. At the end, the advantages and disadvantages of alternative sources of heat including wood/biomass, heat pumps and solar water heating are set out so that readers can select the most appropriate and cost-effective solutions.

REGULATION CORNER

The Approved Document L1B (2010) requires that "reasonable provision shall be made to ensure that fixed building services are energy-efficient, have effective controls and have been commissioned to optimise fuel use." Fixed building services include:

■ internal and external lighting systems;
■ heating and hot water;
■ air-conditioning and mechanical ventilation.

ADL1B states that whenever a fixed building service is extended or provided, 'reasonable provision' would be demonstrated by following the guidance set out in the Domestic Building Services Compliance Guide (CLG, 2010). The Guide covers heating, ventilation, cooling, internal and external lighting and renewable energy systems, including Heat Pumps and Solar Water Heating.

For heating systems, the requirements in the Guide are lengthy and complex so the input of an experienced and qualified heating engineer would generally be required to ensure compliance.

Comparison of available fuels

All combustible fuels are based upon carbon in one form or another. Burning carbon gives rise to carbon dioxide emissions and the CO_2 emitted from burning fossil fuels such as gas, oil or coal simply adds to that already present in the atmosphere. The burning of carbon from renewable fuels such as wood or biomass has the advantage that CO_2 has been captured in the growing of the fuel by the

process of photosynthesis. If growing plants or trees for fuel simply displaces other crops then there is no net gain to the environment but, where land is under-utilised, the switch to renewable sources of fuel will reduce the CO_2 burden if it displaces fossil fuel consumption.

Almost all domestic properties in the UK are served

by mains electricity and most are served by mains gas. Where gas is unavailable, the choice of primary fuel for heating rests on a trade-off between price, convenience, the local supply chain and environmental impact. Alternative and renewable sources of heat are discussed later in this chapter.

The following table ranks fossil fuels in terms of their CO_2 emissions for a given heat output.

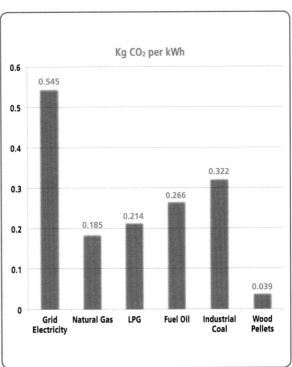

FUEL SWITCHING

When a boiler or a complete heating system is being replaced, there is an opportunity to reassess the choice of primary fuel used for heating. The selection of system and fuel depends on what is available locally but the potential for subsidy under the Renewable Heat Incentive (see later in this chapter) will also have an impact.

It is clear that the CO_2 emissions from electric heating are triple those from gas for a given heat output. Of all the available fuels, electricity is one of the most expensive and least efficient for space heating or water heating. This is largely due to the energy losses associated with the generation and distribution of electricity. Some 40% of the UK's electricity is currently generated by power stations fuelled by natural gas[1], so it is clear that it should be cheaper and more efficient to burn gas for heat rather than convert it into electricity first and then into heat. Where mains gas is not available, the use of heat pumps can reduce the emissions by around 2/3 – see later in this chapter.

The environmental impact of heating by oil without system replacement can be reduced if it is possible to fuel the boiler with biodiesel rather than diesel. Pure biodiesel used for heating is currently not subject to the duty applicable to ordinary diesel, although most biodiesels used for heating are blended with fossil-fuel diesel. It is ironic that Rudolf Diesel, inventor of the engine which bears his name, originally intended to run it on biodiesel.

The other point to consider around fuel replacement is the cost and impact of installation and servicing of the system. New flue regulations mean that solid fuel boilers (oil/wood) can be expensive to install and oil-fired systems are significantly more expensive than LPG.

The standards to which any new central heating system must conform are set out in 'CHeSS, Basic and Best Practice Specifications for the components of domestic wet central-heating systems that are critical to energy efficiency'.

Central heating systems

BOILER SIZING

It is important to size the boiler correctly for each particular house, taking into account any improvements that have been made in the insulation of the property. If the boiler is oversized, it will run less efficiently, resulting in higher heating bills and higher CO_2 emissions. Check with your heating engineer to see whether your boiler is oversized, particularly if you have recently added insulation.

BOILER EFFICIENCY

To look up how efficient your existing gas or oil boiler is, visit the SEDBUK (Seasonal Efficiency of Domestic Boilers in the UK) website (**www.sedbuk.com**). The SEDBUK rating represents the average annual efficiency achieved in typical domestic conditions and the website lists most current and obsolete boilers.

With rare exceptions, newly installed gas boilers are now required to be condensing boilers, which means that they achieve efficiencies of around 90%. Condensing boilers are so named because they recover and use some of the heat present in the hot flue gases. At this point, water vapour in the combustion gases will condense and then be drained away. (This water is very slightly acidic.)

To get an idea of how much you would save by upgrading a gas boiler, first work out your consumption of fuel for heating over the course of a year. For example, assume you used 20,000 kWh of gas and the price of gas is 4p/kWh so the cost is £800. You then need to deduct other gas uses (cooker, gas fires etc) to arrive at an estimate of the fuel cost for space (and water) heating. Say £700. Ignore any standing charges. If you replace a 75% efficiency boiler with a 90% efficiency boiler you would then expect to save £117 per year. There is a helpful cost calculator available on the SEDBUK website. To work out the payback period in years, divide a quote for boiler replacement by the expected saving per annum calculated as above. At £1,500 for a replacement boiler, this would pay back within 13 years – or less, if the cost of reduced servicing is taken into account.

However, once a house has been thoroughly draughtproofed and insulated the demand for space-heating will be greatly reduced, but there are several other ways to reduce heat demand before making costly alterations such as boiler replacement:

TURNING DOWN THE THERMOSTAT

Centrally-heated houses are often kept well above generally

accepted comfort temperature levels, so energy can be saved simply by turning down the thermostat (if fitted) by a degree or two, without noticing the effect.

The old advice to put on a sweater rather than turn up the heating saves money and reduces CO_2 emissions. Comfort levels do, of course, vary according to how active you are, according to age and to state of health, so it would be dangerous to suggest absolute levels, but the following table is useful as it illustrates the typical contrast between rooms.

Guide temperature for the living room is higher than for the bedrooms – many people prefer a slightly cooler temperature for sleeping and believe it to be healthier – and lower for the kitchen, where people tend to be more active. A higher temperature in the bathroom is generally preferred.

Room	Design Temp (°C)
Lounge/sitting room	21
Dining room	21
Kitchen	18
Kitchen/Breakfast	21
Hall	18
Cloakroom	18
Utility room	18
Study	21
Bedroom	18
Landing	19
Bathroom	22

THERMOSTATIC RADIATOR VALVES

The best way to set different temperatures for each room is to fit thermostatic radiator valves (TRVs) to radiators. This is now standard practice for new central-heating systems and it is not an expensive job to fit them to an existing system.

Standard valve

Thermostatic radiator valve

The TRVs can then be adjusted to sense and deliver the correct temperature for each room.

After draughtproofing and introducing good levels of insulation, heat demand will be much lower, so existing radiators may now be oversized. Fitting TRVs will also help to solve this problem without having to replace radiators. Modern slim-line radiators may be more efficient than the existing radiators but TRVs are less costly and disruptive to fit. There is also an embodied energy cost in replacement radiators which needs to be offset against any energy savings obtained by replacement.

If a TRV is fitted to *every* radiator (or every radiator within a zone) then it will also be necessary to fit an auto-bypass at the boiler. This is a specialist job for a plumber and no alterations to heating systems should be made without consulting a qualified professional.

If the system already has a thermostat, TRVs should not be installed in the same room (usually the sensor is built into the control panel).

HEATING CONTROLS

The aim of any heating control system is to provide heat when there is a demand for it and to avoid wasting money and energy when there is not. Occupancy patterns vary so it is difficult to generalise. For a household which is unoccupied during the day, a simple timer which sets the heating system to come on in the morning and again in the evening will deliver space heating when it is required. More sophisticated is the programmable room thermostat which allows for different temperatures to be set at different levels over the course of a 24-hour period.

Weather compensators not only measure the temperature outside but also 'learn' how the heating system functions and adjust accordingly to make it run more efficiently. Primarily they do this by predicting when the external temperature will rise sufficiently to warm the building so they can shut off the boiler earlier, saving money and energy. Opinions vary as to their effectiveness but they are certainly more sensitive than a simple room thermostat.

SYSTEM MAINTENANCE

Central heating systems as a whole run less efficiently if they are not maintained – that is, if sludge from lime-scale and/or corrosion deposits builds up in the distribution pipes and radiators. The system can be flushed out with chemical additives to break up this sludge, but treating the water with inhibitors will help to prevent this problem from occurring in the first place. If you find that inhibitors are needed, ensure that they are non-toxic and biodegradable and that sludge is disposed of safely.

HEAT RECOVERY

One way to reduce space heating demand is to recover the heat lost through ventilation and the provision of fresh air. Mechanical and passive ventilation and heat recovery are covered in Chapter 3 – Insulation.

Alternative heat distribution systems

UNDERFLOOR DISTRIBUTION

Warm air rises, so the most efficient means of delivering heat through water-based distribution systems is by means of underfloor heating. Radiator-based distribution

systems need to be at a high temperature to radiate and convect heat to all corners of a room but a complete underfloor heating system can be run at a lower temperature to deliver the same degree of thermal comfort. This in turn means that the boiler can operate more efficiently, so saving money and greenhouse gas emissions.

Underfloor heating is not practicable for most refurbishment projects as it involves raising the floor level. If you are considering an extension, it may be possible to add an underfloor heating system to the existing boiler and radiator circuit without having to install a new boiler. It is also possible to connect solar water heaters to underfloor heating systems (see the section on Solar water heating later in this chapter).

Underfloor heating is normally arranged by laying pipes in formwork or clips and then pouring a cementitious screed over the top to form a slab, which then stores and dissipates the heat. There are other systems available which do not require a screed, as a finished floor surface can be laid directly over the pipes if they are laid in channels within load-bearing insulation. Screeded systems incorporate a degree of thermal storage, so they are slower to warm up (longer response time) but hold the heat more effectively.

Photo: Jupiter Heating Systems

AIR-BASED SYSTEMS

Air requires much less energy to heat than water, so air-based heating systems produce a much faster response time. Air-based systems are common in the USA and Canada, partly because they can also provide cooling as well as heating, which cannot be achieved via radiators. Generally, air-based

Photo: Unico System International

systems are more expensive to install than water-based systems due to the large duct sizes required, but they typically use 25–30% less energy in operation.

Warm air systems can be combined with air conditioning and ventilation systems to provide an integrated atmospheric control system. Air can be heated in the same way as water – usually by a gas- or oil-fuelled boiler, but warm air systems are often connected to heat pumps in addition to, or instead of, a fossil fuel source (see the section on 'heat pumps').

ELECTRIC STORAGE HEATING

In highly insulated homes, where gas is not available and electricity is purchased via a green tariff, modern electric storage heating can be a relatively efficient means of space heating. It is also worth bearing in mind that the carbon intensity of electricity used at night is less than electricity used in the daytime when demand is higher.

Electric storage heating systems are designed to take advantage of the fact that electricity is cheaper to purchase at night than in the daytime under an Economy 7 pricing tariff. Heat generated at night is stored in bricks or other dense material and released during the daytime and evening. Modern electric storage heaters may be fitted

Photos: Applied Energy Products

with automatic charge controls which detect the rate of temperature fall during the night and adjust the amount of heat input accordingly, making them even more efficient.

Storage heaters give out heat by radiation and by convection. Heat radiated from electric storage heaters is difficult to control, but the rate of convected heat can be varied according to demand. Modern heaters may be fitted with thermostats to control heat output and may be fan-assisted to improve the warm-up time in rooms that are intermittently occupied. As with most other heating systems, temperature and time controls are essential to the economy of the system.

Electric underfloor heating is effectively a form of storage heating but is less responsive than modern storage heaters so it is more expensive to run; like other forms of electrical resistance heating it has fallen out of favour as energy prices have risen.

INDIVIDUAL ROOM HEATERS

Individual electric fires (direct acting heaters) are one of the most expensive forms of heating. Unlike storage heaters, direct acting fires cannot take advantage of the relatively lower cost of electricity during the off-peak period. If a property is heated primarily by means of direct acting electric heaters, an alternative system will save money and reduce emissions.

Individual gas-fuelled room heaters (wall heaters and fires) are becoming less common. However, in contrast to some decorative-flame gas fires they are a relatively efficient form of heating, as they warm up rooms quickly and allow heat to be delivered when and where needed. Once insulation has been installed, depending on layout, it may not be necessary to fit gas heaters in all rooms in order to heat the whole property.

AIR-CONDITIONING SYSTEMS

One of the effects of climate change is thought to be the increasing incidence of heat waves. New buildings are required to be designed to prevent summer overheating and therefore reduce the demand for air conditioning. Air conditioning can consume a surprising amount of energy. During the heat wave of 2006, electricity supply companies became seriously concerned about their ability to meet the high demand for power resulting from the surge in the use of air-conditioning plant. However, energy demand for air conditioning can be reduced by a number of methods.

Heat pumps can be operated in reverse during hot weather to provide cooling. The most energy-efficient system during hot weather would be ground-based or water-based, as the source temperature is lower than the air temperature (see the section below on Ground source heat pumps).

Ventilation systems can be operated at low energy to provide summer cooling. Passive stack ventilation (see 'Ventilation and heat recovery systems' in Chapter 3) uses no energy at all, although fan-assisted systems are likely to be more effective during a heat wave.

Good design and summer shading will both reduce

overheating. Planting a tree on the southern side of the property will provide shade and projecting awnings will prevent the sun from shining directly into the house when at its highest, while allowing plenty of natural light to penetrate the interior – this is known as 'solar shading'. Overheating is also exacerbated by a lack of thermal mass in modern buildings – the heat has nowhere to go, so the interior heats up rapidly in warm weather (see the section on 'Passive solar design' at the end of this chapter).

> **REGULATION CORNER**
> The 2010 Approved Document L1B of the Building Regulations sets out standards to which any installed air-conditioning plant must conform.

AGAS AND RAYBURNS (AND OTHER RANGE COOKERS)

Range cookers (such as Rayburns) are designed primarily for cooking but many can also supply hot water and some provide central heating, and some even also. They can be fuelled by oil, gas or coal (a few stoves can use wood and some are capable of using several types of fuel). Although they are an excellent source of heat in winter they are an inefficient and expensive means of cooking in summer, when there is no demand for heat, unless the functions are separated.

See space heating decision tree on page 76.

Water heating systems

Water can either be heated and stored in a cylinder or heated 'on demand' and delivered directly from the heating unit to the tap. Water heating systems vary widely so first it is necessary to work out what kind of arrangement you have in your house and then you can see whether anything can be done to improve the efficiency of the system.

STORED WATER – IMMERSION HEATER ONLY

It is increasingly rare for an immersion heater to be the only method of water heating in a home and an immersion heater is now more often used as a backup. An immersion heater is simply an electric element which is fitted into the hot water cylinder. Temperature is controlled by means of a thermostat.

The 'Economy 7' tariff encourages users to heat their water at night (12:00pm–7:00am) when electricity prices are lowest. The hot water can then be stored and used throughout the day. A timer and a sufficiently large well-insulated cylinder are required for this process to be energy-

DECISION TREE FOR SPACE HEATING SYSTEMS

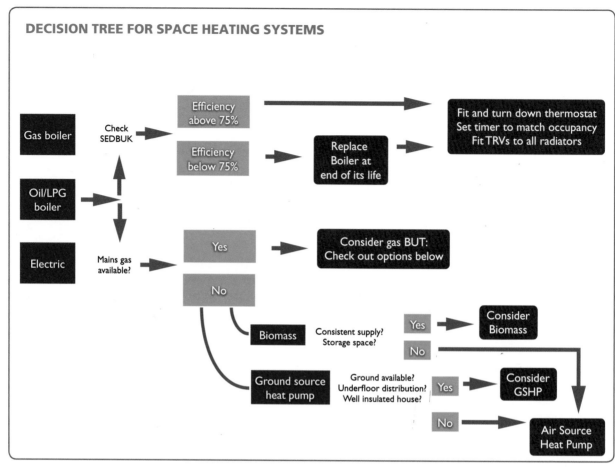

DECISION TREE FOR WATER HEATING SYSTEMS

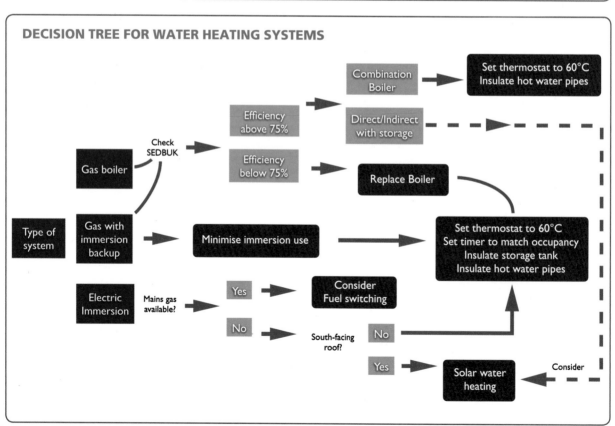

efficient. Transferring electricity demand from daytime to night-time makes more effective use of the capacity of the electricity generation and distribution system, which is why rates are cheaper at night.

Even if the cylinder is well-insulated, an alternative means of water heating would provide savings as electricity is an expensive method of heating water and generates a high level of CO_2 emissions per kW of useful heat. If your water comes out of the tap hotter than you need and you find you always add cold water to the sink or bath then you can save energy by turning down the thermostat a little. This may take a couple of attempts to find the right balance and remember you will have to wait a while for the temperature to adjust, as a well insulated cylinder should remain at the same temperature for some time.

STORAGE CYLINDER WITH DIRECT BOILER SYSTEM (VENTED)

Water is fed from the bottom of the cylinder to the boiler, which heats it and returns it to the cylinder higher up. When a tap is opened, hot water is drawn from the top of cylinder and is replaced by cold water lower down. Water is heated directly, either by the boiler or by an immersion heater, and is then used. The cylinder simply stores the hot water before use.

Direct vented system

Mains water

STORAGE CYLINDER WITH INDIRECT BOILER SYSTEM (VENTED)

With an indirect water system, the water that is heated by the boiler circulates in a loop through a heat exchanger (coil) in the cylinder, and then back to the boiler. This is known as the primary loop. The water actually used is fed into the cylinder, heated by means of the heat exchanger and fed out again without passing through the boiler.

Indirect vented system

Mains water

Both the direct and the indirect systems described above are known as 'vented' systems. Vented systems operate at atmospheric pressure, so flow rates tend to be low. They also require feeding from a separate cold water tank which takes up space, generally in the attic.

STORAGE CYLINDER WITH INDIRECT BOILER SYSTEM (UNVENTED)

In an unvented system, the cold-water inlet comes directly from the mains rather than via a header tank (cold water cistern), so flow rates are normally much higher than vented systems are able to deliver. Otherwise, the principles are similar to vented systems.

Indirect unvented system

Mains water

RENOVATION RECOMMENDATIONS FOR STORED WATER SYSTEMS

The recommendations for upgrading the three types of system described are as follows:

- Insulate the hot water cylinder or replace with a high-performance cylinder
- Ensure that timer controls are fitted to the boiler
- Ensure that a thermostat is fitted and is turned down to the optimal level.

Boiler efficiency is discussed in the next section. If you are considering replacing the cylinder, note that a dual coil cylinder will allow a renewable source of energy such as solar to be added in the future at substantially reduced cost (see the sections on 'Wood-pellet heating' and 'Solar water heating'). Building Regulations require that replacement hot water storage vessels meet the same requirements as in new buildings and have an adequate control system in place.

COMBINATION BOILERS

Combination boilers combine the functions of a central-heating boiler and an instantaneous multi-point water heater. Priority is given to the supply of domestic hot water so heating will not operate while a hot tap is open.

As there is no wastage of stored water, combination boilers were originally more efficient than conventional boilers. However, advances in insulation and boiler technology have narrowed the gap. Hot water cylinders may also enable the connection of renewable heat sources such as solar water heaters, woodburners or heat pumps,

whereas it is difficult or impossible to do this with a combination boiler.

SINGLE-POINT WATER HEATERS

Single-point gas heaters provide hot water on demand. They operate by sensing the arrival of cold water in the internal reservoir when a tap is opened. This triggers the ignition of the burners that heat the water. The hot water rises to the top and is available almost immediately. Generally they are sited near to the point of use, so the 'dead leg' is very short.

Single-point gas heaters are becoming increasingly more rare as they have largely been replaced by gas combination boilers which can serve more water outlets and also provide central heating. Single-point electric heaters are more common – an electric shower is a good example. As with any electric device that requires rapid heating (for example a toaster or a kettle), the demand for power is high and these are the energy guzzlers of the water-heating world.

THERMAL STORE SYSTEM

A British invention, the thermal store system uses the principle of indirect water heating in reverse. The water heated by the boiler is stored in a highly insulated cylinder – the thermal store – from where it is taken to the central heating radiators. Mains water is fed through the cylinder via a heat exchanger (coil) and on to the hot water outlets.

Thermal store capacities range from 170 to 500 litres and systems can deliver flow rates of between 18–30L/min. Thermal store systems are ideal for the future connection of alternative heat sources – woodburners, heat pumps and solar – which are discussed next in this chapter.

Combination boilers

Mains water

Thermal store systems

Bypass

Mains water

Renewable Heat Incentive

The Renewable Heat Incentive (RHI) is a subsidy scheme which aims to provide long-term support for renewable heat technologies. The RHI is being introduced in 2 phases.

- Phase 1 – Non-domestic – 2011
- Phase 2 – Domestic – 2013

PHASE 1: NON-DOMESTIC RHI SUBSIDIES

Phase 1 of the RHI provides a subsidy payment for each kWh of "renewable" heat produced but this is limited to non-domestic heating schemes. At present, the subsidy is funded out of general taxation and the amount of subsidy is dependent on the technology:

Technology	Subsidy (p/kWh)
Biomass (Small)	Tier 1 - 7.6
	Tier 2 - 1.9
Ground Source Heat Pumps	4.3
Solar Thermal	8.5
Biomethane	6.5

Source: DECC Publication 1387 March 2011

For biomass, the higher tier subsidy will be paid up to the tier break. This break is defined by multiplying the installed capacity (in kW) by 1314 (peak load hours). So a 20kW system will receive the Tier 1 subsidy of 7.6p/kWh on the first 26,280kWh and the lower Tier 2 subsidy on any heat generated in excess of that figure.

PHASE 2: DOMESTIC RHI SUBSIDIES

At the time of going to press (2012), **Phase 2** of the RHI – for **domestic** building – has not yet been finalised but it is expected that the support will take the same form – a payment per kWh of heat generated from renewable sources.

This will be important in many ways and will significantly reduce payback times for investments in renewable heat sources.

RENEWABLE HEAT PREMIUM PAYMENT

Before the domestic RHI is introduced, small subsidies are available towards the capital cost of installation of certain technologies. This is known as the Renewable Heat Premium Payment (RHPP) which is due to run until March 2013. The subsidies available at the time of writing (2012), subject to available funding, are as follows:

Technology	Voucher value
Solar thermal hot water	£300
Air-to-water heat pump	£850
Ground-source or water-source heat pump	£1,250
Biomass boiler	£950

Readers are advised to check the latest situation with the RHPP and RHI by visiting the websites of Ofgem or DECC.

Woodburning stoves

WOOD AS FUEL

Wood is considered a carbon-neutral fuel as the CO_2 emitted from burning wood is the same as (or slightly less than) the CO_2 which is absorbed as the tree grows. Even allowing for emissions of fossil carbon dioxide in planting, harvesting, processing and transporting the fuel, replacing fossil fuel with wood fuel will typically reduce net CO_2 emissions by over 90%. Wood produces negligible amounts of sulphur dioxide or nitrous oxides, unlike fossil fuels, so burning wood does not contribute significantly towards the problem of acid rain.

Logs must be dry and well seasoned, so if you are planning to install a woodburner you must make provision for storage of the fuel – a well-ventilated dry space is ideal, as it is the air which does the work in drying timber. Depending on the time of year when it is cut and the species of timber, it can take up to three years to season wood before it is ready for burning. Burning wet or unseasoned wood is not only less efficient but can also cause harmful deposits to build up in the chimney. When wood is fully dry, the bark should come off easily and splits should be visible in the end-grain. Another tip is to bang the ends of two logs together: unseasoned wood gives out a dull thud whereas good, dry, seasoned wood rings like a bell.

Wood varies by species in terms of its calorific (heat) value. Hardwoods are denser than softwoods so they will burn for longer and give off more heat, but it is important to ensure that the wood is split to no more than 4in (100mm) in order to burn efficiently.

Wood (fully air dried)	Weight (per m³ in kg)	Gross heat value kW/kg (btu/lb)	% Moisture when green	Seasoning time in summers
Ash	674	4.1	35	1
Beech	690	4.3	45	1–2
Birch	662	4.1	45	1
Elm	540	4.6	60	2–3
Oak	770	4.5	50	2–3
Poplar	465	2.6	65	1
Pine/Fir	410	2.6	60	1

Source: Solid Fuel Association

In order to remain carbon-neutral as a fuel, it is important that the wood is grown close to where it is used and that the local distribution system is efficient. Timber that is harvested for fuel must be replaced so that the equivalent CO_2 emitted during combustion will be reabsorbed by new trees as they grow.

Waste wood often ends up in landfill, so burning waste wood for heating is a good use of a sometimes free resource, although painted or treated timber should not be burned, as this would release a number of toxic chemicals. Pallets have often been treated so burning these should also be avoided, although treated pallets can be reused for many other purposes.

At the time of going to press (2012), it is not known how wood will be treated under the Renewable Heat Incentive Phase 2 (Domestic) but a subsidy may be available.

STOVES

A woodburning stove is much more efficient than an open fire – i.e. it produces more heat than an open fire from a given amount of fuel, primarily because an open fire loses a great deal of its heat straight up the chimney, especially if it consists simply of a dog grate in an inglenook. Woodburning stoves are not to be confused with cooking stoves.

Photo: Stovax Ltd

Many woodburners have built-in secondary and tertiary burn systems which ensure that very little smoke is produced (smoke contains particles of unburned fuel).

Clean-burn systems have the added advantage that they produce very little tar. The build-up of tar deposits is a common cause of problems with chimneys.

Photo: Stovax Ltd

REGULATION CORNER

Any installation of a heating appliance, or modification to a chimney, such as relining, has to be carried out in accordance with Building Regulations (Part J in England and Wales and Section 3 in Scotland). In England and Wales there is also a requirement that Building Control consent is obtained for such work unless the work is carried out by a Competent Person. For solid fuel and woodburning appliances a Competent Person is defined as someone who is registered with HETAS. Where there is a radiator from a fossil fuel boiler in the same room as the woodburner, it should be fitted with a TRV. Any solid fuel appliance requires an adequate supply of air. The requirements for ventilation are set out in the Building Regulations Approved Document J – this varies depending on whether the stove is larger than 5kW.

INSTALLATION AND MAINTENANCE

When burning wood, it is important to have the chimney swept regularly; twice a year is the current recommendation. Failure to sweep regularly can lead to build-ups of material within the chimney which may later ignite and cause chimney fires, leading to structural damage and the production of toxic fumes. Slow burning (or banking up to keep the fire 'in' overnight) can also lead to the build-up of harmful deposits.

Wood actually produces very little ash – less than 1% is common. The ash is high in potash and therefore a useful garden fertiliser; this can be mixed with other composted material in order to disperse it evenly.

For further information see:
- British Flue and Chimney Manufacturers Association, **www.feta.co.uk/bfcma**
- The Solid Fuel Association, **www.solidfuel.co.uk**
- HETAS, **www.hetas.co.uk**

SMOKE CONTROL AREAS

Many parts of the UK are designated as Smoke Control Areas, which means that emissions of smoke from domestic properties are banned. If you do live in a smoke controlled area, this need not prevent you from using a woodburning stove. Some stoves burn wood so efficiently that they are designated as 'Exempt Appliances'.

For a full list of exempt appliances (by region) and to find out whether you live in a smoke controlled area visit **http://smokecontrol.defra.gov.uk/index.php**

CONNECTING TO WATER HEATING SYSTEMS

Woodburners may include an integral back boiler which which is used to provide hot water. As with indirect fossil fuel boiler systems, the back boiler on a woodburner is generally linked to a coil in the cylinder. A pump is

Woodburner with back boiler

Heat leak radiator

Mains water

normally used to circulate the water, although gravity (hot water rises) may be sufficient to induce movement around the loop. For advice on pumps visit the British Pump Manufacturing Association website at www.bpma.org.uk

Radiators can also be connected to woodburners which have back boilers, though this may require the addition of an accumulator. An accumulator simply stores the heat

Woodburner with boiler and neutraliser

Heat leak radiator

Neutraliser

Solid fuel room heater or cooker

Gas or oil fired boiler

Mains water

produced by a wood-fuelled boiler and delivers it to the radiator system in a controlled manner. The introduction of an accumulator into the system means that the woodburner may only need to be fired up twice a day, eliminating the need to feed it constantly. Where no accumulator is fitted there is the danger that excessive heat will build up in the back boiler, so at least one radiator connected to the back boiler must be left without a TRV to ensure that the heat is dissipated when the burner is operating while the rest of the radiator system is switched off.

If a stove used primarily for space-heating also provides the hot water, in warm weather it would be an inefficient use of fuel to fire the stove simply to heat water, so it may be useful to have a backup water heating system.

It is also possible to combine woodburning stoves with fossil fuel boilers and solar water heaters to create a highly efficient multi-fuel system which takes best advantage of the natural and renewable sources of heat and minimises fossil fuel use. This will mean the addition of a neutraliser and a considerable amount of additional plumbing and control equipment will be needed. A neutraliser prevents a pumped circuit from a fossil fuel boiler setting up an induced circuit through an alternative heat source (such as a solid fuel boiler) when it is not in operation.

This is a specialist area, and if you are making alterations to an existing heating system the services of a heating engineer will be required. It is impossible to make general recommendations as even standardised systems may have been altered.

For further information see:
■ The Solid Fuel Association, **www.solidfuel.co.uk**

Wood-pellet heating

PELLETS
Wood pellets are manufactured from waste wood products such as ground wood chips, sawdust and bark, all of which are created by the wood processing industry. No chemical additives are needed as the natural lignin in the wood serves as a binder when the pellets are compressed. They have a

Photo: Rural Energy

low moisture content and a relatively high energy content for their volume. Typically they are about 20mm long and 8mm wide.

As pellets have a higher energy density, they require fewer deliveries and less space to store than wood in its natural state. Effectively, they can be made to flow like a liquid, so the consistency of their size and moisture content mean that automatic feed systems can deliver controlled heating on demand.

At the time of going to press (2012), it is not known how pellets will be treated under the Renewable Heat Incentive Phase 2 (Domestic) but a subsidy may be available.

PELLET STOVES

Stoves have been designed specifically to burn wood pellets. They can be fed from a hopper that will hold enough fuel for up to three days and the ash pan only needs to be emptied monthly or even less often, depending on usage. Many people consider them to be more convenient than a conventional woodburning stove.

Firefox pellet boiler.

of pellet boilers from Europe and North America are available and a few models are now manufactured in the UK.

Heating with pellet boilers is almost as convenient as using oil. A simple push-button ignition starts the boiler and no supervision of the equipment is required, although the pellet burner will need cleaning about once a month. The ash must be removed at the same time although, like stoves, the quantity is small as the pellets burn very thoroughly. As with oil or LPG, storage space is required for the pellets. Depending on demand and the size of the storage facility, delivery might be required approximately once a month.

Wood chips (as opposed to wood pellets) are only used for larger installations which fuel district-heating systems for groups of houses or for commercial property.

PELLET SUPPLY

The cost of energy supplied by wood pellets is at present comparable to that supplied by natural gas. In order to consider using a pellet boiler, you need to be confident of having a long term supply of pellets. To access a list of pellet suppliers in your area visit: **www.nef.org.uk/logpile**

BIOMASS, BIOGAS AND COMMUNITY HEATING

Biomass is a generic term that covers any material grown to provide fuel. Two of the most common plants grown for this purpose are miscanthus grass and short rotation coppice willow, although it is common for forestry waste to be used in biomass schemes. There are plenty of examples of small groups of houses or even whole communities which have a shared heating (or combined heat and power) system, including several household waste incineration schemes where the heat produced is used to provide hot water to the surrounding community, or to generate electricity. Biomass can also be fermented to make ethanol, which can be blended with gasoline.

While pellet stoves look similar to modern woodburners, they use built-in microprocessors to achieve optimal efficiency and a clean burn. Thermostatic controls and fans distribute warm air around the room where they are situated, whereas conventional woodburners rely on radiated heat, resulting in uneven temperatures.

PELLET BOILERS

Pellet boilers have been mostly used to heat larger systems such as those in schools and factories. Recently, however, domestic-scale pellet boilers have been successfully developed and are an excellent substitute for fossil fuel boilers, although they are still significantly more expensive. The small size of pellets means that the boiler response time is fast and the heat output is easily controlled. It also allows them to be fed into a boiler automatically. As with pellet stoves, microprocessor technology controls the air and fuel intake rates to achieve efficiencies up to 90%. Several makes

Biogas is most often produced from processing farm waste via anaerobic digestion and this can be a very efficient way to produce heating fuel if the transportation distances for the waste are kept to a minimum.

Although this book is aimed at the individual householder, there are many situations in which it may be beneficial for people to club together to set up biomass-fuelled community heating (or CHP) schemes, particularly in the countryside where mains gas is unavailable. The available land area in the UK for biomass production is limited and there are ecological issues to be addressed, but the use of renewable fuels may yet be the most environmentally attractive solution for heating older properties where insulating to modern standards is impractical. Grant schemes are constantly evolving; in some cases it may be possible to get support with the feasibility and/or installation phases of community schemes.

At the time of going to press (2012), it is not known how community biomass schemes will be treated under the Renewable Heat Incentive Phase 2 (Domestic) but a subsidy may be available.

Solar water heating

Solar water heaters collect energy from the sun and use this to heat water. (People often refer to 'solar panels' when they mean photovoltaic panels, which generate electricity. These are explained in Chapter 6.)

Solar collectors are commonly mounted on a south-facing slope of the roof but they can operate just as effectively on the face of a building or even on the ground as long as they have an unobstructed view of the sun during the warm parts of the day.

Even in the UK's temperate climate, solar water heaters work reasonably well, generating heat even on sunny winter days. On average, domestic systems will provide around 50% of the energy required to deliver hot water over the course of the year, allowing for heat losses from stored water. (This is known as the 'solar fraction'.)

Much of the energy required to heat water is used to take it from cold to lukewarm temperature. A smaller additional amount of energy is then required to raise the temperature to that which is comfortable for a bath or a shower. On hot or even warm days, solar panels can collect sufficient energy to heat water from cold to normal bath/shower temperature, while on duller days they can still do most of the work by heating the water to a lukewarm temperature. Solar water heaters are therefore normally used in conjunction with another heat source, such as a woodburner or a fossil fuel boiler, which can bring the warm water up to the required temperature using very little additional energy.

In this system, both heat sources work indirectly via heat exchangers in the cylinder. The lower coil is connected to the solar water heater on the roof or face of the building and the upper coil is connected to the boiler. Water is circulated through the boiler circuit coil via the normal

Photo: www.aranservices.co.uk

pump, whereas liquid is circulated through the solar panel by a second pump which is switched on automatically by a controller. The controller works by means of sensors which measure the temperature in the cylinder and in the panel. The controller switches on the solar circuit pump when the water in the solar collector is warmer than the cylinder.

As with conventional indirect water heating systems, the usable water is heated as it passes through the cylinder. The boiler loop and the solar loop are independent and sealed. In the case of the solar loop, antifreeze is normally added as the panels are exposed in all temperatures although some systems automatically drain back the water from the solar collector to avoid frost damage and prevent summer overheating. It is also possible to power the pump which runs the solar loop by means of a photovoltaic panel, making the whole system carbon-neutral in operation. Although it is not as sophisticated as other systems, there is added advantage that the collector loop can only circulate when there is sufficient sunshine and can reduce the need for control equipment.

Photo: Imagination Solar

TYPES OF COLLECTORS

There are two main types of solar collector – flat plate and evacuated tube. Evacuated tubes are slightly more efficient than flat plate collectors, so smaller panels can be used for the same heat output if space is at a premium. Evacuated tube systems tend to be more expensive than flat plate collectors as the technology is more complex. For a three-person household, a solar water heater with an area of 2–4m^2 should be sufficient.

Flat plate collector.   Evacuated tube collector.

Photo: www.aranservices.co.uk

Photo: Sol Heat

ORIENTATION

South-facing roofs are ideal but solar collectors can work efficiently up to 45° either side of due south.

PLANNING PERMISSION

Planning permission is not normally required for solar water heaters, although there may be restrictions in Conservation Areas or in other architecturally sensitive locations. Some flat plate collectors look very similar to a conservation roof light, so they will not necessarily look obvious when mounted on an old building. Listed buildings are special cases and consent would be required for any visible alterations.

SPACE AND SYSTEM REQUIREMENTS

Where there is a hot water storage cylinder and water is presently heated indirectly (see 'water heating systems' earlier in this Chapter) it is simpler, less disruptive and less costly to install a solar water heating system.

For many types of installation, single-coil cylinders will need to be replaced but the existing pipework to the boiler can be reused. It is important to note that the coils within the cylinder must be sized correctly for the boiler and panels to be attached to them, so make sure that this is discussed with your solar panel/cylinder supplier and heating engineer. Recently, a number of devices have been developed to enable solar water heating to be installed without cylinder replacement. These are unlikely to be quite as efficient as a twin-coil cylinder but the associated reduction in cost may make this a more attractive proposition.

Combination boilers heat water directly, which makes it difficult or in some cases impossible to combine them with a solar water heating system. If a solar water heater is used to preheat water before it passes through a combi, the boiler would need to be fully modulating – that is to say, it would need to sense the temperature of the incoming water and adjust the burn rate accordingly, otherwise the boiler would overheat with potentially serious consequences. If a heat store is introduced into the system it is possible that some combi boilers can be converted and retained. Some systems incorporate a valve to add cold water to reduce the temperature of solar pre-heated water before if reaches the boiler, although it will still be more efficient than heating from mains temperature. All systems vary, so it is essential to consult an experienced heating engineer who is familiar with solar water heating and thermal storage.

PAYBACK PERIOD

The payback period is the amount of time it takes for the cost of the installation to be repaid through savings in fuel bills. This payback period has been worked out purely as an example and you will need to insert up-to-date figures in order to work out the actual payback period.

This example is based on a gas-heated property and would typically include cylinder replacement:

Fossil fuel	Gas
Installed cost including new cylinder	£3,500
Gas price	4.0p/kWh
Annual (small family) water heating cost	£200
Solar fraction	50%
Annual fuel saving: 50% x £200 =	£100
Simple payback period: 3,500 ÷ 100 =	35 years

(For convenience it has been assumed that the discount rate for future savings is the same as the rate of fuel price increases.)

It is expected that a subsidy for domestic solar water heating will be provided under the Renewable Heat Incentive (RHI). If the subsidy were 10p/kWh, for example, this would reduce the payback period to 10 years. This may make the investment more attractive financially but does not alter whether it is the best thing to do for the environment. Irrespective of who is paying for the system, the amount of energy generated per £ needs to be compared with other sources of heat, taking into account the fact that solar water heating is low-carbon once in operation. If the existing fuel is electricity, the saving would be greater so the payback period would be significantly shorter.

The payback period can be dramatically reduced if you build and install your own solar water heater. For further information see: *Solar Water Heating: A DIY guide* – Paul Trimby, published by the Centre for Alternative Technology. However, check whether DIY installation is eligible under the Renewable Heat Incentive (RHI) – as a subsidy will make a significant difference to payback.

SOLAR WATER HEATERS AND UNDERFLOOR HEATING

It is also possible to provide an element of space heating by linking up solar water heaters to underfloor heating systems. Underfloor heating runs at a lower temperature than radiator-based systems so it is well-suited to the lower temperatures obtainable from solar water heaters at times when there is a demand for space-heating. However, another energy source will still be required. If you already have underfloor heating or are thinking of installing it, a specialist contractor would be required to link it up to a solar water heater.

Heat pumps

Heat pumps are classed as renewable energy (by the Department of Energy and Climate Change) but they are effectively an electrical form of heating as electrical energy is required to run the pump. The UK Government plans to 'decarbonise' the national grid by increasing the proportion of mains electricity generated from nuclear and renewables (mainly wind farms) rather than fossil fuels (coal and gas) over the next 20 years. It is therefore possible that heat pumps may eventually become more attractive in carbon terms but at present they have similar emissions to gas central heating systems. Where gas is not available, heat pumps present a useful saving in running costs and emissions over oil and much greater saving when compared to storage or direct acting electrical heating.

TECHIE CORNER: HEAT PUMPS

The great majority of heat pumps work on the principle of the vapour compression cycle. The main components in such a system are the compressor, the expansion valve, and two heat exchangers referred to as the evaporator and the condenser. The components are connected to form a closed circuit, through which a volatile liquid, known as the working fluid or refrigerant, is driven by the pump.

When the fluid is forced through the compressor it increases in temperature. This heat is then given off by the heating circuit (the 'condenser') as it travels around the house. When the fluid passes through the relief valve, the rapid drop in pressure results in a cooling of the fluid. The fluid then absorbs heat from the ground collection loop (the 'evaporator') before being re-compressed.

Expansion valve

Condenser (heat distribution system)

Evaporator (ground loop)

Compressor

GROUND SOURCE HEAT PUMPS

Ground source heat pumps take low-grade energy from the ground and convert it into usable energy at a higher temperature for space- and water heating. They work on the same principle as a refrigerator but operating in reverse. The ground in the UK is heated to a temperature of approximately 12°C by the sun, so ground source heat pumps are actually making use of solar energy. In this sense they are renewable but they still require electricity to run the pump.

Open-loop systems take groundwater and pump it to the surface, extract the useful heat energy and return the water

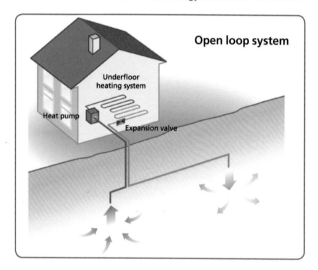

to the ground. These systems tend to be used on large commercial applications where the initial exploratory costs, environmental concessions and long-term maintenance issues can be justified.

In a closed-loop system the heat exchanger in the ground consists of a sealed loop of polyethylene pipe which is buried approximately 1.5m deep in horizontal trenches or vertically in a borehole. Typically, boreholes are between 50m and 90m deep.

Drilling borehole for vertical collector.

The ratio of the kW of heat energy produced by the system to the kW of electrical energy needed to power the pump is known as the coefficient of performance (CoP). Most systems have a CoP of between 2.2 and 4, which means that several times the amount of energy is produced than it takes to run the system. In other words, for 1 unit of electrical energy input, you might get 3 units of heat energy output.

Electricity costs about 3 times as much as gas, so ground source heat pumps are similar or slightly more expensive to run than natural gas but still a cheaper form of heating in operation than oil, LPG or electrical resistance heating. If there is a consistent and reliable source of renewable electrical energy available then the system could be almost carbon-neutral in operation but, in practice, electricity from the grid will normally be required. In terms of CO_2 emissions the situation is similar – electricity has approximately 3 times the emissions of gas per kWh so little or no emissions savings would be achieved unless the National Grid is substantially 'decarbonised'.

For large heat pumps replacing gas or other non-electrical heating, the additional electricity demand may require upgrading of the local grid.

The performance of the system is critical to working out the savings (if any) that can be achieved. Manufacturers often claim higher CoPs than are achieved in practice – this can be due to poor design of the collector loop or poor control of the distribution system so it is worth bearing in mind that it is the efficiency of the whole system which is important. Recent tests by the Energy Saving Trust revealed that most systems they tested had a CoP of between 2.3 and 2.5[2]. When summed over an entire heating season, the ratio of total energy input to total heat output is known as the Seasonal Performance Factor or SPF.

Ground source heat pumps are normally only appropriate for new buildings because they require either a substantial area of ground (approximately 10m of trench per 1kW of heat energy produced) or the drilling of a deep hole. The sizing of the ground loop will be determined by the following variable factors:

- Annual heat demand for the building, including hot water if required
- Mean ground temperature at the location
- Local ground conditions/geology
- The selected heat pump.

The cost of installation is relatively high, particularly where a vertical ground loop is necessary but, for detached houses with no mains gas supply, ground source heat pumps can be an economically viable option. As they contain very few moving parts they may be expected to last for many years and require only minimal maintenance.

Ground source heat pumps work best when combined

Laying 'slinky' pipe for horizontal collector loop.

Photos: EarthEnergy Ltd

with an underfloor heating system, as they start off by capturing low-grade heat. Since underfloor heating runs at a lower water temperature than conventional radiator systems, less energy is required via the pump to concentrate the heat to a useful level.

In the summer the ground temperature is lower than the required internal temperature. Some systems can be reversed to supply cooling and air conditioning by taking heat out of the building and depositing it into the ground via the ground loop. This increases annual system efficiency slightly as the ground becomes a heat store and will be at a higher temperature when the heating season commences again.

While there is currently no subsidy available for domestic heat pumps, ground source heat pumps have been included in the Renewable Heat Incentive Phase 1 (non-domestic) so it is expected that heat pumps will be subsidised under Phase 2 and a payment made for each kWh of heat output. The current level of subsidy for non-domestic installations means that it is possible to run a commercial heat pump almost for free but this will change if fuel price rises outstrip the wider rate of inflation in the economy.

For further information contact the Ground Source Heat Pump Association **www.gshp.org.uk/**

AIR SOURCE HEAT PUMPS

Air-source heat pumps (ASHPs) work on the same principle as ground source heat pumps, taking low-grade energy and converting it to useful energy by means of the vapour compression cycle. ASHPs are in common use in commercial scale Heating, Ventilation and Air Conditioning (HVAC) systems as they can supply both heating and cooling. They are starting to become more common in housing where gas is unavailable.

Compared with ground source heat pumps, ASHPs have the advantage of being cheaper to install, but the disadvantage that in cold weather the air (i.e. the source of heat) will be at its lowest temperature when space heating is needed most. The pump thus has to work harder to supply the heat required, so the efficiency of the system drops rapidly. However, if an ASHP is combined with another source of heating, the system can be programmed so that the pump only works when it would operate above a pre-set coefficient of performance. The overall efficiency of the heating system will thus have been improved.

Photo: Sol Heat

WATER-SOURCE HEAT PUMPS

Water-source heat pumps harvest their low-grade energy from nearby bodies of water. The heat can be collected, as in ground source systems, either by an open loop or a closed loop. Water abstraction from rivers or other public bodies of water for use in open-loop heat pumps would require permission from the Environment Agency.

GEOTHERMAL ENERGY

Ground source heat pumps should not be confused with geothermal heating. Geothermal heating is rare as it relies on heat generated from within the earth, rather than solar energy stored near the surface of the earth. The temperature of the earth rises approximately 2.5°C with every 100m of increasing depth. Where geological conditions lead to hot springs arising, this energy can be harnessed cheaply for heating and power systems, but normally it is necessary to drill very deep wells and pump in water under high pressure to take advantage of this resource. Rare examples in the UK include Southampton city centre and the Roman baths at Bath.

Passive solar design

Newly-built houses can be designed to admit and collect the heat of the sun during the day and radiate it back into the living environment during the evening and night. Glass is a particularly useful material for generating solar gain, as it allows short-wave infrared frequencies through, but not the low-frequency heat waves which are radiated back out from the building fabric.

The houses illustrated require very little space-heating as the large glazed southern facade allows the energy of the sun to flow directly into the building. Heat received

rooflights for good daylight

highly insulated building envelope

solar shading (to reduce sun penetration during summer months)

passive solar design south facing sun space pre-heat air entering adjacent rooms

good daylight

SUN SPACE

easily openable windows thermal chimneys & open plan layouts aid natural ventilation

existing vegetation buffers cool north winds

reduced openings on north face

thermal mass to absorb heat

double glazed facades

Image: Stride Treglown Architects

in this way is known as 'solar gain'. The internal walls are built of dense masonry in order to absorb the heat – a technique known as 'thermal mass' construction.

Where a complete renovation is planned, locating the rooms to be lived in on the warmer (southern) side of the house will reduce heat demand by taking best advantage of solar gain. Cooler rooms such as kitchens are best located on the northern side of the house. Reducing glazing on the northern side or improving the insulation of the glazing will reduce heat loss. By contrast, increasing glazed areas on the southern side will increase heat gain. However, this also accelerates the rate of heat loss, as walls are better thermal insulators than glass, so a balance

must be struck depending on the building's heat (and light) demand and its orientation. An absence of thermal mass can lead to problems of overheating in buildings designed for solar gain so it is essential to include plenty of heavyweight fabric within the insulated shell in order to soak up the available heat during the day.

Existing housing, however, can do nothing to alter its aspect and little to alter the size and shape of the windows. Where houses overlook each other, people also tend to use net curtains for privacy, which further reduces the solar gain. Passive solar heat gain can be increased without making alterations to the

windows by adding a conservatory or other heavily-glazed structure on the southern side of the property.

The internal wall then becomes a heat store which can radiate the heat back out after the sun has set. The extra room can also act as a heat store and as a buffer between the internal and external space, in effect providing additional insulation. A considerable amount of heat can be collected in a conservatory even on a winter day if the sun shines.

Conservatories cost nothing to heat but can reduce heating bills. This is negated, of course, if a radiator is situated in a conservatory, although the Building Regulations require any heat source in a conservatory to be independently controlled.

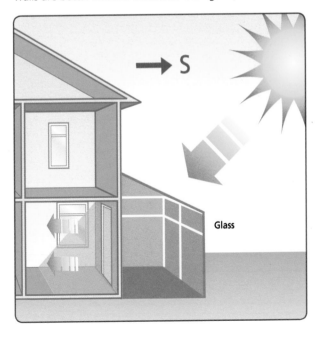

S

Glass

5 ELECTRICITY DEMAND

This chapter begins by explaining how electricity is measured and can be monitored and provides a description of the forthcoming smart metering programme. It then examines the most significant sources of demand for electricity in the home – namely appliances and lighting, and provides a range of options for reducing this demand – thereby saving energy, emissions and money.

Terms and measurements

It is useful to understand the basic units and terminology of domestic electricity in order to put into context the various savings that can be achieved. This is also helpful when considering the installation of any kind of electricity-generating equipment.

At the domestic level, the *rate* of electricity consumed is measured in watts or kilowatts (thousands of watts). A 60W light bulb uses 60W per hour; a single-bar electric fire uses 1,000W (1kW) per hour.

The *amount* of electricity used is the rate multiplied by the time. The amount of electricity used by a single-bar fire switched on for an hour is therefore 1kW x one hour, or one kilowatt-hour (1kWh). The amount of electricity used over days, months or years is based on this measure and is always quoted in kWh.

AVERAGE UK DOMESTIC ELECTRICITY

Type of property/occupation	Quarterly	Yearly
Flat	707	2,829
Semi-detached house	962	3,847
Terraced house – med/large over 70m²	1,100	4,399

Source: Powering the Nation - EST June 2012

CONSUMPTION FIGURES IN KWH

Note that these are only average figures and actual consumption will vary widely depending upon lifestyle and the efficiency of electrical goods in the house.

To get a better idea of your own electricity consumption, take a look at some recent electricity bills. Bills that correct an underestimation or overestimation on previous bills will

not give an accurate picture and ideally the bills should cover a period of a year as consumption will probably be higher during the winter months. Normally 1 unit equals 1 kWh.

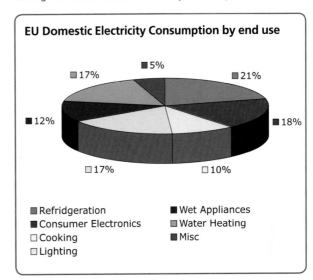

EU Domestic Electricity Consumption by end use

■5% ■21% ■18% □10% □17% ■12% ■17%

- ■ Refridgeration
- ■ Consumer Electronics
- □ Cooking
- □ Lighting
- ■ Wet Appliances
- ■ Water Heating
- ■ Misc

Source: Carbon Futures for European Households/DETR

For dwellings where neither hot water nor space-heating is supplied by electricity, the breakdown of consumption is as follows:

Smart metering

THE NEED FOR SMART METERING

For most of us, meters are stuck in a dark cupboard and, even when read regularly, they tell us very little about our energy use. On a day-to-day basis we generally have no idea how much energy we are using or what systems or appliances use the most energy and cost the most money to run. Our meters (and our bills) also fail to tell us how consumption varies from one year to the next and whether our consumption is higher or lower than average.

There is a good deal of evidence to suggest that people become more energy efficient if they have better information on real-time and historical energy use so the UK Government has committed to installing smart meters in all homes in England, Scotland and Wales by 2019.

Smart meters have three key features that are lacking from existing meters:

Electricity Statement

Electricity Readings

Meter Serial No.	Read Date	Read Type	Read	Last Read	Units Used
DOOD19977	26/4/2012	Customer	49167	48924	243
DOOD19977	30/4/2012	Estimate	49207	49167	40
Total units					**283 kWh**

Electricity Charges 01 Apr 2012 - 30 Apr 2012

Electricity supply standing charge	30 days	25.0p per day	£	7.50
Electricity total unit charge	283.0 kWh	14.62p per kWh	£	41.37

SMART METERING

In-home display — Comms Hub — Gas — Electric

Via SMS, internet or power lines

Automatic 2-way communications

Utility Company

Example of new 'smart meter' with communications interface

Photo: Sibert Instruments

- Two-way communication with the supplier
- Export metering
- In-home display

Smart metering will cover both gas and electricity supplies but the communications hub may be able to add other inputs if these are required in due course (such as water or perhaps oil).

COMMUNICATIONS

Two-way communications will allow the supplier to read meters automatically, so no more visits from the meter reader, and goodbye to estimated billing. A variety of communication systems may be used, depending on the location, and could include:

- SMS (similar to mobile phones)
- Power line carrier (the supply lines themselves)
- Internet.

At present it is envisaged that a communications hub will accept the inputs from the gas and electricity meters and then communicate with the energy supplier via a centralised communications hub (offsite) and also provide data to the householder's display unit.

EXPORT METERING

At present, most meters do not have the capacity to measure any electricity exported to the grid by households who have microgeneration equipment installed (a separate meter is normally installed for microgeneration but this simply records total production rather than the balance exported). For the purposes of the Feed-in Tariff, the amount of electricity exported is currently 'deemed' at 50%. Comprehensive two-way meters are also seen as a critical first step towards the introduction of smart grids. Smart grids will provide better information to energy suppliers, taking into account microgeneration, and enable suppliers to balance supply and demand across the UK in real time. This should lead to efficiency savings overall across the electricity supply industry.

IN-HOME DISPLAY

Importantly for the consumer, every smart meter will have an in-home display showing real-time and historical energy use. This means that you can see how much consumption

Ecometer.

Photo: Landis+Gyr

jumps when you switch the kettle on but also compare consumption with the same period in previous years. Information is presented in terms of kWh (energy) but also in £, so the cost of energy will become much more obvious. This in turn should help consumers to identify wastage and become more energy efficient, saving money but also reducing carbon emissions, in line with government policy.

PLANS FOR THE ROLL-OUT

The roll-out of smart metering is expected to commence in 2014. The meter replacement programme will be carried out at the expense of energy suppliers and costs will, of course, be passed on to the consumer. However, there should be benefits for suppliers and consumers in the short–medium term so the investment will be repaid fairly quickly. Privacy and data security have also been addressed carefully, so consumers need not fear a spy in the home and the needs of vulnerable people have been taken into account. In advance of the full roll-out, it is possible that some suppliers will offer smart metering on demand as an additional service to their customers.

Seen in the wider context, smart metering will also enable us to carry out large-scale field trials to find out exactly how much different energy efficiency improvements actually save in practice so that cost-effective measures can be prioritised.

For up-to-date information on the smart metering roll-out programme visit **www.decc.gov.uk**

POWER MONITORING

In advance of smart metering, there are several devices available which enable the consumer to monitor the electricity use of appliances in order to work out their efficiency and even CO_2 emissions. Real-time monitoring helps consumers to reduce consumption as they become aware of what items use the most electricity and over what period of time.

Photo: theowl.com

Source: "Household Electricity Survey" Intertek April 2012

STANDBY
Standby power measured between 03:00 and 04:00 All households

Power (W)

Households

Average: 81 W

DECC/Defra/EST

Appliances

Appliances are responsible for a significant proportion of electricity consumption and this has been growing in recent years as the number of appliances in the average home has increased rapidly.

Electricity is one of the most expensive domestic fuels and (at the power plant) it generates a high level of CO_2 emissions, so it is worthwhile taking a few simple steps to reduce consumption. Much can be done to reduce costs and consumption by changing the way we use our homes and our electrical equipment and need not require any significant expenditure.

STAND-BY

Many appliances such as televisions, set top boxes and DVD machines are operated by remote control and switched off by remote as well. This leaves the appliance on 'stand-by', ready for the next time the remote button is pressed. Leaving appliances on stand-by uses a surprising amount of energy – a television consumes 7% of the energy on standby that it consumes when in use.

The hassle of turning off several appliances can be reduced by using a multiple-gang extension lead and switching off the extension lead at the wall socket. Take care not to overload the extension lead but most televisions and stereos do not demand a high current. Some extension leads incorporate switches, as it may be easier to reach the head of the extension lead than the wall socket. A few appliances reset the memory when switched off completely, although internal batteries are increasingly used to maintain the memory and settings.

OTHER ENERGY-SAVING TIPS

Washing machines can be run at 40° or even 30° rather than 60° as most modern detergents work just as well at lower temperatures. It is also more efficient to wash full loads rather than part loads, even if the machine has a reduced load programme.

Fridges lose cold air when the door is open, replaced by warm air that then has to be cooled again, so keep the door open for the minimum amount of time. Allow leftover food to cool before placing it in the fridge. Defrost regularly (self-defrosting machines are more energy-efficient in this respect).

Kettles consume a large amount of energy for a short period of time, so significant savings can be achieved by using them efficiently. Only boil the water that's needed for immediate use, otherwise the energy used to heat the remaining water simply dissipates as the kettle cools. Some kettles have a gauge so that the amount of water to be boiled is clearly visible.

Photo: Product Creation Ltd

In more sophisticated eco-kettles, a push-button transfers water from an integral reservoir to the boiling chamber. Of course the better insulated the kettle is, the more heat will be retained when you next come to use it. Build-up of lime-scale on the element slows down the rate of heat transfer from the element to the water.

The tumble dryer is a good example of an energy-consuming device that it can be possible to do without altogether. Where tumble dryers are not vented directly to the outside, they can be a significant source of unwanted moisture indoors, leading to condensation and encouraging mould growth. If you have a garden or other outside space, drying clothes outside saves energy and money. Even the most efficient dryers available still use up to 3kWh to dry a 6kg load[1], costing 45p per load at the current price of 15p/kWh.

COOKERS

As with space heating, gas is a cheaper and less carbon-intensive fuel for cooking than electricity. A common arrangement is to have a gas hob combined with an electric cooker. However, cooking in an electric oven uses approximately double the energy used by a microwave and certainly for smaller items that simply need reheating, the microwave would use far less energy than an electric oven.

EU ENERGY RATINGS SYSTEM

The EU energy label rates products from A (the most efficient) down to G (the least efficient). By law, the label must be shown on all refrigeration and laundry appliances, dishwashers, electric ovens and light-bulb packaging. Refrigeration equipment has improved even further in recent years so refrigeration labelling now extends up to an A+++ rating.

For refrigeration appliances, the energy consumption is shown in kilowatt hours per year. For washing machines and dishwashers, the energy consumption is shown in kilowatt hours per cycle. To work out the expected annual running cost of a particular machine, simply multiply the kWh consumption figure by the average unit price of electricity. For example, an A+ fridge-freezer using 267kWh per year would cost £40.05 per annum to run at 15p/kWh. Devices which claim to save energy used to run fridges and freezers may not deliver as modern energy-efficient appliances will already have taken advantage of any savings available and built in the necessary technology.

Washing machines and dishwashers also have ratings for washing, spinning and/or drying performance. The A–G indicators are similar to the main efficiency ratings and labels for some models also include information on noise levels – the lower the number, the less noise is emitted. Advanced machines which employ fuzzy logic can monitor conditions during the wash and adjust various inputs such as water intake, wash time, temperature settings, rinse performance and spin speed to deliver optimum cleaning performance while consuming the minimum amount of water and energy.

Replacing appliances purchased new in 1995 with equivalent new efficient models would save the following approximate amounts, based on a family of four and an electricity cost of 15p/kWh (2012 figures):

Appliance	EU energy rating	Saving/year
Fridge freezer	A+	£63
Upright/chest freezer	A+	£49
Refrigerator	A+	£28
Washing machine	A	£14
Dishwasher	A	£28

Savings for A++ refrigeration appliances are, on average, £6 per year greater.[(2)]

'ENERGY SAVING RECOMMENDED' LOGO

The 'energy saving recommended' logo is a UK scheme managed by the Energy Saving Trust. It only endorses the most energy-efficient products available. The logo acts in conjunction with the EU label and means that the product is guaranteed to save energy, cost less and help the environment.

THE EUROPEAN ECOLABEL

Some products are also awarded the Ecolabel. It may appear on the packaging, for example on the EU energy ratings label. This means that the product has been independently assessed to meet strict environmental criteria from production through to packaging, use and eventual disposal. The Ecolabel is a voluntary European scheme which has been in existence since 1992 and is used for a wide variety of products (paint, floor coverings, cleaning products and so forth) in addition to electrical appliances.

HEAT REPLACEMENT EFFECT

All electrical appliances and lights give off heat and this heat contributes toward the warming of a dwelling.

As appliances become more efficient, this heat output is reduced. In summer the heat output from electrical appliances is unwanted, so more efficient products represent an absolute saving in energy and CO_2 emissions. In winter, however, there is a small but significant addition to the heating requirements in a house. This is known as the 'Heat Replacement Effect' and has been studied in some detail.

For further information see the briefing note 'BNXS29: The Heat Replacement Effect – thermal simulation of domestic lighting and appliances', published by the Market Transformation Programme (updated 2006).

Lighting

Conventional tungsten or incandescent light bulbs generate more heat than light. Low-energy light bulbs are designed so that more of the energy produces light rather than heat, so they are a more efficient way of lighting your home, although the quality of light which they produce is not to everyone's taste. An improved range of 'colour temperatures' is now available in some energy-saving lamp designs – the lower the colour temperature the 'warmer' the light.

As lamp technology is still evolving, this may be an ambitious timetable.

REGULATION CORNER

The EU has taken the lead with legislation to phase out less efficient lamps across the community. 100W tungsten lamps have already been phased out and from September 2011, 60W bulbs and above must be category C or better. Remaining less efficient lamps will be phased out according to the following timetable:

Date	Requirement
1 September 2012	Phase out of all remaining clear incandescent lamps (i.e. 40W and 25W).
1 September 2013	Enhanced functionality requirements
1 September 2016	Raising the minimum level to B class for clear retrofit lamps (i.e. phasing out C-class retrofit halogen lamps).

Categories A to G are defined by the lumens per watt achieved by the lamp – i.e. the light output for a given energy input and can be summarised as follows:*

Lamp technology	Energy savings	Energy class
Incandescent lamps		E, F, G
Conventional halogens (mains voltage 220V)	0–15%	D E F
Conventional halogens (low voltage 12V)	25%	C
Halogens with xenon gas filling (mains voltage 220V)	25%	C
Halogens with infrared coating	45%	B (lower end)
CFLs with bulb-shaped cover and low light output, LEDs	65%	B (higher end)
CFLs with bare tubes or high light output, LEDs	80%	A

* EU MEMO/09/368 Brussels, 1 September 2009

HALOGEN LAMPS

Halogen or dichroic lamps are popular as the quality of light they produce is attractive and the angle of focus is appropriate for many domestic locations. They are available in either standard (240V) or low-voltage (usually 12V) versions and they tend to be used in multiples in any room so they normally use more energy in total than centrally positioned tungsten lighting.

The energy used by halogen lamps can be reduced by substitution with CFL lamps or LEDs (see below) but also by more efficient halogen lamps containing an alumimium reflector to prevent heat from escaping upwards thereby improving the efficiency of the lamp. The standard replacement for a 50W halogen GU10 is a 35W lamp, reducing consumption by 30%.

CFLS

Most compact fluorescent lamps (CFLs) take a second or two to light and can take up to a minute to attain their full brightness, so they may not be suitable for all locations – such as staircases, where immediate full illumination is required. They are best suited to areas where lights are left on for long periods – for example in living rooms or in hallways that need to be lit constantly. Outside security lighting that needs to be left on and is not sensor-controlled is a good candidate for low-energy lamps. Typically, energy-saving lamps use a quarter of the energy required by conventional lamps. Note that CFLs may not be suitable for use with some sensors, timers and dimmers.

Of all the improvements that can be made to domestic property, energy-saving lamps have one of the fastest payback times:

Tungsten lamp	60W
Replacement lamp	15W CFL
Cost of CFL	£4.00
Hours per day	6
Price per kWh	£0.12
Cost of use of original lamp per day	60/1000 x 6 x £0.14 = 5.04p
Cost of use of CFL lamp per day	15/1000 x 6 x £0.14 = 1.26p
Saving per day	5.04p – 1.26p = 3.78p
Payback period	400 ÷ 3.78 = 106 days

* Electricity standby consumption only

The payback period for switching from a 60W tungsten lamp to a compact fluorescent lamp (CFL) based on these assumptions would be under 4 months.

As remaining tungsten lamps are phased out, focus will move elsewhere to find further energy savings. It may be worth knowing that there is now a CFL replacment for the commonly used Halogen GU10 spotlight.

All lamps generate heat as well as light so they contribute towards the heating of the house. When moving to a more efficient lamp this 'useful heat' is reduced, so there will be a corresponding increase in heat demand (see Heat Replacement Effect above).

The price of CFLs is up to ten times the cost of tungsten lamps but on average they last ten times longer. The net result is that over a sufficient period of time the cost of the bulbs themselves (rather than their energy use) is similar at current prices.

Look for the 'Energy Efficiency Recommended' logo on the bulb packaging, as there are cheaper 'economy' bulbs around which may not last as long or save so much energy. Also check for the EU Energy label, which should be 'A' for all energy-saving bulbs. Alternatively, the Ecolabel has a wider set of criteria regarding manufacture, packaging and disposal rather than just energy use.

CFLs draw more current when starting up than in operation so, in some cases, where there is more than one fluorescent lamp on the same switched circuit, cables and switch gear may need to be uprated. If in any doubt, consult a qualified electrician.

It should be pointed out, however, that CFLs contain at least 5mg of mercury, which is a toxic chemical and one of the main substances targeted by the RoHS 2006 legislation (see the section on 'Electronic equipment' in Chapter 9). This mercury is released into the domestic environment if the bulbs are broken and the number of lamps which can safely be disposed of via normal household waste is unclear. The recycling of fluorescent lamps is only now (somewhat belatedly) being developed so it is possible that most of the mercury might eventually be recovered in this way.

See also the comments on 'Building Regulations' at the end of this section.

FITTINGS

When changing over to more efficient lighting, it is essential that lamps and lamp-holders (caps and bases) match up correctly.

Some types of lamp-holder can only accept low-energy bulbs, so people are then obliged to use low-energy lighting.

However, most fittings in domestic property are of the

Lamp-holder for low-energy bulbs.

'bayonet cap' type and the most common energy-saving bulbs have been designed to suit this type of fitting. Energy-saving bulbs are now available to suit the smaller bayonet base and both sizes of screw fittings.

LEDS

Light-emitting diodes (LEDs) are still relatively new to the domestic lighting market but many people believe them to be the future of lighting design. They are well known in the electronics industry and are used widely in panel indication applications. There are relatively few LED lights available for use in homes at present but the market is growing steadily.

LEDs are available in a wide variety of colours including a range of different white 'temperatures'. Although the control gear can generate some heat, the lamps themselves

produce very little (and have no fragile filament) so LEDs can be installed in certain locations where fitting other kinds of lights would be impossible.

LEDs also last much longer than other types of light emitters – a typical high-power LED will be emitting 70% of its initial lumen output after 100,000 hours and it will be millions of hours to total electrical failure. As they produce a negligible amount of heat they are highly energy-efficient and comparable at present to the best CFLs. A common use of LEDs in domestic lighting is as a replcement for Halogen GU10 lamps in downlighters.

LED lamps have now been developed to replace fluorescent (strip) lights. This produces a 50% saving in running costs and they last many times longer but at

LED version of Halogen GU 10.

present they are rather expensive – for example, 8–10W 600mm (2ft) LED lamps currently cost anything up to £25 compared to a normal 18W 600mm T8 lamp at £4.

COLD CATHODE FLUORESCENT LAMPS (CCFLS)

Like LEDs, cold cathode lamps are only just being developed for the domestic market. They are mostly used in torches, lightboxes and in electronic goods such as scanners and monitors. Essentially they are discharge lamps and are similar in many ways to fluorescent lamps but they have three main advantages over ordinary fluorescent lamps and CFLs:

- CCFLs use 50% less mercury than CFLs
- CCFLs last several times longer than CFLs (further reducing the mercury use)
- CCFLs are dimmable and lifespan is not affected by repeated switching.

The range of CCFLs is currently limited but, given their advantages, it is possible that they will become more widely available.

EXTERIOR LIGHTING

Security lights are sometimes used more for outdoor space lighting than for security. It is often possible to replace a 500W halogen lamp in a security light with a 150W lamp and find that it does the required job just as efficiently. If not angled carefully, security lights can cause nuisance as they are bright and have a wide beam, even if they are only on for a short period of time. Reducing the wattage of bulbs in security lights will reduce this problem in addition to saving energy and, as less heat is generated, the luminaire units will also tend to last longer, since they can become brittle through extended use.

Also see the comments on 'Building Regulations' at the end of this section.

Several garden light ranges are now available which use low-wattage halogen or LED bulbs. Solar-powered garden lights do not increase electricity consumption, although the cheaper models may not last, so some will turn out to be a waste of money and resources.

LOW-VOLTAGE LIGHTING

There is sometimes confusion over low-voltage lighting, as some people believe that low-voltage systems are automatically low energy consumers. This is not necessarily true, as it is the type of bulb which matters most, not the voltage at which it is operating. In general, low-voltage lamps (for example 12V or 24V) require more current (amps) to deliver the same wattage as the equivalent lamp running at 240V. Put simply, volts x amps = watts.

However, it is worth bearing in mind that battery systems powered by PV or wind are usually running at 12V, so it would be efficient to use 12V CFLs in conjunction with alternative power sources to avoid the need for a separate inverter. (See the next chapter for more information on low-voltage alternative energy sources.)

Note that as low-voltage lighting draws more current on the load side of the transformer (if present), cables and switch gear need to be sized accordingly.

CONTROL SYSTEMS

We have become accustomed to good levels of lighting throughout our houses, but lights are often left on in places where we are not, illuminating unoccupied space and burning energy needlessly. This most commonly occurs in what is known as the 'communication areas' of dwellings – i.e. halls, stairs, landings and corridors. Lights also often get left on in rooms which we visit briefly but regularly such as bathrooms.

Most lights in homes are controlled by simple on/off switches. It can make sense to install sensors in halls or landings so that the lights switch on automatically when you enter the area and switch off automatically after a pre-

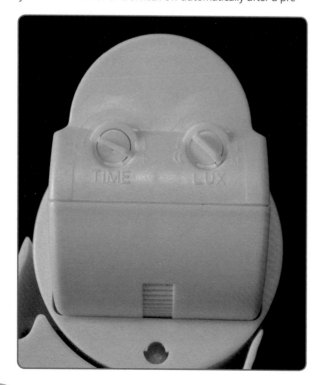

set time. Most people are familiar with this technology as Passive Infra Red (PIR) switching is widely used for security lighting and burglar alarm systems. PIRs are activated by movement in their field of detection.

PIRs can normally be adjusted to suit time overrun and some have a control for sensitivity. Time overrun is simply the time that the light remains on once the switch has been activated by the PIR. Of course a pre-set timer may mean that the light stays on after you have left the area, consuming further energy, so people who habitually turn off the lights as they leave rooms, corridors or stairs would not benefit from installing PIRs. Note that some PIRs are not suited to work with low-energy lamps.

Sensitivity controls allow the user to set the approximate size of signal which is required to trigger the switch. This avoids the light switching on whenever pets, for example, enter the detection field. It has been known for insects to trip PIRs in burglar alarm systems!

Some control units - including all those in exterior lighting, have an integral photocell. This will detect whether there is already sufficient daylight present and avoid switching on the light unnecessarily. The lux control in the model shown can be adjusted to determine the level of light needed to trigger the switch. It is also possible to fit photocells to dim or turn off lights, depending on daylight levels, without the use of a PIR.

CABLE

Most cable sold in the UK is sheathed with a protective layer made from PVC. In the event of a fire, this emits toxic smoke containing hydrochloric acid, among other chemicals. An alternative product, low smoke and fume (LSF) cable, gives off greatly reduced amounts of smoke but still emits halogens, whereas low smoke zero halogen (LSOH) cable is the safest of all in a house fire. Of course, if the LSF cable is distributed through PVC trunking then the additional effort and expense has been wasted, as the PVC content of the trunking would probably exceed that of the cable.

Building Regulations on lighting

The Approved Document L1B (2010) requires that reasonable provision shall be made to ensure that fixed building services are energy-efficient, have effective controls and have been commissioned to optimise fuel use. Fixed building services include:

- internal or external lighting systems;
- heating and hot water;
- air-conditioning and mechanical ventilation.

ADL1B states that whenever a fixed building service is extended or provided, 'reasonable provision' would be demonstrated by following the guidance set out in the *Domestic Building Services Compliance Guide* which is available online. (The Guide covers heating, ventilation, cooling, internal and external lighting and renewable energy systems.)

Whenever fixed external lighting is newly fitted, the lamp capacity may not exceed 100W and must switch off automatically when there is sufficient daylight, or the fittings must have sockets which are only capable of receiving a low-energy lamp. For both internal and external lighting, a low energy lamp is defined as having an efficacy greater than 45W/lumen.

For further information see:
- 'Cost Benefit of Lighting' – Energy Saving Trust CE56
- 'Low energy domestic lighting' – Energy Saving Trust GIL20;
- 'Low energy domestic lighting – looking good for less': case studies – Energy Saving Trust CE81.

Voltage optimisation

Voltage optimisation has been employed as a means of reducing energy usage in the non-domestic sector for some years. Many appliances – especially those containing motors – are designed to work optimally at 220V and, although the supply voltage in the UK is variable, supply at 240V is the nominal voltage and 242V is the average. By using voltage optimisation, a consistent (and normally lower) supply voltage is maintained and equipment runs more efficiently, producing substantial savings in overall energy use.

More recently, voltage optimisation has been developed to serve the domestic market.

While there is not yet a general consensus on the savings produced by these units, it is clear that there are measurable reductions available but also some other effects. If voltage is reduced, some machines may work slower and lights will – in theory – burn slightly less brightly. It has certainly been noticed that kettles take significantly longer to boil after voltage optimisation has been introduced.

Manufacturers recommend that specific equipment should not be covered by this technology – including immersion heaters, cookers and dedicated heating circuits. For many households these will constitute the highest electricity-consuming devices in the home, so predicted reductions in total electricity use must be examined closely. Fundamentally, it is necessary to understand exactly what is likely to be reduced by voltage optimisation and what is not – so the savings and payback can be calculated accurately.

Daylighting

Homes which have plenty of natural daylight are generally regarded as being healthier and easier to live in. As with so many aspects of eco-renovation, when faced with dimly-lit rooms overshadowed by other buildings or suffering from absurdly small windows, the homeowner is entitled to say with hindsight 'I wouldn't have built it this way'. However, there are some steps that can be taken to improve daylighting in existing buildings and reduce the demand for artificial light.

WINDOW CLEANING

Dirty windows can reduce the amount of light entering a room by up to 20%. Dirt on the windowpanes also affects the quality of the light so it is well worth cleaning them regularly.

CURTAINS AND BLINDS

When fixing curtain track, allow for an area either side of the window so that the curtains can be drawn back without covering any part of the glazed area itself.

Blinds vary in size and fixing design but often they are fixed within reveals rather than above them. If fitted above the reveal they can be rolled or pulled up without obstructing the window.

Many old buildings have splayed window reveals to admit more light. Some eco-builders have started to

Above: Blind above window reveal.
Below: Blind within window reveal.

reintroduce this detail into housing – a good example of green building techniques mirroring those which were common before the 20th century. Splayed reveals allow a smaller (thus cheaper) window to be used, with a corresponding reduction in heat loss.

Splayed reveal – above, old; below, new.

glass should be self-cleaning. In terms of saving money or CO_2 emissions. a light pipe would have a very long payback period but it is an excellent way of delivering natural light to dark corners. Light pipes can also be combined with ventilation systems, so they are particularly useful for bathrooms and kitchens.

Where major building work is planned, light wells can be introduced (in place of light pipes), which admit considerably greater amounts of light. Light wells are much more common in commercial buildings than in domestic property.

Photos: Solalighting Ltd

ROOF LIGHTS

Roof lights are excellent at admitting daylight because the view of the sky is usually unobstructed from the roof. Technically, it is usually easier to add a roof light than to add a window, and much less likely to require planning permission. Roof lights are particularly useful over landings – landing lights being the ones most commonly left on when not needed – avoiding the need for electric light altogether for most of the day.

LIGHT PIPES

Some parts of a house are difficult to get daylight into by conventional means. A light pipe takes light from outside (usually the roof) and then transfers it down a reflective tube to where it's needed. The tubes are sized to fit between rafters and floor joists.

Inside the house, a light pipe looks similar to a fluorescent panel light. An electric light can even be located within the tube for night-time use. At roof level the pipe protrudes only slightly through the roof covering; flashing kits are available to suit most kinds of roof.

Light pipes generally need no maintenance as the roof

Installing a tubular daylight system

Tubular daylight systems vary in design so it will be necessary to check the installation instructions provided with any particular system. The following example is based upon the installation of a 'Solatube 250mm Daylight System', courtesy of Solalighting Ltd.

THE SOLATUBE SYSTEM COMPRISES:
- Dome and reflector
- Roof flashing kit
- Pre-assembled adjustable angle top tube
- Pre-assembled adjustable angle bottom tube
- Diffuser
- Sealants, fixings and installation instructions

TOOLS REQUIRED
- Hole Saw
- Hammer
- Tile saw (or angle grinder)/slate cutter
- Drill
- Screwdriver
- Roof access system

Note: *Access to the roof is required to fit the flashing kit and the dome. Ensure that the enclosed health & safety recommendations for roof access are followed. Please visit* **http://www.hse.gov.uk/falls/roof.htm** *and take note of the relevant suggestions before commencing work.*

1 Identify the desired location on the ceiling for the diffuser, ensuring that the path from the diffuser to the roof will be free of obstacles such as joists, pipes or wires. Check also that the roof flashing fits in the desired location. Ideally, the tubing should run as straight as possible between the roof and the ceiling, but pitched roofs, attic obstructions and diffuser location can make this difficult. Adjustable angle adapters allow you to adjust the top and bottom tubes to the degree necessary to allow easy connection between the roof and the ceiling.

2 Mark up the hole to be cut for the diffuser on the ceiling, using the template provided. Carefully cut a hole in the ceiling with a hole saw.

3 Turn the angle adjuster so that the bottom tube points towards the roof flashing. Insert the bottom tube components into the ceiling hole and twist the locking arms to secure the bottom tube to the ceiling.

6 If a light reflector is provided, clip this into the dome and orientate the dome so that the reflector faces south. Ensure that the dome seals are securely placed and fix the dome to the flashing.

7 Within the loft space, join the top and bottom tubes using the extension tubes. Ensure the protective film on the inside of the top and bottom tube and any extension tubes is removed before final assembly. Seal the tubes carefully using the aluminium tape provided to prevent insects and dust from entering the tubes. Self tapping screws may be required to join longer tube lengths securely and support wires should be used if the tubing is travelling any significant distance across the loft space.

4 Establish safe access to the roof. Remove tiles or slates from the location identified for the dome. Fix the roof flashing to the battens. Replace any tiles or slates, cutting as necessary and seal to ensure water-tightness as directed in the instructions for the particular roof type on your property.

5 Now take the pre-assembled top tube components and drop them into the turret of the roof flashing. Check in the loft space that the top tube is pointing towards the bottom tube. Turn the angle adjuster to achieve this if necessary.

8 Finally, attach the ceiling diffuser to the bottom tube assembly to complete the installation.

6 MICRO-GENERATION

Photo: Carymoor Environmental Centre

Micro-generation is the production of electricity at the domestic scale. This chapter looks at the main types of micro-generation available in the domestic market, namely:

- **Photovoltaic panels**
- **Micro wind turbines**
- **Micro hydro power**
- **Combined Heat and Power (CHP)**

In each case, the advantages and disadvantages are laid out and the payback period is calculated making allowance for subsidies via the Feed-in Tariff.

Introduction to Micro-generation

Micro-generation can be independent of the mains supply or linked to it. Where the system is independent, storage facilities such as batteries will be required. The most effective way to use the energy generated is at the same voltage, avoiding the cost of an inverter and the efficiency losses associated with transforming to higher voltages. In practice, however, the output from most micro-generation equipment is used or exported at 240v.

Perhaps the main advantage of micro-generation is that the energy is generated at the point where it is consumed, so avoiding the transmission losses associated with the distribution system for electricity generated in power stations. Decentralised energy also improves energy security, if only marginally. It has the more significant added advantage that people who have micro-generation systems installed tend to become much more aware of their consumption of electricity and use it more efficiently as a result.

A wide range of factors will have an influence when making a decision on whether or not to install micro renewables. This might include:

- Financial impact
- Environmental benefits
- Appearance
- Planning permission
- Perceived risk
- Anticipated disruption
- Availability of installers
- Added value upon sale of the property.

The energy used to manufacture, transport and install any equipment used to generate electricity constitutes the 'embodied energy' of that equipment. In other words, just as there is a financial payback period for micro-generation, there is also an energy payback period, after which it will have generated more energy than was needed to manufacture, distribute and install the equipment. When considering the

environmental benefits it is important to look at embodied energy in the context of the expected life of the equipment. It is equally important to be aware of other impacts in terms of pollution and water use in manufacture.

The examples of payback periods given in this chapter are based on assumptions that are likely to change. When calculating payback periods it is therefore important to make sure that current information is used.

Feed-in Tariffs

Feed-in Tariffs (FiTs) were introduced in Great Britain in 2010. (They are not currently available in Northern Ireland.) FiTs aim to "encourage the deployment of additional small scale low carbon electricity generation, particularly by individuals, householders, organisations, businesses and communities."[1]

FiTs provide a payment for each unit of electricity generated, and a second (smaller) payment for electricity exported to the grid. FiTs will be funded by a levy upon electricity bills, so the cost will be passed on to all consumers. The high generation tariff levels initially set for PV in particular and the reduction in the cost of the equipment led to level of take-up which exceeded government predictions and the FiT for PV was reduced dramatically in 2012.

GENERATION TARIFFS

At present (2012) the most relevant[†] generation tariffs for householders are as follows:

Energy Source	Scale	Tariff (p/kWh)	Duration (years)
Solar PV	≤4 kW new	16.0	20
Solar PV	≤4 kW retrofit	16.0	20
Solar PV	4kW – 10kW	14.5	20
Hydro	≤15 kW	21.9	20
Wind	≤1.5kW	37.9	20
Wind	1.5kW - 15kW	29.3	20
Micro-CHP	<2 kW	12.5	10

Source: Ofgem Tariff Tables 1 August 2012.

[†]There are other (lower) tariffs for larger PV and wind installations. Support is also provided for anaerobic digestion – not included here as it does not apply to most householders.

In order to qualify for the rates of subsidy quoted above for PV, the government has introduced a requirement that the dwelling must meet a certain level of energy efficiency. This reflects the fact that investments in energy efficiency are a much more cost-effective way to reduce emissions than micro-generation. Applicants now need to demonstrate that the building to which the solar PV installation is attached or wired to provide electricity has an Energy Performance Certificate rating of Level D or above. Generators who cannot demonstrate that they meet the energy efficiency requirement will only be eligible for a lower tariff (currently

7.1p/kWh) for the duration of the tariff lifetime. The Government is consulting on proposals to extend this requirement to forms of micro-generation other than PV.

At present, the Generation Tariff, once installed, will be increased each year in line with inflation. Generation tariffs are under review at the time of publication so readers should check the latest FiT levels by visiting the DECC website. It is currently proposed that, the level of tariff for new PV installations will be reduced quarterly by 3.5% dependent on deployment (this is known as the rate of degression) – to reflect the fact that this kind of subsidy is intended to be a transitional measure. Existing installations will continue to receive the generation tariff applicable when the technology was installed.

EXPORT TARIFF

Householders will also receive a payment for electricity exported to the National Grid. The export rate is now 4.5p/kWh for PV and for all other technologies is currently set at 3.2p/kWh though this may well change. Where an export meter has not been fitted, the amount of electricity exported is 'deemed' at 50% – so the householder would receive the payment per kWh multiplied by 50% of the output in kWh (taken from the output meter). When smart meters are installed the method for calculating exports may well change to reflect actual electricity exported.

CONSUMPTION AVOIDED

In addition to the generation and export tariffs, the electricity actually produced and used on site is of course free, so whatever electricity use is offset will no longer need to be purchased, providing a further saving to the consumer.

MICROGENERATION CERTIFICATION SCHEME (MCS)

In order for an installation to qualify for the FiT subsidies, the installer must be accredited under the Microgeneration Certification Scheme (MCS). The MCS is a recognised quality assurance scheme designed to provide confidence that installations will be carried out to rigorous professional standards.

MCS does not have an automatic monopoly over certification of products and in theory other schemes may be used (if they have been correctly certified by the UK accreditation service UKAS).

SUMMARY

To summarise, micro-generation with FiTs now produces three types of financial benefit to the homeowner:

Benefit	Level
Generation Tariff: small PV, wind and hydro (less for CHP)	Varies by technology and date of installation
Export Tariff	Based on 50% of electricity generated
Reduction in demand from supplier	Based on 50% of electricity generated

In addition to payback, there are some other factors which may be worth considering when deciding on an investment in micro-generation:

Although the energy companies will be paying the subsidy, FiTs will be funded by consumers. Those who can afford the capital outlay will then benefit while those who do not invest will end up paying, for up to 25 years. This increases fuel poverty for the least well off (albeit marginally at present but the costs will increase) so it has been described as a form of regressive taxation.

In comparison to other methods of generating electricity, micro-generation and PV in particular is relatively inefficient and therefore expensive. If we need to generate renewably to reduce CO_2 emissions for the country as a whole, we need to encourage the technologies that give us the best value for money at least overall environmental impact. These are likely to be larger scale generation systems such as biomass, hydro, offshore wind, clean coal, wave/tidal and even nuclear.

Most of the equipment currently installed for micro-generation is imported. This does little to stimulate the UK economy or develop new manufacturing jobs and weakens the balance of payments and hence the pound.

Micro-generation offers an attractive investment at present due to the FiT. However, it will do relatively little to reduce our carbon footprint or to stimulate the economy. To compare with other means of reducing carbon emissions:

Photovoltaic panels

Photovoltaic cells convert the energy in light (photons) into electrical energy (volts), hence the name. Individual

Installation in progress.

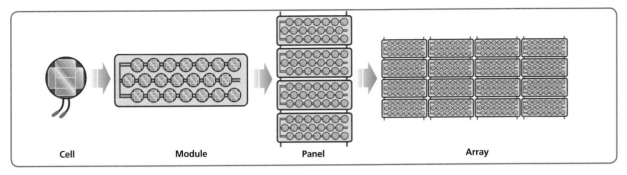

Cell   Module   Panel   Array

photovoltaic cells produce very small amounts of electricity so they are grouped together into modules. A panel consists of several modules linked together. Where several panels are grouped together this is known as an array.

The power generated by photovoltaic cells is direct current at low voltage. Unless the power is being used solely to run low-voltage d/c appliances, it needs to be converted to 240V a/c by means of an inverter. Apart from the inverter, photovoltaic generation systems do not take up any internal space. A cable connects the panels to the inverter and the system is then connected into the mains.

Inverter.

TECHIE CORNER: PHOTOVOLTAIC CELLS

A photovoltaic cell consists of a junction between two thin layers of dissimilar semiconducting materials. These materials are usually based on silicon, although photovoltaic cells can also be made from other materials.

The first layer, known as the 'p' type layer, is created by doping the silicon with tiny amounts of boron. This effectively causes a shortage of electrons and hence a positive charge. The second layer, known as the 'n' type layer, is doped with small amounts of phosphorus, which creates a surplus of electrons and hence a negative charge. The barrier between these two layers is known as the p–n junction. When energy in the form of light is applied at this point, the electrons are given enough energy to move across the junction. This in turn creates a 'potential difference' or 'voltage'. If the circuit is completed, this potential difference drives the flow of electrons around the circuit and an electrical current is produced.

There are four main types of PV cell:

Monocrystalline cells are the most expensive and efficient cells presently in mass production. A single silicon seed crystal is drawn into a cylinder and cut into thin wafers which are then doped to create the 'n' and 'p' type layers described above. Monocrystalline cells are considered to be the most durable of currently available PV cells.

Polycrystalline cells are cut from a mass of silicon which has been melted and re-crystallised. The rest of the process is similar to that used to create monocrystalline cells. Polycrystalline cells are slightly cheaper to produce but approximately 20 per cent less efficient.

Thick film silicon is formed by depositing a layer of polycrystalline silicon onto a prepared base material by means of a continuous process. The result is a cheaper but much less efficient system.

Amorphous silicon is not based upon crystalline structure. Instead a thin homogenous layer of silicon is used to absorb the light, so these type of cells can be spread on a range of substrates. Although they're much less efficient than crystalline cells, they perform well in diffuse light and have the added advantage that they can be used on curved surfaces.

Illustration: solarcentury.com

Photo: solarcentury.com

Generation of electricity by means of photovoltaic panels is silent and they do not require direct sunlight to operate, which means that they still generate some power even in the UK's frequently cloudy conditions. Once panels have been installed, the electricity which is produced is free. Panels may be expected to last 25–30 years and require little or no maintenance. The electricity is non-polluting and generates no CO_2 or other emissions while the system is in use. Inverters may require replacement once or twice during the life of the panels but there is not enough data available to be more specific.

MOUNTING AND ORIENTATION

Panels are normally mounted on south-facing roofs, although any roof facing south-east to south-west will perform relatively well. Any overshading from trees or surrounding buildings will reduce the power output. The ideal slope for mounting panels is 30° to 40° which works well with roof pitches commonly used in the UK.

Flat roofs are also suitable for PV installation. Suitably angled mounting brackets will be needed to compensate

for the fact that the sun is not high enough in the sky for a long enough period in the UK for the panels to be laid flat.

For installations on pitched or flat roofs, it is necessary to check that the roof can support the additional weight of the panels. Installers should address this question but, if there is any doubt, the opinion of a structural engineer should be sought.

ROOF TILES

Photo: solarcentury.com

PV cells can also be made into roof tiles. These are more expensive than panels and the output is lower per square metre so it is really only worth considering this option if you are building an extension or carrying out a major refurbishment which includes re-roofing, as the cost of the omitted roof covering can be offset against the cost of the tiles. PV tiles can be fully integrated into a roof covering, so they may be preferable to panels for both technical and aesthetic reasons.

PLANNING PERMISSION

Planning permission is not normally required to fit PV panels or tiles to a pitched roof but may be required for flat roofs. However, it is always best to check with your Local Authority. Permission would probably be required for houses in conservation areas and conservation consent would be needed in order to fix PV panels to a listed building.

OUTPUT

The output from PV panels varies significantly over the course of the day, peaking at around 1:00pm if the sun is out and falling sharply whenever there is cloud cover. Output from PV panels is measured at the peak rate of production, shown as kWp – kilowatts produced at peak.

A 1kWp system in a good location may be expected to produce 800kWh of usable electricity per year. This is equivalent to approximately 25% of the average (non-heating) annual consumption of electricity per household in the UK. To meet a total household demand of 3,300kWh over the course of a year, a 4kWp system would therefore be required.

GRID CONNECTION

PV panels generate most of their electricity during the daytime when domestic demand is generally low, which is the opposite of what is needed, so mains electricity will still be required. Unless the property is off-grid or the system is designed to be independent and used primarily to run low-voltage applications, it makes sense to connect the PV panels to the grid.

Surplus electricity that is not used immediately in the household is exported to the grid. During the time when the panels are not generating, electricity will have to be imported and paid for as normal.

It is the installer's responsibility to inform the local distribution network operator (DNO) that a new PV system has been connected to the grid and this is usually carried out as part of the standard installation service.

FEED-IN-TARIFF (FIT) FOR PV

The following tariffs apply to PV at the time of writing (2012)

Tariff	Level
Generation Tariff	16p/kWh
Export Tariff (currently applied to 50% of the power generated)	4.5p/kWh

The generation tariff available is expected to be reduced regularly as panel prices fall. However, once fixed for any particular installation, the generation tariff will be increased annually in line with inflation. The payments are guaranteed for 25 years from the date of commissioning.

However, FiTs have been reviewed twice – so it is wise to check the current rates. (See the section on FiTs at the beginning of this chapter.)

PAYBACK PERIOD

The simple payback period is the amount of time it takes for the cost of the installation to be repaid. Without subsidy, the payback on PV exceeds 40 years but the introduction of the FiT has radically altered that equation.

The details given here have been worked out purely as an example and you will need to insert up-to-date figures in order to work out the actual payback period.

System size	2kWp
Total cost	£5,000
Amount of electricity produced p.a.	1,600kWh
Generation tariff @16p/kWh	£256
Export tariff (deemed at 50%) @ 4.5p/kWh	£36
Electricity saving (50% of production) at 15p/kWh	£120
Total benefit	£412
Payback period = £5,000 ÷ £412 =	**12 years**

In order to justify the expense of installation, the payback period must be less than the expected life of the system. Susidised as in the above example, the payback period is well within the expected life. Without subsidy, the payback probably exceeds the life of the system.

We do not yet have enough long-term data to establish how PV systems will perform over 10 or 20 years. Some degradation in performance is expected and when working out longer-term paybacks it might be wise to allow for a 10% drop at 10 years and 20% after 20 years. It is also necessary to factor in the cost of inverter replacement at least once during the life of the system.

ENVIRONMENTAL IMPACT

The payback period may not be the only issue to consider when deciding on investment in a PV system. It takes energy and raw materials to build, transport, install and maintain any energy generation system and the end-of-life impacts must also be considered. Research indicates that it will take 3–4 years [1] for a small PV system in Mid Europe to repay the energy cost of manufacture and installation although some estimates are higher. Some rare or toxic materials are used in manufacture there have been incidents of the release of toxic waste from PV plants in China so it will be necessary to monitor the production impact closely if PV is to be deployed more widely in the UK. Research is only now being carried out on how spent modules should be recycled at the end of their economic life – the impact of recycling is excluded from the energy payback period quoted above, as is the impact of reconditioning or replacing the inverter at least once.

There are also wider social and economic impacts of FiTs to bear in mind – see the section on FiTs at the start of this chapter.

FREE SOLAR PV OFFERS

The size of the subsidies for PV has led to a situation whereby private companies offer to install PV for free on houses and the householder continues to benefit from the free electricity generated. Of course the company carrying out the installation keeps the subsidies available under the FiT. This is sometimes referred to as rent-a-roof – where the householder receives a small sum per annum in addition to the free electricity.

Consumer guidance on free solar PV offers is provided on the EST website.

Wind turbines

Wind has been used to generate power in the UK for centuries. Like photovoltaic systems, wind turbines generate electricity from a clean and renewable source of energy, in contrast to fossil fuels.

BUILDING-MOUNTED MINI WIND TURBINES

Many people associate mini wind turbines with their much larger cousins which have been the source of much controversy, as older models are noisy and they all have a very significant visual impact on the landscape. Mini wind turbines produce comparatively little noise and are not much larger than a satellite dish. Horizontal axis wind turbines have blades like a propeller.

Vertical axis wind turbines are less common in the UK although they do have some advantages in terms of performance at low wind speeds. Opinions differ as to their efficiency overall and at present there is a shortage of performance data for a useful comparison and there are few models available in the UK at the domestic scale. At present most VAWTs are independently mounted.

Not all buildings are structurally suitable for mounting mini wind turbines. The manufacturers have obviously gone to great lengths to ensure their mechanical and electrical safety but a weak or defective building should be checked carefully. In some circumstances a bespoke support structure will be required.

At present, in Northern Ireland an application to Building Control is required for building-mounted wind turbines. However, approval from Building Control is not currently required for free-standing wind turbines unless structural changes are made to the building which benefits from the output of the turbine. The situation in the rest of the UK is still unclear and the turbine installer should clarify the updated position on Building Control requirements.

Photo: Courtesy of QRS

Vertical Azis Wind Turbine.

Photo: Carymoor Environmental Centre

Horizontal Azis Wind Turbine.

Photo: Renewable Devices Swift Turbines Ltd

SMALL WIND TURBINES

Small wind turbines (for example 2.5kW to 25kW) are the next size up from mini wind turbines. Whether horizontal or vertical axis, they are usually independently pole-mounted as they need to be sited sufficiently high and far away from obstacles to avoid turbulence. They are therefore only suitable for houses with sufficient land but are very useful in rural areas. Some turbines require guy ropes to provide stability and therefore have quite a significant 'footprint'. Turbines over 5kW can also be used for small shared power schemes, as they can generate more power than is needed for the average UK domestic property. Shared schemes normally involve setting up an ESCO (Energy Services Company) through which the shared source of energy can be purchased and managed and costs can be allocated. Any independent pole-mounted turbine will probably require planning permission.

OUTPUT

For horizontal axis wind turbines, the power of a wind turbine is proportional to the square of the diameter of the rotor blades and to the cube of the wind speed:

Where : **D** = air density
A = area swept by the blades
V = wind speed
C = capacity factor
Power = **C** x **D**^{2} x **A** x **V**^{3}

So, for a given wind speed a turbine with a diameter of 2m will be producing four times as much power as a turbine with a diameter of 1m. Similarly, a turbine will produce almost double the amount of power at a wind speed of 6m/s compared to a wind speed of 5m/s. Not all the energy available in the airstream can be harvested by the turbine or the air would have no energy left to blow away downstream; the theoretical maximum is 0.59, known as the Betz limit but for the purposes of calculation it is realistic to assume a capacity factor of 0.5.

Wind turbines are rated by comparing their output at a given wind speed of 12m/s (27mph). This does not mean that average wind speeds are expected to be at this level; it is purely a means of rating the turbines. Given a wind speed of 12m/s, a 1kW wind turbine will be generating at 1kW. Typical wind speeds in the UK are much lower than this, so the turbine will normally be operating at a greatly reduced rate, producing no power at all at wind speeds below 3m/s. At very high wind speeds, wind turbines have safety cut-outs to prevent damage to the system.

The actual output of any particular wind turbine is therefore sensitive to three factors: geographical location, obstructions and turbulence, and height of mounting. The last two are similar – at greater height there are, of course, fewer obstructions, but average wind speed also increases significantly with increasing height, quite independently of obstructions. Annual output figures quoted by manufacturers in terms of kilowatt hours are very sensitive to local wind speed and conditions, so many sites can be expected to produce much less than the quoted figures. If it appears that your home is unsuitable for a mini-wind turbine, a similar reduction in environmental impact might be achieved by investing the equivalent sum in a wind farm. Local co-operatives can also be formed to invest in medium-sized turbines on sites nearby which have a better wind resource.

WIND SPEEDS

Wind speed varies widely across Britain. Data on wind speeds for every part of the country is available from the NOABL database. This can presently be accessed via the British Wind Energy Association at www.bwea.com/noabl/

index.html. Average wind speeds are also available from the Met Office website at **http://www.metoffice.gov.uk/ climate/uk/averages/19712000/index.html.** This will be updated with data from 1981–2011 during 2012.

The available wind speed data takes no account of turbulence which will be thrown up by neighbouring buildings, trees and other obstructions. Speeds are also quoted for heights that are greater than those at which an average building-mounted turbine will be operating, so the figures must be treated with some caution.

Where average wind speeds are less than 5m/s, the economic viability of a wind turbine should be calculated carefully and will be very dependent on the site and the height of the mounting. Other areas with higher wind speeds may still be unviable if there is significant turbulence in the location selected.

A report [3] into performance of mini wind turbines by the Energy Saving Trust stressed the output is highly sensitive to location and local wind speeds. "The NOABL database was found to significantly overestimate the wind resource at urban sites. It should not be used for wind speed estimation unless the site is very remote. The new Microgeneration Certification Scheme installer standard has incorporated an adjustment to NOABL that is now used by accredited installers. This method provides a more accurate prediction of wind speeds than NOABL at domestic locations, especially for urban and suburban sites. The Carbon Trust tool for wind speed estimation was found to be the most accurate method to predict wind speeds at potential sites of both free-standing and building-mounted turbines." **www.carbontrust.co.uk/wind-estimator**

GRID CONNECTION

In grid-connected systems, the output from the turbine is converted to 240V a/c by means of an inverter and the power generated is used primarily to serve the domestic electricity demand by means of a direct connection to the distribution system within the house. However, wind turbines generate power at rates which are completely independent of

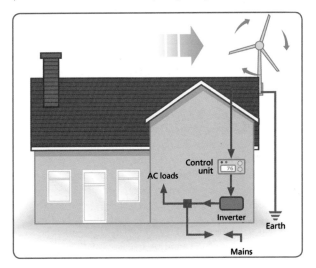

consumption patterns, so during the time when the turbine is not generating (in excess of consumption), power will have to be imported and paid for as normal.

As with a PV system, it is the installer's responsibility to inform the local distribution network operator that a mini-wind turbine has been connected to the grid and this should be carried out as part of the standard installation service.

FEED-IN-TARIFF (FIT) FOR MICRO/MINI WIND

The following tariffs apply to wind turbines at the time of writing (2012)

Tariff	Level
Generation Tariff ≤5kW	37.9p/kWh
Generation Tariff 1.5kW–15kW	2.9p/kWh
Export Tariff (based on 50%)	3.2p/kWh

These tariffs are guaranteed for 20 years from the date of commissioning. However, FiTs are under review – see section on FiTs at the start of this chapter.

PAYBACK PERIOD

The simple payback period is the amount of time it takes for the cost of the installation to be repaid.

The details given here have been worked out purely as an example and you will need to insert up-to-date figures in order to work out the actual payback period. These figures are for a 1.5kW wind turbine in a good area:

Rated system output at 11m/s:	1.0kW
Total cost	£5,000[1]
Amount of electricity produced p.a.	975kWh [2]
Generation tariff @37.9p/kWh	£369
Export tariff (deemed at 50%) @ 3.2p/kWh	£16
Electricity saving (50% of production) at 15p/kWh	£73
Total benefit	£458
Payback period = £5,000 ÷ £458 =	**11 years**

[1] Dorset County Council 2009
[2] Reference: Location location location – EST 2009

*Annual output is subject to testing and to local wind conditions. Actual output may be less than the quoted figure, which will extend the payback period accordingly.

PLANNING PERMISSION

Planning permission is currently (2012) required for mini-wind turbines. Parliament is considering removing this restriction in order to encourage the take-up of micro-renewables and to allow turbines to be installed under 'permitted development' rules. Planning permission will probably be needed in any case for installations where the rotor diameter exceeds 2m. Permission will also almost certainly continue to be needed for conservation areas or for listed buildings.

CHP engine.

Images: Calor Gas

Micro-CHP

Combined heat and power (CHP) systems take advantage of the fact that heat is produced during generation of electricity by means of burning fuel. The excess heat generated by CHP systems has so far been used primarily for district-heating and commercial applications, as the pooling of demand leads to greater efficiencies. Shared schemes also allow for CHP to be run from renewable power sources such as biomass or wood-chip, with the result that both the power and the heat generated are close to being CO_2 neutral and the consumption of fossil fuels is avoided. Even given the energy used in harvesting and transportation, biomass schemes deliver net carbon reductions of up to 90% in comparison to burning fossil fuels.

CHP technology has now been adapted to operate on a domestic scale, so every house with a gas supply has the potential to become a mini power station, generating its own electricity and heat simultaneously. Micro-CHP engines are based on the Stirling external combustion engine, patented in 1816. They are quite unlike internal combustion engines and produce a similar amount of noise to a conventional boiler. From the householder's point of view, a micro-CHP engine is simply a boiler which also generates electricity. When operating, a domestic CHP unit will generate approximately 1,000W (1kW) of electrical power. While this will be sufficient to power lights and some small appliances, a mains electricity supply will still be required.

The micro-CHP engine converts gas into electricity very efficiently and any electricity produced is used at the point of generation, avoiding the transmission losses associated with electricity provision through the national grid. Decentralised generation without transmission losses is one of the main advantages of micro-CHP and why the UK Government is keen to see it deployed more widely.

It is expected that micro-CHP units will be purchased when replacing boilers, as the cost of installation will then be offset by the cost of a new boiler. CHP engines are more expensive than boilers but, based on an electricity saving of £150 per annum, they would repay the *additional* investment (i.e. over and above a replacement boiler) within a few years. They will, however, require additional maintenance as they are more complicated than a boiler, which only generates heat. The basic design of the heating side of a micro-CHP system is similar to a conventional vented system with a hot water cylinder (see 'water heating systems' in Chapter 4).

In contrast to gas boilers, which are designed to heat water quickly and then to shut down, CHP engines are designed to run for long periods to maximise the amount of electricity generated so they are ideally suited to situations where there is a heat demand over a relatively long period.

CHP engine housed outdoors.

A micro-CHP engine has a relatively low heat output and the heating system will take longer to reach full temperature than a system fuelled by a conventional boiler. A micro-CHP engine will therefore need to run for longer periods – for example, starting earlier in the morning – to deliver the same level of thermal comfort. They are designed to be free-standing or wall-hung in the same way as a conventional boiler. They can be located outside – but additional plumbing work would be required if the unit is located in an outhouse or a purpose-built exterior shelter.

From a system designer's point of view it is best to think of a CHP engine as an electricity generator which happens to produce useful heat. As micro-CHP engines are designed to run for long periods, the heat output is ideally suited to running a thermal store system (see 'water heating systems' in Chapter 4). Thermal store systems require a lower-rated source of heat supply than a conventional boiler but the thermal store allows the central-heating system to provide a much faster response time than a conventional heating system which is connected to a CHP engine.

Micro-CHP technology is still under development but the government has a commitment to encourage micro-CHP as it delivers undoubted benefits in efficiency and therefore reductions in CO_2 output, even though it is still consuming a fossil fuel (gas).

FEED-IN TARIFF (FIT) FOR MICRO-CHP

Only one product is currently licensed under the MCS and therefore eligible for the FiT but others may be expected to follow. The following tariffs apply to micro-CHP at the time of writing (2012):

Tariff	Level
Generation Tariff	12.5p/kWh
Export Tariff (based on 50%)	3.2p/kWh

These tariffs are guaranteed for 10 years from the date of commissioning. However, FiTs are under review – see the section on FiTs at the start of this chapter.

For further information see: The Combined Heat & Power Association, **www.chpa.co.uk**

Hot water cylinder system

Micro CHP unit

Mains water

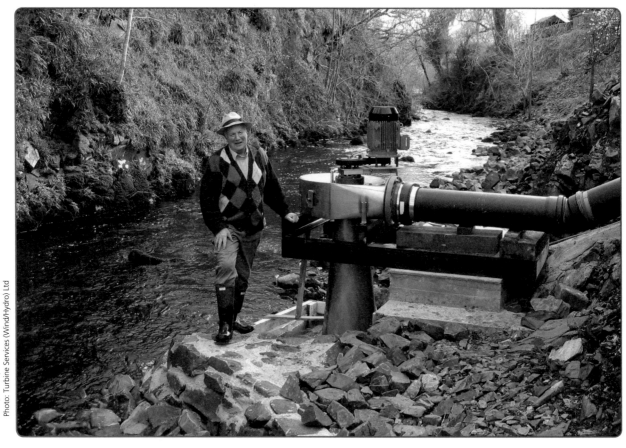

Micro-hydro

Water wheels were once widely used across the UK and streams can now be harnessed as a reliable and consistent means of generating electricity. Unlike wind turbines and photovoltaic panels, micro-hydro generators can operate constantly throughout the day and night. Even if the flow-rate of a stream is reduced in the summer months, these are the times when energy demand is likely to be lowest. In the winter months, when demand is higher,

flow rates and energy generation are also likely to be at their maximum.

Electricity is produced from water flowing from a high level to a lower level, making use of the potential energy of water that falls on high ground. This change in elevation is called 'head' and supplies the pressure that drives the turbine. 'Flow rate' is the other factor contributing to power production and is limited by the size of the stream. The amount of electricity produced is directly proportional to the head and the flow. If the head or flow is increased the power output increases proportionally. The hydro power in a stream or river can be calculated as follows:

Hydro power (kW) =
    head (m) x flow (m³/s) x acceleration due to gravity

For example, if the head is 3.0m and the available flow is 0.12m³ per second, the hydro power is:
    3.00 x 0.12 x 9.81 = 3.5kW

At 50% equipment efficiency, in this example the turbine would generate electricity at the rate of 1.75kW. Turbine efficiencies can be as high as 90%, depending on the degree of sophistication. No abstraction is required – the water which is used to drive the turbine is returned to the stream and, if correctly designed and installed, the equipment should have negligible environmental impact.

Distance from the stream to the property where the energy is to be used need not be a problem as voltage drop over moderate distances is not excessive.

Various different types of turbine are available:

Turbine type	Head range
Propeller, Water Wheel	1.5–5m (ultra low)
Crossflow, Propeller, Kaplan	5–20m (low)

For most of us, sadly, the opportunity to harness hydro power does not arise, so we are limited to PV, Wind and Micro-CHP if we want to reduce our carbon footprint through micro-generation.

FEED-IN TARIFF (FIT) FOR MICRO-HYDRO

The following tariffs apply to micro-hydro at the time of writing (2012):

Tariff	Level
Generation Tariff ≤15kW	21.9p/kWh
Export Tariff (based on 50%)	3.2p/kWh

These tariffs are guaranteed for 20 years from the date of commissioning. However, FiTs are under review – see the section on FiTs at the start of this chapter.

For further information see the British Hydropower Association **http://www.british-hydro.org/index.html**

Green electricity suppliers

One simple way for householders to make a contribution towards improving the environment and reducing their CO_2 emissions is to switch to an electricity supplier which generates some or all of its power from renewable sources such as wind or hydro.

However, this market has been affected more than any other by 'greenwash'. Often, major suppliers offer products based on renewable electricity which they purchase from existing suppliers. While this may take advantage of people's natural desire to be green, it does little towards actually generating any new renewable electricity other than forcing up the price as suppliers compete for a fixed output.

In some cases the companies (or their parent companies) offering the tariffs have a highly questionable environmental record, so it pays to do your research if you really want to make a difference by switching your electricity supplier. By contrast, some suppliers actually dedicate a proportion of their income towards investment in new sources of renewable power, thus actually reducing the carbon intensity of grid electricity.

There is a useful comparison service provided by a leading green energy supplier – Ecotricity – available at **http://www. whichgreen.org/**. It should be stressed that as this emanates from a supplier it cannot be considered impartial, but they are completely transparent about their data sources and methods of calculation and final ranking of suppliers.

Photo: Ari Liddell

This chapter first explains why water conservation is an important subject even in a country where the weather is often much wetter than we would like. All the basic techniques of domestic water conservation in the home and garden are then explained, together with suggestions on how to work out how much you will save by specific measures. The chapter concludes with a section on rainwater harvesting and, for the more adventurous, there are sections on composting toilets and reed beds.

Water – a scarce resource

In most countries, water is treated as a precious and valuable resource. The temperate climate and more than a century of piped mains water have led to a relaxed attitude towards water consumption in the UK, but supplies are now under increasing pressure.

RAINFALL

Statistics indicate that rainfall in the UK is stable in the long term and there appears to have been no statistically significant change for the past 50 years.

The frequency and intensity of rainfall is also important, as sudden heavy downpours may now be more common. Water from this kind of rainfall tends to be washed away rapidly, often causing flooding, rather than soaking into the groundwater system and replenishing underground aquifers. This problem is exacerbated if the ground is very hard after a long period of dry weather, or if the ground is already saturated.

For example, in 1998, after two very wet months, several parts of the Severn and Wye valleys were flooded when heavy rain fell and the ground could not absorb any more water. The problem had been exacerbated by developments upstream on land which once absorbed water, so rain that fell on the hard surfaces was channelled swiftly to the rivers, which ultimately could not cope with the additional discharge.

April Rainfall in the UK

Legend: Data — 1971-2000 Average — Smoothed Kernel Filter; Highest; Lowest; Most recent value

Rainfall (mm) vs Year

Illustration: © Crown copyright 2012, the Met Office

The rainfall pattern is skewed regionally in the UK, with the south and east receiving less water than the north and west.

DEMAND FOR WATER

Nationally, the consumption of water can be broken down into three main sectors:

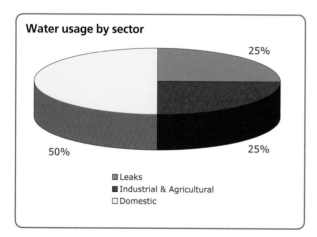

Water usage by sector

- 25%
- 25%
- 50%

■ Leaks
■ Industrial & Agricultural
□ Domestic

The domestic demand for water has been rising steadily over the past century, partly due to population expansion and associated development, but also due to the increasing amount of water used daily by the average person.

Water supply companies thus find themselves having to face the dual problem of increasing demand and decreasing supply. For example, the Bewl reservoir on the Kent/Sussex border was only 37% full in February 2006, a time of year

when it is normally 90% full. This was principally due to low rainfall in the winter months, but water demand per head in the South-East appears to be 10% higher than in the wetter North of the country.

The water companies themselves have a clear responsibility to reduce leaks in supply pipes and to invest in the infrastructure. The 'economic level of leakage', regulated by OFWAT, is that which is defined by comparing the cost of providing a megalitre of additional water resource with the cost of reducing leaks by the same amount. In other words, it would appear to make economic sense to accept a certain level of leakage within the distribution system. As water is no longer a public utility we are obliged to rely on government to regulate the water industry, but there is much that can be done in domestic property to reduce consumption, as the current level of demand is clearly unsustainable. However, it is curious to note that, while water bills have soared, water companies in general spend little effort or money on water-saving initiatives for their customers.

Reducing water demand in the home

Domestic water consumption can be broken down as follows:

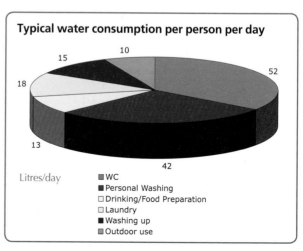

Typical water consumption per person per day

- 10
- 15
- 18
- 13
- 42
- 52

Litres/day

■ WC
■ Personal Washing
□ Drinking/Food Preparation
□ Laundry
■ Washing up
■ Outdoor use

These are only average figures and much depends on lifestyle and the equipment which is already installed in our houses. The increase in single-person households in the UK is also thought to have contributed to an increase in demand per person. Many of the methods by which we can save water involve simply changing the way in which we live and how we use water, rather than any costly purchase of new equipment.

In addition to water used directly in the home, we also consume water indirectly through the food and other products we buy. As with energy, information on embodied water consumption is not readily available to consumers.

REGULATION CORNER

Water use in existing dwellings in England and Wales is not presently regulated directly. Part G of the Building Regulations originally only covered Sanitation but it was amended in 2010 to include hot water safety and water efficiency. The regulations apply primarily to new buildings but a requirement has also been introduced to achieve water efficiency for refurbishment projects if there is a material change of use including where:

- the building is used as a dwelling, where previously it was not;
- the building contains a flat, where previously it did not.

In either of these cases, the specification for internal water-using equipment must aim for a use of 120 litres per person per day (125l including outside use). This calculation is based upon frequency of use assumptions employed in the Water Calculator underpinning both Part G and the Code for Sustainable Homes. Designers for major retrofit projects are therefore required to specify water-using goods which will in theory achieve this stated maximum consumption.

The Water Fittings Regulations 1999 (or Scottish water Byelaws 2004) are national requirements for the design, installation and maintenance of plumbing systems, water fittings and water-using appliances. Their purpose is to prevent misuse, waste, undue consumption or erroneous measurement of water and, most importantly, to prevent contamination of drinking water. From 3rd August 2009 revised Water Fittings Regulations apply in Northern Ireland which are technically very similar to those in England and Wales. Copies can be downloaded from **www.drdni.gov.uk/index/water_policy**

In Scotland, Guides to the regulations may be obtained from WRAS – the Water Regulations Advisory Scheme. **www.wras.co.uk.**

WATER METERING

If the supply is metered there will be a financial incentive to save water. It is thought that one of the most effective ways to reduce water consumption is to install a meter, as awareness that water has a cost tends to make consumers more careful. High users, however, might find that metered water is more expensive than paying a fixed price for water and sewerage services. When comparing charges, it is always necessary to remember to take into account the charges for both supply and sewerage – in some cases a single rate is quoted – known as a a combined charge.

As smart metering is being introduced in the UK by 2019 (see Chapter 5), customers with water meters will also be able to see their water use clearly on the in-home display, making consumption even more transparent.

LEAKS

Leaks account for the greatest wastage of water so, before introducing water-saving measures in a property, it is first important to address any leaks.

One drip per second	wastes	4 litres per day
Drips breaking into a stream	wastes	90 litres per day
1.5mm (1/16in) stream	wastes	320 litres per day
3mm (1/8in) stream	wastes	985 litres per day
6mm (1/4in) stream	wastes	3,500 litres per day

If there is a meter fitted and a leak is suspected, the 'night-flow test' may prove useful: read the meter before going to bed and, as long as no water is used overnight, the meter reading in the morning will indicate whether or not there is a leak.

The supply pipe is that part of the service pipe which runs from the boundary of the property to the rising main. Technically, owner responsibility for leakage begins at the boundary of each property but most water companies offer a free supply pipe leak detection and repair service. OFWAT clearly states that it regards

Stain caused by leaking overflow.

this as a responsibility of the water companies, especially as 75% of the water saved by *all* water efficiency measures was achieved by carrying out supply pipe repairs.[1] If the opportunity arises to replace an old lead supply pipe in the process, this will eliminate a potential source of toxins. Although this is at the expense of the homeowner, the water company will normally replace the section of the pipe (the communication pipe) which runs from the property boundary to the water main in the street at the same time, at its own expense.

TOILETS

As approximately one third of the water used in domestic property is accounted for by toilet flushing, this is a good place to start looking for savings. Cotton wool and tissues can be disposed of by means of a waste bin in the bathroom rather than using the toilet to flush them away. Older cisterns use 9 litres or more for each flush. To reduce the flush volume without changing the cistern, solid objects can be put in the cistern to displace water that would otherwise be flushed through. It is important that any object placed in a cistern does not interfere with the operation of the flush or siphon assemblies and does not introduce unwanted chemicals into the system. For example, bricks will eventually decompose and cause problems. However, all water companies offer free displacement devices designed for this purpose.

When replacing a toilet or fitting a new bathroom, dual flush cisterns can be installed which enable the user to select between a limited flush and a full flush. These come in either 2/4, 3/6 or 4/6-litre versions.

Photo: Hippo UK

Flushes on new toilets are not permitted to exceed 6 litres and most now incorporate the dual flushing facility set at 4/6 litres. For siphonic toilets (compulsory in the UK until 2001) the siphon can be replaced with one which allows air into the siphon, thus reducing the flush volume. Questions have been raised about the leakage in imported valve systems, although all UK-manufactured valves will have passed the WRAS test (see below) and are of sufficient quality.

Ifo Cera ES4 4.5 litre.

Photo: Green Building Store

Retrofit kits are available which enable a single flush to be replaced by a variable flush. This can be achieved either by a dial change, manually setting the flush lever to control the volume used, or by the use of an interrupt button, which flushes until the handle is released. It is important to note that if a variable flush or a displacement device results in the need to flush more than once, then the saving is lost and the actual water consumption may even be increased. If this occurs, the best course of action is to revert to the previous arrangement.

For further information see 'Retrofitting variable flush mechanisms to existing toilets' (Environment Agency 2005).

The critical measure, which takes into account all these variables, is the 'effective flush volume'. When a flush volume is quoted by manufacturers it tends to under-measure the amount used. When a toilet is flushed it immediately starts to refill, so water is flowing into the cistern while it is still draining. This can be avoided by the use of a delayed action inlet valve. This type of valve has a small evacuating bowl beneath the float that operates the valve. When the flush is operated, the water level in the cistern drops but the valve is held shut by the water remaining in the bowl. As the water drains slowly, the valve can open and the cistern can refill. When used with a 7-litre cistern the valve can save about 1.4 litres per flush at 3 bar and 3.5 litres at 10 bar, when compared to the same valve without the bowl. Delayed action inlet valves are currently not available as a retrofit option but may ultimately become compulsory in new installations.

DEAD-LEGS

A dead-leg is the amount of water drawn off from a hot tap while waiting for the water to come out hot. If the distance from the cylinder (or from the boiler if a combi has been fitted) to the point of use is minimised, the dead-leg will be shorter so the use of both water and energy will be reduced. Insulation of the hot water pipe that runs between the boiler/cylinder and the tap may keep the water warm enough to be used without waiting for freshly heated water from the boiler or cylinder.

SINKS AND HAND BASINS

Mains pressure can run at 20l/min or more, so it is possible to save water by restricting this flow where the full pressure is not needed – for example in hand basins. Flow restrictors are available which can be plumbed in near the point of use and smaller bore piping would reduce both the flow and the dead-leg.

In-line flow regulator suitable for basins.

Spray tap heads or aerators can reduce water flow from a tap by up to 50% while still providing an effective flow of water for washing hands. Spray taps may require more regular maintenance than conventional taps to ensure that nozzles are not blocked by soap, grease or lime-scale and that water does not become trapped.

Note, however, that 'there has been concern that spray fittings and aerators might introduce a risk of legionella. The temperature of the water is an important factor in the occurrence of legionella outbreaks. Sufficiently hot water will kill off the legionella, as they cannot survive in very high temperatures. Descaling regularly and reducing the pressure of water to taps will reduce the production of aerosol droplets, which is how legionella usually enters the body.'[2]

Taps are used for filling the sink or basin as well as rinsing so it is useful to be able to fill the basin quickly without the spray switched on. Inserts are available which can be fitted to taps with a round outlet or standard metric thread. These inserts deliver a spray at low pressure and an unrestricted flow as the tap is opened more fully.

When fitting any kind of tap attachment it is necessary to maintain the gap between the bottom of the tap outlet and the overflow of the basin in order to guard against the risk of back contamination of the mains supply.

Some single-lever mixer taps contain a cartridge which produces resistance as the lever is lifted to a preset flow rate – 6l/min, for example. The full flow can be obtained by lifting the lever further than this stop point.

In commercial applications, sensors and push taps are effective at saving water where there is a risk that taps may be left on. Sensors are also more hygienic as they avoid the need to touch the tap with dirty hands to turn it on and then to touch it again with clean hands to turn it off. There is no reason why these should not be used in domestic applications.

Lastly, cleaning your teeth with the tap running uses an average of 9 litres of water whereas turning off the tap whilst brushing can reduce this to less than a litre.

Adopting one or more of the measures described in this section will reduce the volume of water used, but otherwise this is one example of the ways in which we may have to adjust our habits to reflect the increasing scarcity of water resources.

WASTE DISPOSAL UNITS

Waste disposal units use power and drinking quality water to dispose of food waste via the public drainage system, which seems to be a poor use of resources in every sense. In many Local Authorities, cooked food waste is now collected directly. Uncooked vegetable peelings can be added to the compost heap, saving water and energy while producing useful compost.

SHOWERS

Water-saving shower heads can deliver the effect of a power shower while using considerably less water. This effect is achieved by introducing air just before the point of delivery. They require pressure of at least 1 bar, which is usually produced by mains-fed combination boilers but is not always available from vented systems. Water-saving shower heads are not appropriate for electrically-heated showers as they can lead to overheating and the risk of scalding.

Photo: H2O Building Services

As a rough guide, most people find a flow of 10l/min comfortable for a shower, although a water-saving shower head can give the same level of comfort with a reduced flow.

SHOWER WATER USE

Conventional wisdom has it that showers use less water than baths. This is not necessarily true. The average length of a shower is said to be between five and six minutes. At

	7.2kW elec	9.5kW elec	Water saver	Power shower
Flow rate*	3.5l/min	4.6l/min	4–10l/min	12l/min+
Water use for 5-min shower	17.5l	23l	20–50l	75l
% of 70l bath	25%	32%	28–71%	107%

*At 30°C rise in temperature.

10l/min, a seven-minute shower would use 70l whereas a bath may use as little as 60l, depending on the design. Power showers consume even more than this as they are pumped from the tank at high pressure and if flow rates exceed 12l/min then technically it is necessary to inform the water supply company. On the other hand, if you share a bath, the water usage per person is halved.

BATHS

Bath sizes vary considerably. Shaped or narrow baths take less water to fill up to the equivalent height of a conventional bath. Volumes of new baths should be stated in the manufacturer's brochure and these are generally quoted to the centre of the overflow.

Bath sizes can be deceptive: above 290 litres; below 185 litres.

It is necessary to ensure that an accurate comparison can be made as some manufacturers subtract the volume of a submerged adult (usually around 70 litres) when quoting the volume to overflow level. If a bath size is quoted as 100 litres this would probably mean that the overflow is reached when adult + water = 170 litres. Available data suggests that people tend to fill the bath to approximately 40% of volume – in this example, therefore, using 68 litres per bath. Insulated baths keep water warm longer and reduce the need to top up when enjoying a long soak, saving both energy and water.

Technology for the extraction of energy from waste water is not yet fully developed, although trials are being carried out in the USA to make use of this recycled energy to pre-heat the incoming supply to the boiler. It has been pointed out that simply waiting for bath water to cool before disposal allows the 'useful heat' to dissipate inside the property rather than within the drainage system.

Bath water can be reused for garden watering. However, if considering doing this, it would be necessary to use soaps that contain only plant-based ingredients and to allow the water to cool before distributing it in the garden. Storing and recycling greywater raises various issues which are covered in the section on storage tanks later in this chapter.

DOMESTIC APPLIANCES

Washing machines and dishwashers are steadily becoming more efficient in terms of their water use as well as their energy use. Experts calculate that dishwashers use less water and energy than washing by hand, although they do produce noise over a more extended period. It is more efficient to avoid half loads in either machine, even if a half-load button exists, as this uses more than half the energy and water required by a full load. Water can also be saved by scraping food off dishes rather than rinsing before loading the dishwasher.

Even given the energy and water savings available from more technologically advanced machines, it usually only makes economic sense to replace a machine which is nearing the end of its life (typically eight years), due to the embodied energy of the appliance and the environmental impact of its production and disposal. Water consumption is now mentioned on the EU energy labelling of relevant domestic appliances (see the 'Appliances' section in Chapter 5). The following table illustrates the water savings to be gained by using a more efficient machine:

	Washing machine		Dishwasher	
	Old	New	Old	New
Litres per wash (full load)	100	50	25	16
Annual use (m³)*	37.4	18.2	9.1	5.8
Annual water cost**	£72.80	£36.40	£18.20	£11.60

*Based on seven full-load washes per week for both washing machine and dishwasher.
**Based on combined average UK water and sewerage charges of £2.00 per m³.

Reducing water demand in the garden

It is possible to have a beautiful and productive garden with minimal use of mains water. The peak demand for garden watering tends to be in high summer when water supplies are under greatest pressure, so measures to reduce garden water use can have a very significant effect.

PLANTING

Examples of plants that thrive in hot and dry conditions once established include:

- African Lily (Agapanthus africanus)
- Buddleia (Buddleja)
- Californian Lilac (Ceanothus thyrsiflorus)
- Californian Poppy (Romneya)
- Catmint (Nepeta)
- Daisy Bush (Olearia)
- Evening Primrose (Oenothera)
- Foxtail Lily (Eremurus)
- French Honeysuckle (Hedysarum coronarium)
- Lavender (Lavandula)
- Peruvian Lily (Alstroemeria)
- Pink (Dianthus)
- Red-hot Poker (Kniphofia uvaria)
- Rock Rose (Cistus, Helianthemum)
- Rosemary (Rosmarinus officinalis)
- Straw Daisy (Leucochrysum Albicans)
- Thyme (Thymus)
- Tulip (Tulipa).

There are many other shrubs and herbs of Mediterranean origin which require little or no watering, although some may struggle in soils which are not well drained. Ornamental grasses come in many varieties and sizes and thrive in arid conditions.

WATERING

Most established trees and shrubs do not need watering. Vegetable seedlings need to be watered with a rose-head attachment on the watering can. For established vegetables it is more effective to water the base of the plant directly without the rose-head and to avoid soaking the leaves.

Watering in the early morning or late evening will reduce evaporation so a higher percentage of the water will penetrate to the roots. Watering cans direct water more efficiently than hoses and reduce the risk of damage to plants, which is a common problem with trigger jets on hoses. Occasional soakings are better than regular light watering as a good soaking encourages the roots to go deeper to seek out the water stored in the ground.

LAWNS

Lawns are probably the greatest cause of water wastage in a garden. A sprinkler uses as much water in an hour as the average family uses in two days. Although lawns will turn brown during a prolonged dry spell, they will not have died; the roots are deep and lawns will quickly recover once rain returns. As with vegetables, occasional soakings are much better than regular light watering. Allowing the grass to grow longer provides shade, which reduces soil temperature, cuts down evaporation and reduces the need for watering.

Same lawn during and after drought.

Photos: Kent & East Sussex Railway

SOIL AND MULCHES

Soils containing a good quantity of organic matter will tend to hold water best. Organic matter reduces the frequency at which watering will be required, in addition to providing essential nutrients for plants.

Mulches and bark placed over the topsoil will help

water to be retained in the soil and will greatly reduce evaporation. If you are laying gravel to reduce evaporation, the use of a liner avoids mixing the gravel with the soil.

HARVESTED WATER

Water butts are the most familiar form of harvested water. These are simple to install and are usually filled directly from the downpipes, which convey water from the gutters to the drainage system, by means of a diverter.

The simplest form of water butt allows a watering can to be filled from a tap near the bottom of the butt. This requires mounting at sufficient height for the can to be placed easily under the tap. A stand can be made simply from old bricks and offcuts of timber and need not require a bespoke unit – but beware, water butts are very heavy when full. Butts vary in size up to 220 litres and many are made from recycled plastic. Some incorporate child safety lids.

When the butt is full – which will be the case for much of the winter when rainfall is high and demand is low – the overflow must be connected to the drainage system. It may be possible to connect into the downpipe below the overflow point, or to a drain or gully below. Submersible pumps can be installed in water butts, which means that a hosepipe can be run directly from the harvested water, even during a hosepipe ban.

Some plants will benefit from a winter soak to make use of the abundance of stored water. This is particularly important for plants that lie in a 'rain shadow' against a fence or building which shelters them from the prevailing wind and rain.

Rainwater harvesting

The basic principle behind rainwater harvesting is to collect the water that falls on the roof and store it for use in flushing toilets. It is also possible for washing machines to use harvested water – rainwater is soft and therefore ideal for clothes washing, eliminating the need to use conditioners.

If water efficiency has already been addressed and the effective flush volume of toilets has been reduced to less than 4 litres, the demand for non-potable (non-drinking) water may be so low that there is little to be gained by installing such a system. There is also at present a considerable debate about the environmental effectiveness of rainwater harvesting as it takes energy to construct, install, run and maintain a rainwater harvesting system. As has been noted, embodied energy calculations are potentially extremely complex but recent research has drawn attention to the fact that the mains water system is actually a very energy-efficient

way of delivering water to our homes and businesses. Further research is evidently needed but instinctively it feels wasteful to purify water to drinking quality and then to utilise it as a waste-disposal mechanism. If water shortages become more common as a result of climate change, this may also affect the way in which rainwater harvesting systems are assessed.

STORAGE TANKS

Rainwater storage tanks may be sited above or below ground. Above-ground systems require protection from freezing.

Communal systems (usually underground) that pool the rainfall from several properties are slightly more efficient than individual systems and should require less mains backup in prolonged periods of low rainfall.

Water is pumped from the storage tank, either directly to the points of use in the property or to a secondary header tank in the loft. The main disadvantage with direct-pumped systems is that toilets have to be flushed with a bucket of water if the pump fails. By contrast, rainwater harvesting provides a source of water for toilet flushing at the very least during the occasional interruptions to the mains supply.

MAINS BACKUP

There are several ways of arranging mains backup but the most common for direct-pumped systems is to use a float switch inside the storage tank to sense when the level reaches a critical low point and then to open the mains water feed to refill with a limited amount of mains water.

As the tank only partly refills there will be plenty of room for rainwater to be collected when it starts raining again, so the system will always favour the use of harvested water. Mains backup must be correctly installed in accordance with the Water Regulations (1999) to prevent back contamination of the mains supply and there are legal standards of how pipes must be marked up to identify rainwater or greywater pipes clearly.

FILTRATION AND CLEANING

Filtration is necessary to prevent leaves and other debris from entering the tank via the gutter system. There are sophisticated filtration systems available which are self-cleaning and some even reject the first flush of water when rain commences as this tends to contain the most debris.

When the tank is full, excess water drains off to the surface-water drainage system as normal. This overflow will also remove floating contaminants, which is a good reason not to oversize the tank.

TANK SIZING

Tank sizing is subject to the law of diminishing returns. The larger the tank, the fewer the occasions when mains backup will be required, but the effect decreases as tank size is increased. A tank size of 1,500 to 2,000 litres will supply most of the toilet and washing machine requirements in the average house. As a guide to volume, one cubic metre contains 1,000 litres.

To work out the amount of water that could be collected from a domestic property, first calculate the area of the roof in plan – the effective area of the roof is independent of the slope, so it should be similar to the ground floor area of the house. Next, find out the expected annual rainfall per square metre – average rainfall figures for all areas of the country are available on the Met Office website (**www.met-office.gov.uk/climate/uk**). For example, a house in the West Midlands would receive an average rainfall of 669mm p.a. If the ground floor measured 5m x 9m the available water would be calculated as follows:

Average rainfall (m) x area of roof (m^2) = available water (m^3)

Ground floor area = 5m x 9m = $45m^2$
Available rainwater = 45 x .669 = $30.1m^3$

As some is lost to evaporation and overflow, not all of this water is collected, so multiply by 0.75 to gain an approximate idea of the yield (0.75 x 30 = $22m^3$). Terraced housing with the ridge running parallel to the street will only realistically allow harvesting on one side of the property unless costly alterations are made to convey water through or under the building.

PAYBACK PERIOD

Most water bills charge for supply of water and for disposal. For metered properties, the amount billed for both supply *and* disposal is calculated from the supply meter. As the water which is harvested displaces mains water supply but is still drained eventually via the toilet, it has been argued that rainwater harvesting is unfairly depriving the water companies of revenue. On the one hand, this fails to account for the fact that the water which is harvested is stored when rain falls rather than being transferred directly to the drainage system, so there is indeed a net reduction

Wisy filter.

Illustration courtesy of Rainharvesting Systems

Discount rate p.a.	5%
Water price escalation p.a.	5%
Installed cost of system	£2,500
Tank size	1,500 litres
Mains water saved p.a.	$22m^3$
Combined cost per m^3	£2.00
Saving per annum	£44
Payback period: 2,500 ÷ 44 =	**56 years**

in the volume of water which is drained away. On the other hand, the amount of pollutants which water companies are required to treat remains the same.

Note that if interest rates and water price escalation are unequal over the long term this significantly affects the calculation. If water prices rise more quickly than the absolute level of long-term interest rates, the payback period for rainwater harvesting will be shorter. The calculation also ignores the cost of maintaining the system, and takes no account of the small amount of energy required to run the pump (unless the system is gravity-fed).

Payback periods will vary across the country. In the South-West, where rainfall is higher, water charges are double those in the South-East. This leads to the bizarre conclusion that the payback period for installations in the South-West may be far shorter than for installations in the South-East.

Rainwater harvesting also has a beneficial, if minor, effect on the drainage system as it serves to hold water when it rains, rather than conveying it directly to the storm-water drains. With the increasingly evident effects of climate change, periods of heavy rain are expected, so widespread harvesting and storing of rainwater could reduce the risk of local flooding.

For further information see: The Chartered Institute of Water and Environmental Management, **www.ciwem.org**; and The UK Rainwater Harvesting Association, **www.ukrha.org**.

GREYWATER REUSE

Greywater is defined as that which is recovered from hand basins, baths and showers and, like harvested rainwater, it is normally used for toilet flushing. Using greywater on the garden is not recommended unless biodegradable detergents have been used, and only then in small quantities.

Unlike rainwater, greywater requires a settlement tank and filtration treatment to remove contaminants, and biological cleansing or disinfectant chemicals or UV filtration to deal with organic compounds. It is not recommended that greywater is stored for long periods.

PRIVATE WATER SUPPLIES

There is a common misconception that boreholes are a water-saving substitute for mains supply. Boreholes abstract water from the same underground reserves that are used for the public mains supply – 75% of the water supply in the South-East is already taken from underground reserves. Energy is also required to drill and operate boreholes, whereas the mains supply performs the same function very efficiently in energy terms. An Environment Agency licence is required for abstraction of more than 20m³ per day.

Greywater system

Reed-bed systems and composting toilets

COMPOSTING TOILETS

The basic concept of a composting toilet is to allow natural processes to break the waste down into a safe and essentially inert form so that it can be disposed of safely as a fertiliser. This process may need encouragement – sometimes shredded cardboard is added to the waste in order to prevent the mixture becoming too wet for the natural mouldering process to operate properly. It is not uncommon to add tiger worms to the mixture to accelerate the process.

Two basic varieties are available – self-contained toilets are larger as the waste is stored in the bathroom. The alternative, if space and layout permit, is to collect the waste in a tank which is situated below the bathroom floor, effectively on a different level. Vent fans are fitted to most units but, at an average of 5W, their power consumption is surprisingly low (under £7pa at 15p/kWh).

Smaller models require regular turning in order to aerate the mixture and some models even incorporate heaters to acclerate the process of decomposition. The energy consumed by heaters would partly offset the environmental benefits of using a dry toilet system.

It is possible to obtain Building Regulations approval for composting toilets. It is worth noting that as there is no connection to the mains water, the Water Supply (Water Fittings) Regulations 1999 do not apply.

Waterless self-contained.

Waterless remote tank.

Photos: www.envirolet.com

Compost toilets require no drainage, they are silent to operate and, thanks to the fan, odourless. They do not freeze, which can be a great advantage in a remote location without power and even for outdoor toilets in parts of the UK. Their only disadvantage is that the compost which is produced at the end of the process will have to be removed and spread on the field or garden.

REED BEDS

Reed beds are simply ponds into which liquid effluent, such as the outflow from a septic tank, is channelled and which then convert the effluent to harmless plant material and gases. They work by using three principal methods:

- the ability of plants to convert waste matter
- the chemical properties of the gravel or soil
- the action of microbes which live in the soil.

The microbes, flora and fauna in the soil are the most effective and important ingredient in these systems and the function of the reed is in part to introduce oxygen to the root system and to provide an environment for the microbes to flourish and do their work.

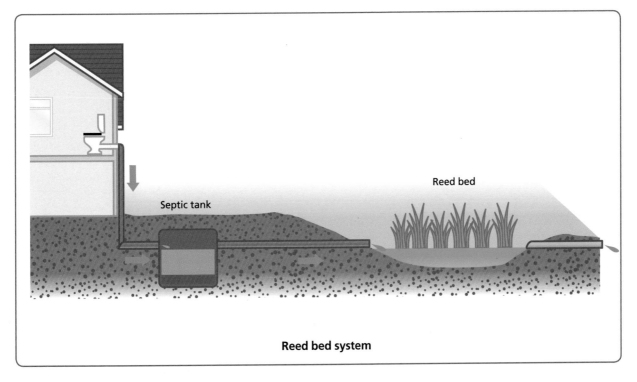

Reed bed

Septic tank

Reed bed system

Ponds are generally lined in order to prevent any seepage into the adjacent ground and then filled with gravel and soil which acts as a base for the plants and reeds. The effluent is then normally delivered by means of a feeder trench below the surface – this is known as a horizontal flow system. Where the effluent is delivered above the surface this is known as a vertical flow system, which is more common in the USA than in the UK.

Installing a water butt

Water butts vary in design so it will be necessary to check the installation instructions provided with any particular system. The following example is based upon the installation of a 190l recycled plastic butt and the diverter kit can be fitted to standard 68mm round or 65mm square downpipes.

THE RAIN SAVER WATER BUTT COMPRISES:
- Butt with pre-installed tap
- Diverter kit with connecting hose
- (Stand)

TOOLS REQUIRED
- Bricklaying tools
- Spirit Level
- Drill and 25mm hole cutter
- Hacksaw (plastic pipe can be cut with a wood saw but it harms the teeth so use an old one)
- Screwdriver

1 Identify a downpipe which carries the downflow from a significant portion of the roof.

2 Identify the required height of the installation – you will need to be able to get your favourite watering can under the tap at the bottom of the butt.

3 Construct a plinth for the butt to rest upon. Water butts are extremely heavy, so it is important that the plinth is strong and level.

4 Place the butt on the plinth. Some water butts come with a prefabricated stand. If using such a stand it is equally important to ensure that the stand is placed on firm level ground.

5 Measure and mark the height of the diverter. In this system, the diverter also acts as an overflow, so the height of the diverter will govern the level of water in the tank. Be careful not to set the diverter too high or the tank may overflow. For this water butt and diverter kit the cut should be made 20mm below the height of the top of the water butt.

6 Slacken off or remove the downpipe clips. Cut the downpipe and then cut off a further 30mm from what is now the lower section of the pipe.

7 Drill a 25mm diameter hole in the side of the butt, 50m below the top.

8 Fit the connector and washer from the inside and tighten the nut on the outside.

9 Assemble the diverter tube and the downpipe and connecting tube. Retighten or refit the downpipe brackets.

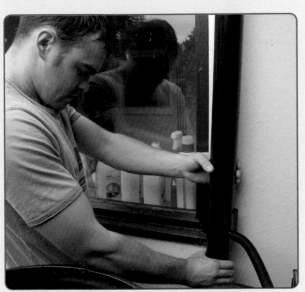

10 Fit the lid – in this case a childproof lid has been provided.

11 Sit back and wait or, if you're impatient, do a rain dance.

12 Enjoy your free water supply.
NB – Ensure that the overflow is working correctly when the butt is full.

INTERIORS

Photo: Alternative Flooring Company

Interiors are replaced or upgraded far more often than building fabric so the environmental impact of paints and furnishings can be substantial. At the same time, many common products contain chemicals which are unhealthy and give rise to poor air quality within the home. This chapter explains the main issues to consider when selecting products for interiors and sets out the environmentally friendly alternatives which are available.

Carpets

It is well known that fitted carpets harbour dust mites, allergens, moulds and animal dander. In particular, the dust mite allergen triggers asthma, eczema and other allergic illnesses, affecting the health of children and other vulnerable people. Hard flooring does not harbour dust in the same way as carpets do.

What is less well known is that the chemicals used in many fitted carpets are a source of indoor air pollution, principally arising from the pesticides, stain inhibitors and fire retardants with which they are commonly treated. Fitted carpets can also act as a reservoir for toxic substances used in the home. Children are most at risk from this concentration of chemicals as they spend more time near or in contact with the floor and their immune systems are not fully developed.

For further information on this subject see: 'Poison Underfoot' – Greenpeace/Exeter University, **www. healthyflooring.org.**

Alternative natural carpet materials are now widely available which, combined with regular cleaning, can significantly reduce this risk. In terms of hygiene they are most effective if used as rugs placed over hard flooring, as rugs are easier to remove and clean and hard flooring avoids the dirt traps that exist in the corners of carpeted rooms. It is also worth noting that natural materials do not generate static electricity in the same way as synthetic products, so they attract and retain less dust. Natural carpets are usually backed with natural latex rather than PVC or other synthetic products. If produced abroad, there is a significant embodied energy in natural carpets but this has to be offset against their many advantages and the fact that conventional carpets use a much larger amount of energy and water in their production.

JUTE
Jute is derived from the stems of the cochorus plant, a herb grown in tropical areas. At present it is mainly available in natural colour. As jute is soft, it can be closely-woven, giving the carpet a fine texture

and making it ideal for use in bedrooms. Its use is not recommended in areas of heavy traffic such as entrance halls and stairs.

SISAL
Sisal is made from the leaves of the agave plant, which is a type of cactus. It is extremely hard-wearing and can be finely woven, making it suitable for living rooms and stairs. It accepts dye better than other natural carpet fibres so is available in a wider range of colours.

COIR
Coir consists of fibres taken from the outer husk of the coconut – the coconuts we normally see are just the inner shell of the seed pod. These fibres are soaked and softened and then spun into a yarn. It produces a rugged, tough and inexpensive flooring material.

SEAGRASS/MOUNTAIN GRASS
Seagrass is harvested from tall grass-like plants which grow in wetland areas. The weave tends to be quite coarse and open and there are plenty of natural colour variations. Grass carpets are hard-wearing and inexpensive. but they tend to have a natural sheen which make them unsuitable for use on stairs.

WOOL
Wool is a much more familiar natural carpeting material, widely popular as it is softer than all the materials described above. Lanolin acts as a natural stain inhibitor so there is no need to add the chemical stain inhibitors used in synthetic carpets.

However, wool carpets commonly have the same synthetic backing which is applied to non-natural carpet

Photo: Alternative Flooring Company

Photo: Natural Carpets

materials, which includes synthetic latex. This contains a vulcanising agent known as styrene, which is a known carcinogen.[1] Styrene is one of the chemicals responsible for the 'new carpet smell'. Many wool carpets are also treated chemically and may therefore contain some of the fire retardants, pesticides and other chemicals mentioned above.

Some of the UK's wool carpeting is made from wool which is imported from New Zealand, which greatly increases the embodied energy of the product, while there is a plentiful supply of British wool for which farmers presently receive a low return.

Soft furnishings

Foam furnishings can add to the cocktail of synthetic substances present in the indoor environment and they give off highly toxic fumes when burnt. Polyester-filled furnishings are routinely treated with a variety of chemicals including fire retardants, which have given rise to various health concerns. Rugs and other soft furnishings manufactured in more remote areas, by contrast, contain none of these chemicals and seem to perform perfectly well without them.

Polybrominated diphenyl ether (PDBE) is one of a family of brominated fire retardants commonly used in computers and other household electronic equipment. A recent US study has shown that PDBEs are now occurring in abnormally high concentrations in breast milk.[2]

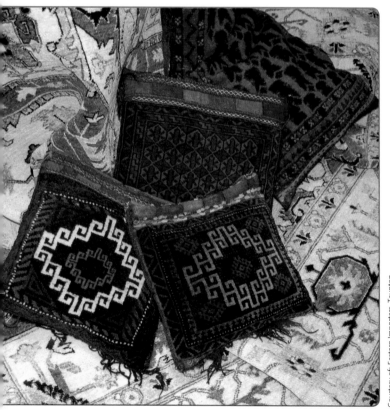

Imported traditional furnishings.

Courtesy of: Eastern Importers, Taunton

Hard flooring

WOOD FLOORING

A wide selection of wood flooring is now available. Care is needed as there are also products which imitate wood but are made from different materials – some are plastic with a photograph of wood grain printed on the top. Hybrid products, sometimes known as 'engineered boards', have a real wooden surface attached to a core of MDF or plywood (see the section on 'Composite/particle boards' in Chapter 2). These may not last as well as solid wood and are difficult or impossible to repair if a scratch occurs. Some engineered boards consist of small sections of solid wood laminated together to form a board or tile, although lamination frequently involves the use of formaldehyde resins.

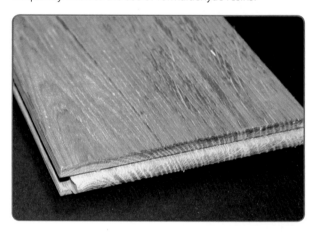

Above: Solid oak flooring.
Below: Wood sections glued together.

The presence of the FSC (or PEFC) logo on solid wood flooring indicates to the consumer that the wood has been sustainably harvested from well-managed forests. Ash, birch, cherry, maple, oak, and beech are all used for flooring and it can be possible to obtain timber grown in the UK, although most of the timber available is European and North American. Hardwood flooring specialists and timber merchants may be able to help if local products are not available from DIY stores.

Adhesives are frequently employed when fitting wooden floors. Many of these adhesives are toxic and continue to emit fumes for months or even years. Non-toxic adhesives have recently become available but they will need to be ordered via a builders' merchant until they are used more widely and stocked on the shelves.

Photo: Rewmar

Floor finishes are another source of concern for the environment as many substances contain VOCs (volatile organic compounds). However, natural oils or wax provide an excellent finish for hardwood floors. They are less hard-wearing than some factory finishes or varnishes and will need periodic reapplication to maintain their lustre, but they have the great advantage that scratches can be simply

Oak flooring finished with UV oil.

repaired by sanding and then adding a little of the oil/wax originally used. UV oils (made from soy and sunflower oils) harden under exposure to ultraviolet light to form a natural lacquer which provides an attractive and tough floor finish. Natural oils and waxes also have a better smell than products containing high levels of VOCs.

CORK

Cork is derived from the bark of the cork oak tree, mainly grown in Portugal and other parts

Photo: Western Cork Ltd

of the Mediterranean. The bark is harvested every nine years and then grows back without harming the tree so it is a completely sustainable product. In addition to being an excellent insulator, it regains its shape well after being compressed under furniture, due to its cellular structure. Cork can also be used in bathrooms and kitchens; the natural presence of suberin, an inherently waxy substance, means that cork is resistant to water and therefore to rot. Many cork flooring products have already been sealed with polyurethane products but it is still possible to buy unsealed cork. Alternative sealants are also available including low-VOC wax.

LINOLEUM

Linoleum was originally manufactured from linseed oil, hence the name. However, during the second half of the 20th century this natural product was often substituted by petrochemical-based plastic products (vinyls) which appropriated the name 'lino'. Genuine linoleum is still made and is rapidly regaining popularity. It is available in a wide variety of colours and textures and is made from linseed oil, wood flour, rosin, jute and limestone. The pigments used are also sourced in an environmentally responsible manner.

Marmoleum.   Photo: Forbo-Nairn

Natural linoleum is ideal for use in bathrooms and kitchens. It needs little or no maintenance, is easy to clean, and it smells good. In terms of environmental life-cycle assessment, natural linoleum has one of the lowest environmental impacts of all flooring materials.

BAMBOO

Photo: Dain Sansome

Bamboo is a plentiful and fast-growing plant which is excellent for flooring, being very strong and hard-wearing. Bamboo is produced in thin strips which are laminated together to be used as flooring. As adhesives are used in this process, it may be necessary to check which chemicals have been used for lamination – and for finishing.

As bamboo is fast-growing it is a good alternative to hardwoods (hardwoods are extremely slow to grow and have a limited supply which cannot respond quickly to increased demand). Bamboo is grown primarily in South-East Asia, so it has a relatively high embodied energy compared to locally grown timber, but its durability helps to offset the energy costs of transport to the UK.

TILES, STONE AND ADHESIVES

Ceramic tiles are generally considered to have a low environmental impact, being fired from clay, which is a plentiful resource. Tiles are also very durable and inert so they can be safely recycled as hardcore at the end of their use. Like stone, the main environmental impact of ceramic tiles is the transportation required, as most tiles sold in the UK are manufactured abroad. It is still possible, but not easy, to source locally produced stone and tiles.

Solvent-based tile adhesives, like conventional paints, contain a variety of toxic substances, including VOCs and synthetic resins. Water-based latex adhesives are not widely

available in the UK at present and some water-based adhesives are not suitable for use in bathrooms. However, good quality non-toxic tile adhesives can be purchased from the USA or via the Internet.

RUBBER FLOORING

Underlay is now available which is made from recycled car tyres, or rubber crumb. Rubber underlay has excellent sound attenuation and thermal properties and can also help to prolong the life whatever carpet is laid over it, as it is more resistant to compression than many other underlays.

Photos: Interfloor

Paint issues

Paint consists of four primary ingredients – pigments, fillers, solvents and binders.

- **Pigments** are colours of either synthetic or natural origin. Inorganic pigments come from minerals of varying types – as opposed to organic pigments – which contain carbon.

- **Fillers or extenders** – these give the paint its solidity of colour (opacity) and are normally chalk (calcium carbonate) or talcum powder, both of which are plentiful and sustainable.

- **Solvents** allow the paint to be spread thinly and then evaporate as the paint dries. Water or white spirit are the most common, although turpentine, citrus oil and de-aromatised white spirit are also used.

- **Binders** are essentially glues whose primary functions are to stick the paint to the surface being painted and to form a finished surface film.

Many paints also contain additives – these include thickeners to improve flow but also chemicals designed to protect against decay – such as fungicides, biocides and in-can preservatives.

ECOLOGICAL ASSESSMENT

There are issues associated with all of these ingredients and the ecological assessment of paints is a complex subject.

Much attention has been focussed on the impact of paints on indoor air quality but the manufacturing process is equally important. Relevant factors include:

- Embodied energy and CO_2 emissions
- Volatile organic compounds (VOCs)
- Air pollution
- Land and sea pollution
- Resource use
- Environmental impact of extraction
- Toxicity of preservatives, biocides and fungicides.

The long-term persistence of paint and its consituents in the environment should also be taken into account but it can be difficult to get information on this from many paint manufacturers.

It is important to choose the right paint for the job. If a paint does not perform as required the effort and expense has been wasted, so the environmental impact is significant. Similarly, coverage per litre and the number of coats required to achieve opacity are highly relevant, so it is only realistic to compare the impact (including labour time) of one coat of a thick paint that covers well with the impact of several coats of a translucent paint. For external paints, concerns about air quality are less pressing but performance is still important, as the longer a paint lasts – the lower will be its impact relative to products of a similar toxicity and embodied energy.

There are two methods by which paint dries or cures – depending on the type of paint.

Natural/Physical drying – water or solvents evaporate and dry chains of molecules link together. Most emulsion paints dry in this manner.

Chemical drying – solvents evaporate and allow oxygen to react with the paint surface, causing a chemical reaction to take place. Oil and wax finishes tend to use chemical drying.

SOLVENTS

The growing market in eco paints has arisen partly due to concerns about the high levels of volatile organic compounds (VOCs) including formaldehyde that are to be found in the solvents in many paint products. They are called volatile because they evaporate rapidly in normal conditions. The fact that ventilation is advised by the manufacturers during and after application, together with the appearance of reduced VOC paint in conventional paint ranges, indicates that the industry recognises that there are health problems associated with some of these compounds, especially toluene and xylene. VOCs also tend to have high Global Warming Potential (GWP) and contribute to petrochemical smog. Including car paints and industrial coatings, paints contribute about 10% of the solvents present in the environment.

By contrast – the ideal solvent is water as this has minimal impact as it evaporates. In some paints – especially exterior gloss paints – chemical solvents are necessary

to provide the required performance; in this case, the environmental impact can be reduced by using paints that have less toxic VOCs – for example citrus oil.

TITANIUM DIOXIDE

It appears that the greatest environmental impact in paint production comes from the use of titanium dioxide (TiO_2). Without this chemical it is difficult to achieve opacity (solidity of colour), but TiO_2 did replace more toxic substances (such as lead oxide and zinc oxide) when it was introduced. The Ecolabel report produced for the EC states that the four environmental problems to which paints and varnishes contribute most are:

- Non-renewable resources depletion due to petroleum consumption for the production of T_iO_2, resins and solvents
- Global warming through release of CO_2 and VOCs resulting from T_iO_2 production and from solvents in paints and varnishes respectively
- Atmospheric acidification due to SO_2 released from T_iO_2 processing
- Discharges of waste into water essentially due to T_iO_2 mining.

Many alternative paints are designed to have a reduced T_iO_2 content or to eliminate this substance altogether. Some accept that it is a necessity for performance but reduce the content of other environmentally damaging chemicals in their paints.

PRESERVATIVES

Many paints contain preservatives. In the concentrations at which they are present even in conventional paints they are not regarded as a health hazard, but they are designed to be toxic to certain micro-organisms, which is the reason for their inclusion. Several brands of alternative paints are free of preservatives.

BREATHING WALLS

In addition to their reduced environmental impact, many natural or organic paints are breathable. Most old buildings and some new eco-buildings are designed to breathe. Old buildings are frequently prevented from breathing by cement renders and a variety of paint skins on both sides of walls – this can on occasion lead to damp and other associated health issues or even structural problems. The re-emergence of natural paints therefore gives homeowners the opportunity to allow walls to breathe again, as long as all the impervious material is first removed. It is worth noting that paints can be resistant to water while still being vapour permeable.

For further information see: 'Paints and Ecology' by Neil May (2005), article accessible via **www.natural-building. co.uk**; and EC ecolabel research, **http://ec.europa.eu/ environment/ecolabel/product/index_en.htm.**

To recycle paint visit **www.communityrepaint.org.uk.**

Alternative paints

Wax finish.

LIME PAINT

Lime is an alternative and traditional binder used in paint. Cheap and simple to produce, lime paints are most commonly used on lime-plastered or lime-rendered walls in order to maintain breathability or vapour permeability and to ensure an effective union between paint and substrate. In some recipes a small amount of linseed oil is added to the mix in order to stabilise the finished surface.

LINSEED PAINT

Linseed oil is another traditional binder for paint. Linseed paints last much longer on exterior joinery than many modern paints and limited maintenance will only be required approximately every seven years. Most traditional linseed paints currently available contain significant levels of titanium dioxide, although generally they are free of solvents and other toxic chemicals. Linseed-based paints have a longer drying time than 'conventional' paints due to the reduced solvent content but this is easily offset by their excellent performance. Although normally used on woodwork, they can be mixed with water into an emulsion for use on walls and ceilings.

SILICATE MASONRY PAINT

Previously unpainted mineral surfaces such as cement render, lime render or stone are ideal for the application of silicate paints, which are based upon stabilised sodium silicate. The paint forms a chemical bond with the substrate, which makes it extremely hard-wearing and resistant to weather and ultraviolet light, so it is most useful as an exterior masonry paint. Available silicate paints are non-toxic and free from solvents and biocides; surprisingly they are also vapour permeable, which helps to prevent the accumulation of moisture.

DISTEMPER

Distemper is an ancient paint formulation. The principal traditional ingredients are powdered chalk and animal skin glue, although modern mixes use linseed oil in place of the glue. It is still used today, as very subtle colours may be obtained from this base. However, it is not hard-wearing and is ineffective on damp surfaces. The addition of oil as a binder and borax as an emulsifier improves its durability while reducing its porosity – these are known as oil-bound distempers.

CLAY PAINT

Natural clay can also be used as a base for paint. Clay paints are breathable and contain mainly natural ingredients, although vinyl acetate is normally used as a binder. They are slightly different to apply in comparison to conventional paints and can result in a more textured surface.

WAXES, OILS AND VARNISHES

The main function of wax, oil or varnish is to protect timber while enhancing the grain. Lacquers and varnishes became popular because they appeared to offer more durability than wax or oil, but once a lacquered surface has been scratched or dented it is more difficult to repair than wood treated with natural coatings. Many lacquers and varnishes also contain a high level of VOCs and other synthetic materials.

There are plenty of natural oils and waxes which will perform the same function as a varnish while penetrating into and enriching the wood rather than simply coating it. Oils can be combined with vegetable wax and beeswax to form highly durable surface finishes.

DIY PAINTS

Using the base paints outlined above you can mix your own paints by adding pigments that are becoming more readily available in shops and online. Natural pigments produce a much more natural tone than synthetic pigments and, if the paint is not mixed absolutely perfectly, there will be slight variations in the finished colour, which many people find more attractive and interesting than large areas of perfectly consistent colour.

PAINT STRIPPERS

Most paint strippers used over recent years are highly toxic and do not biodegrade. The EU has (finally) banned the use of Dichloromethane (DCM) – a class 3 carcinogen – in paint strippers. From December 2011 strippers containing DCM are no longer available to consumers.

Home Strip.

Removable joinery items such as doors are often dipped in sodium hydroxide to remove paint. This method can cause damage to the door as it has been known to raise the grain and can also dissolve whatever glue may remain in the joints.

Photo: Eco-Solutions

Photo: The Green Shop

However, there is an alternative stripping product available which is water-based, solvent free and biodegradable.

Once you have done the job safely without the use of toxic chemicals it is just as important to dispose of the waste properly to avoid contaminating the environment. Even if the stripper is biodegradable, disposal via the drains would spread contamination via the removed paint layers, often containing lead.

PROPRIETARY PAINT BRANDS

Eco-friendly paints vary widely – some have reduced environmental impact in every aspect of paint production, application and recycling but others simply boast reduced VOC content. A selection of more eco-friendly paint brands currently available in the UK is provided below so that readers can research the paint that is right for the job, and decide on their own priorities for reducing the impact of decorating.

Paints that have truly natural ingredients are rare – market leaders include Auro, Biofa and Aglaia. The best tip is to check whether manufacturers declare all their ingredients, as transparency is the key to achieving sustainable materials use.

Photo: The Green Shop

- ■ **www.auro.co.uk** (Auro)
- ■ **www.biofapaint.co.uk/**
- ■ **www.naturalpaintsonline.co.uk** (Aglaia)
- ■ **www.natural-building.co.uk** (NBT own range)
- ■ **www.greenshop.co.uk** ('Green Paints' and others)
- ■ **www.ecospaints.com** (Ecos)
- ■ **www.holkhamlinseedpaints.co.uk** (linseed oil-based)
- ■ **www.earthbornpaints.co.uk** (clay-based)
- ■ **www.stastier.co.uk** (lime paints)
- ■ **www.limeearthpaints.com** (lime earth paints)
- ■ **www.osmouk.com** (Osmo) natural wood finishes
- ■ **www.ecosolutions.co.uk** (less toxic paint strippers)

MAJOR PAINT MANUFACTURERS

Encouragingly, major paint manufacturers are beginning to offer ranges that address some of the issues raised above, borrowing from the specialist green paint companies who have blazed a trail here, as in other areas of the green building movement. However, in most cases only one or two issues are addressed (and then only in part)

so proprietary 'green paints' do tend to be less harmful. It is also worth noting that while major manufacturers are cashing in on a market where people are increasingly conscious of health and environmental issues, they are still causing the same problems with the majority of their products – i.e. the non-green range.

Kitchens

The kitchen is a great consumer of energy in the house. Electrical appliances are discussed in some detail in Chapter 5 so this section will focus on design and on the materials used to build kitchens.

LAYOUT

The layout of a kitchen can have some effect upon energy consumption. Good daylighting is useful for preparing, cooking and for washing up and can reduce electricity consumption. It therefore pays to design to make the best of the available windows (or skylights). Task lighting for the remainder is usually more effective than central lighting.

Fridges and freezers work more efficiently together if the freezer is below the fridge. This also reduces the need to bend down as fridges are opened more often than freezers. It makes sense to position fridges out of direct sunlight if possible and not to site them next to the boiler, the cooker or a radiator, as they would have to consume more power to maintain a low temperature.

CARCASSING

Carcassing is the kitchen manufacturer's term for the basic structure of wall- and floor-mounted cupboards which typically make up a kitchen. It does not include doors or worktops. Normally the material used for carcassing is chipboard or MDF. In addition to the health issues raised in connection with these materials in Chapter 2, they have the great disadvantage that they swell up when in prolonged contact with water. Chips and scratches are also difficult to repair.

It is an unfortunate fact of life that leaks occur from time to time and there is often more than one potential source of leaks in a kitchen. It is a considerable waste of resources

Chipboard swollen by water.

to have to throw away base units as a result of leaks, so when replacing a whole kitchen a tougher material such as (certified) plywood or softwood should be considered. Beech ply and birch ply provide an attractive and hygienic finish and need only occasional oiling. Natural materials such as these are also easier to repair if scratches or dents occur – simply sand, fill any deep dents and then re-oil.

Plywood carcassing.

For existing kitchens which have become 'tired' or simply unfashionable, the major visible items such as worktops and doors can be changed without having to throw away the carcassing, as long as it is in reasonable condition. Often this can be done without major disruption, depending on how tiling has been fixed and the presence of any services penetrations through the worktops.

Freestanding kitchen units are generally more expensive than fitted kitchens but last considerably longer. They can also be removed when a house is sold and be taken to the next property.

WORKTOPS

The most common construction for worktops is a thick layer of MDF or chipboard finished (usually only on the top) with a thin layer of formica. As with carcassing, the MDF and chipboard do not stand up well to water ingress. Damaged worktops are a common reason for complete kitchen replacement, which is an expensive and energy-intensive exercise. Conventional worktops also combine materials with glues, which makes them extremely difficult to recycle.

Polished granite or smooth slate worktops are tough and durable and, if sourced from the UK, have a relatively low embodied energy. They are extremely hygienic and

require little or no maintenance. Mosaic tiled surfaces are somewhat less hygienic as dirt often gets trapped in the grout joints.

Above: Chipboard.
Below: Polished granite.

Wooden worktops such as beech have low embodied energy and, if the timber is sustainably harvested, are probably the most eco-friendly worktops currently available. Whether it is the end grain or the side grain which is left exposed, the timber used is in small sections, so this can be an excellent use of offcuts which are not suitable for structural or joinery work.

Solid wooden worktops can be sanded and refinished if the surface becomes damaged, which is why they are more durable than other types of worktop. Danish oil is a well-recognised treatment for solid wood kitchen worktops but there are other natural products such as tung oil, boiled linseed oil and teak oil that will all do a similar job. Beech, cherry, walnut, iroko, maple and oak can all be used for worktops.

End grain (above) and side grain (below).

RECYCLING FACILITIES

In the course of everyday living, the majority of waste produced by a home is generated in the kitchen. This waste stream can be reduced by choosing products that have less packaging, choosing paper rather than plastics (especially hard plastics), and purchasing vegetables loose rather than in packets.

FSC Timber Recycling Storage Compartment

Photo: Cannock Gates Ltd

By providing convenient recycling storage facilities in the kitchen for fruit and vegetable peelings, cardboard, paper, glass, cans and recyclable plastics (usually milk and drinks containers), the weekly task of recycling can be made much simpler and more efficient.

Photo: The Bin Company

Generally the small kitchen storage facilities can feed the larger recycling boxes kept outside or in porches. Uncooked fruit and vegetable matter can be added to the compost heap along with modest amounts of cardboard. Paper, cardboard, glass and cans are increasingly disposed of via kerbside recycling collections and schemes to recycle plastics are developing.

Home office

An increasing number of people have the opportunity to work from home either full or part time. Working from home has the huge advantage of cutting out the commute, for some or all of the week, saving time, money, stress and pollution (car sharing schemes and community car clubs can reduce the environmental cost of personal transport). Timing of work can also become more flexible

and allow other domestic responsibilities to be undertaken at the same time as putting in a full working day.

To set up a home office, all that is required is enough space for a desk, some shelving, a computer and printer, power and a telephone connection. The provision of a home office need not require the sacrifice of an entire room, as the office can also be used as a guest room or dining room. It is even possible to fit a home office into a cupboard that can be closed when not in use.

The advent of portable computers, bluetooth data exchange and wireless internet connection means that the home office can function without power or a telephone connection, although power is useful for task lighting and for connecting printers.

A home office could also be set up in a bespoke building sited in the garden. Planning permission may be required for garden buildings over a certain size and it is important that services connections to exterior buildings are carried out by suitably qualified professionals. Think carefully about the heating strategy for independent home offices in order to avoid heating badly insulated buildings with fossil fuels for long periods. It would be all to easy to buy a cheap shed and then use electric heating without ever getting round to insulating the building.

The internet is changing the way in which we do business, enjoy our leisure, order goods and even conduct relationships. Without doubt its full potential has yet to be realised but it may hold the key to more sustainable living in the future, so it is likely that a home study area will become an increasingly important feature of modern living. The Code for Sustainable Homes (the Government's methodology for assessing the sustainability of new homes) awards credits for the provision of a home office so some modern dwellings already have this facility.

For further information see the *Working from Home Manual* by Kyle MacRae, Haynes.

Photo: Oak-Apple Frames

141

9 WASTE AND POLLUTION

This chapter begins by looking at construction waste and how to minimise it, including rethinking our attitudes and designing out waste. Where waste is unavoidable, the aim is to maximise the percentage that is reused or recycled and minimise the residual amount sent to landfill. Information is provided on the disposal and recycling of specific forms of domestic renovation waste including electrical equipment and hazardous substances. This chapter also examines how to minimise pollution, and how best to clean up if you are taking on a polluted site.

"When you build a thing you cannot merely build that thing in isolation, but must also repair the world about it, and within it, and the thing which you make takes its place in the web of nature." *Christopher Alexander* (A Pattern Language)

Construction waste

Some 32% of the UK waste stream is generated from the process of construction and demolition. This constitutes over 86 million tonnes of waste per annum.

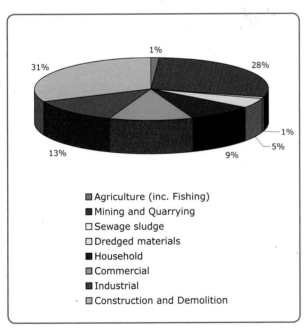

- ■ Agriculture (inc. Fishing)
- ■ Mining and Quarrying
- □ Sewage sludge
- □ Dredged materials
- ■ Household
- ■ Commercial
- ■ Industrial
- ■ Construction and Demolition

Approximately 60% of construction and demolition waste is currently recycled, mainly in the form of hardcore which is crushed and reused, for example as road base. This is a significant improvement over the last decade as the impact of taxes and other waste initiatives starts to take effect. The UK has excellent resources of aggregates but it is less energy intensive to use recycled materials for aggregates than to mine and transport them afresh.

WASTE HIERARCHY

The environmental impact of available means of dealing with waste can be ranked as follows:

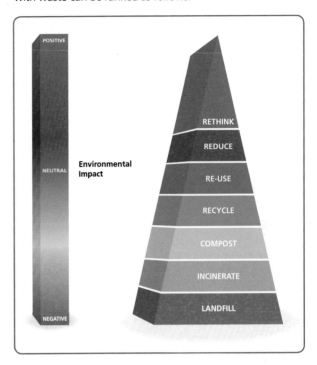

RETHINK

Before starting any construction project, the most effective way to reduce waste is to rethink the job – otherwise known as 'designing out waste.' Does that outhouse really need to be demolished or can it be retained, repaired and upgraded? Are you massively extending a house only to move out of it in 2 years time as the garden is no longer big enough? Designing out waste starts with the justification for the project itself and continues by finding uses for the maximum proportion of the material to be removed.

Ideally, waste is best recycled and reused where it is generated, in order to reduce transport costs. Developers and renovators can assess the probable waste generation at the start of a project and design to reuse some of the materials in the finished building. Heavy items provide the best opportunities for reuse on site. The reuse of bricks and roof coverings also helps to keep a building looking consistent with its surroundings. When demolishing an outbuilding to build an extension, the bricks can often be reused, especially if they were laid originally in lime mortar.

REDUCE

Some 13% of waste generated on building sites is made up of materials which pass directly from the manufacturers to the waste stream without ever being used. While it may be more efficient to order a small amount more than the estimated requirement – to avoid having to leave a job unfinished through lack of materials and deal with the consequent delays to other trades – the sheer size of this wastage implies that manufacturers or merchants cannot deal with returned items cost-effectively.

Packaging also forms a high percentage of materials on building sites, which implies that much packaging is not easily returnable or recyclable. Under the Producer Responsibility Obligations (Packaging Regulations), businesses over a certain size are now obliged to recover and recycle specified amounts of packaging waste each year and to certify that this has been achieved. In the domestic renovation sector, the main contribution that can be made by householders or small contractors is to select products which have the minimum of packaging and to order the correct amount of materials.

REUSE

The reuse of materials does not require energy to transform them into other materials, which is why reuse is above recycling in the environmental impact hierarchy. To encourage reuse, it is important to avoid spoilage by storing goods safely on site until they are needed. (It's also helpful to keep on good terms with the local builders' merchant, in order to be able to return surplus materials in good condition, and to accept any percentage restocking charge which may be applied.)

Surplus timber can be reused in any number of ways either inside or outside the home although, as with all plans for reuse, the ability to store materials until the need arises is critical.

It also pays to see what materials can be reused locally. For example, waste topsoil is usually generated when constructing a patio. By talking to neighbours, it is often possible to discover that someone in the district has a need for topsoil. This is what management consultants would call a win–win situation and saves on the transportation. Keeping it local also makes ecological sense as topsoil varies so much even over comparatively short distances.

The demise of local reclaim yards (often in favour of housing development) makes this kind of reuse more difficult to achieve, but the internet is an ideal method of advertising the availability of materials and a network of locally based sites would be a good way to promote low-energy reuse.

Waste bins made from reclaimed timber.

RECYCLE

Municipal household waste facilities now encourage recycling, after decades of dumping unsorted waste into landfill.

All waste sorted into the following categories can be recycled so, when carrying out renovation projects, householders can reduce the amount of waste which goes into landfill by keeping waste separate:

- Hardcore
- Timber
- Garden waste
- Metals
- Cardboard
- Plastics
- Electrical
- Batteries
- Paper
- Textiles
- Tyres.

The Waste and Resources Action Programme (WRAP) is responsible for a range of innovative schemes which make use of recycled material. Through their website it is also possible to research the various uses for materials which are collected via recycling centres. New uses for recycled products are being developed all the time. This represents a fundamental and welcome change of attitude – from viewing waste as a problem, to considering its potential as a resource.

For further information visit **www.wrap.org.uk**; **www.wastewatch.org.uk**; and **www.salvo.co.uk**.

PAINT RECYCLING

Each year approximately 80 million litres of paint are stored in garages and sheds or simply thrown away. In some parts of the country there are now schemes to enable the recycling of paint. To find out whether there is a paint recycling scheme in your area, visit **www.communityrepaint.org.uk**.

SKIPS AND SEGREGATION

At present the municipal waste facilities are not generally open to building contractors, so if you are planning a larger renovation project it is likely that you will need to hire a skip. Although different types of waste are mixed together in skips, the skip hire company will take the waste to its own transfer station and segregate it there. This is achieved by a combination of hand and mechanical sorting, all of which takes energy. Builders can take pre-sorted waste directly to skip companies' transfer stations, where they are charged by volume or weight.

For small builders, waste is a significant problem and expense – and many jobs do not merit hiring a skip. Just as car breakers (scrap yards) store, dismantle and ultimately recycle cars, the same can be done with construction waste. Schemes are needed to enable contractors to take pre-sorted waste to local holding areas – this is important as builders normally have better vehicles than their customers in which to transport the waste. A pilot scheme in Peterborough (The Ecotrade Centre) was successful, so

Segmentation process for waste from mixed skips. Mechanical sorting through to hand sorting.

145

there is no reason why this could not be repeated across the country, perhaps contributing towards community regeneration projects and helping people back to work. The cost of disposal at such sites would be less than the equivalent cost of skip hire, although the additional cost of transport and time for the builder has to be factored in – so it is important that there is a wide network of local holding sites. The accrued waste can also be sold on cheaply for direct reuse, such as topsoil or timber, or added to the waste stream for recycling, such as glass or aggregates. If cheap and simple methods of disposing of waste are provided, we could achieve a reduction in fly tipping which would be a further welcome result.

For larger construction sites it is more efficient not to

mix the waste but to segregate it as it arises on site. Skips filled with only one type of waste can be cheaper than mixed-waste skips.

The SmartWaste programme helps managers in construction and other industries to audit and improve their waste-handling procedures. For further information visit **www. smartwaste.co.uk.**

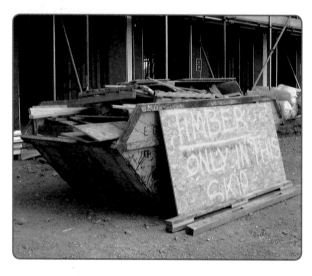

COMPOSTING

Composting is covered in the section on 'Eco-friendly gardening' in Chapter 10. It's often pointed out that composting releases methane (a potent greenhouse gas) but it is otherwise an efficient way to recycle household and garden green waste. Home composting also avoids the use of energy to transport small quantities of green waste to the local municipal site, as the waste itself is usually minor in comparison to the weight of the car and the occupants being transported on the same journey.

INCINERATION

Incineration is the next-to-last resort when handling large amounts of waste. It has the advantage that it reduces the volume of waste but, despite measures to reduce emissions, a variety of toxins is still released into the atmosphere. Approximately two million tonnes (9% of the total) of municipal solid waste is presently incinerated at 13 sites in the UK each year.[1] The environmental impact is somewhat reduced as the heat created is used either to generate electricity or for district-heating.

LANDFILL

Landfill is the last resort for waste disposal. The UK is running out of landfill space in many areas and the present rate of landfill is unsustainable. Leachate (liquid leaking) from active or closed sites poses a considerable threat to groundwater as it contains high concentrations of heavy metals, ammonia, toxic organic compounds and pathogens (organisms which cause disease).[2] Modern landfill sites are engineered to prevent contamination of groundwater, and methane can be collected and used for power generation and district-heating.

The EC landfill directive was introduced in 2002. The landfill regulations aim to reduce the impact of landfill by reducing the amount of waste disposed of in this manner, by banning certain substances from landfill altogether, and by classifying landfill sites according to what type of waste they are permitted to accept. Attitudes towards landfill are finally beginning to change but perhaps one day we will dig up old landfill sites to recover anything from precious metals to bricks.

Above: Methane capture from landfill site.
Below: Power generation plant from methane.

Photos: Canymoor Environmental Centre

Electronic equipment

When renovating property it is not uncommon to dispose of out-of-date electronic equipment. The average age of electronic equipment when it is discarded is as follows:

Electric cookers	12 years
Refrigerators and freezers	11 years
Televisions	10 years
Washing machines, dishwashers and tumble dryers	9 years
Hi-fi and stereo	8 years
Vacuum cleaners and carpet cleaners	8 years
Microwave ovens	7 years
Video equipment/radio, personal stereo and CD	6 years
Home and garden tools	6 years
Telephones, faxes, answer machines	4 years
Computers/small work or personal care appliances	4 years
Mobile phones and pagers/toys	2 years

Given the short life of these items, their collection and recycling will have to be improved markedly, especially in the light of the following items of EC legislation:

WEEE

The Waste Electrical and Electronic Equipment (WEEE) Directive aims to minimise the impact of electrical and electronic goods on the environment by increasing reuse

and recycling and by reducing the amount of WEEE going to landfill. The directive seeks to achieve this by making producers responsible for financing the collection, treatment, and recovery of waste electrical equipment, and by obliging distributors to allow consumers to return their waste equipment free of charge.

ROHS

The Restriction of Hazardous Substances (RoHS) is an EC directive which came into force in the UK in July 2006. This directive restricts the use of heavy metals and flame retardants in electrical equipment, thereby aiming to reduce their environmental impact. Products placed on the European market on or after 1 July 2006 may not contain more than the specified limits of lead, cadmium, mercury, hexavalent chromium, polybrominated biphenyls (PBB) and polybrominated diphenyl ethers (PBDEs). Note that some compact fluorescent lamps (CFLs) have mercury content that does not permit disposal via landfill.

BATTERIES

Increasingly, domestic and automobile batteries can be disposed of via kerbside recycling or in special bins at municipal sites as they contain a variety of heavy metals and other toxic substances. The 2006 EC Batteries Directive requires a gradual increase in the percentage which must be collected, thereby avoiding disposal in landfill sites, but also prohibits the sale of batteries which contain more than specified limits of mercury and cadmium.

Pollution

AVOIDING POLLUTANTS

When refurbishing or upgrading domestic property, a variety of toxins and pollutants are often introduced into the home environment. Chapter 2 highlights some of the issues relating to the manufacture and use of building materials, while issues relating to interior furnishings are discussed in Chapter 8. It is also possible that toxins are released during the manufacture or disposal of products and, while their impact on the home environment is negligible, the pollution occurs elsewhere.

CLEANING PRODUCTS

Having gone to the effort of refurbishing your home with healthy materials, maintaining it and keeping it clean runs the risk of introducing a new set of toxins which can be found in everything from air fresheners to oven cleaners. In many cases, the chemicals in the cleaners are more toxic than the dirt at which they are aimed. Older products such as vinegar are surprisingly effective cleaning agents, and bicarbonate of soda is a useful oven cleaner. There are plenty of alternative ways of dealing with household cleaning and there is a growing range of products that are both biodegradable and much safer for humans to handle.

Photo: Ecover

ACCIDENTAL POLLUTION

Carrying out refurbishment work can itself give rise to pollution. Care needs to be taken with the use of construction materials to prevent contamination of the dwelling being refurbished, or of neighbouring properties. Hazardous substances such as brick acid or paint strippers need to be handled and stored with great care. Nature is no respecter of property boundaries, so products used or spilled in one garden may soon leach out and pollute another.

Cement and lime-based mixes (mortar, render, concrete) should be thoroughly diluted when being washed out as they can cause visible staining if allowed to set on hard surfaces or cause damage to plants and trees if washed out over soft landscaping.

White spirit has gradually replaced turpentine (a natural product distilled from the sap of pine trees) as a thinner and brush cleaner. White spirit contains toluene and xylene so should not be added to the drainage system but disposed of safely at the local municipal refuse site. An alternative natural solvent which is less damaging to the environment is d-limonene – which is distilled from the peel of citrus fruit and a common constituent of eco-paints.

RADON

Radon is a radioactive gas which comes from uranium and exists naturally in very small quantities in soils and rocks. In certain areas of the UK, particularly in parts of Cornwall, radon readings can be abnormally high; if an individual property is tested and found to have a high radon level, the Health Protection Agency recommend a series of remedial measures, depending on the ground-floor construction. If the construction is solid then the recommendation is to build a radon sump. The radon is then extracted by means of a fan. If there is already a sub-floor void, mechanical ventilation will suffice provided that all the vents are open and unobstructed.

In areas where the risk is significant, new buildings are required to incorporate a damp-proof membrane which is vented to the outside via a cavity tray. In high-risk areas, sumps and mechanical ventilation may also be required. The same precautions should be followed for extensions or whenever a ground floor is completely rebuilt.

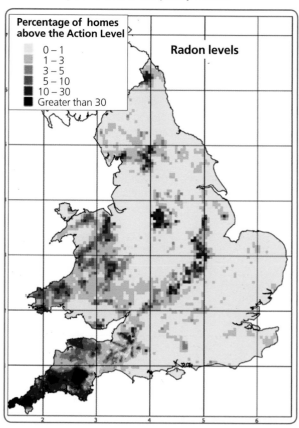

Percentage of homes above the Action Level
- 0 – 1
- 1 – 3
- 3 – 5
- 5 – 10
- 10 – 30
- Greater than 30

Radon levels

For further information visit **www.hpa.org.uk/radiation/ radon/index.htm.**

CLEANING UP CONTAMINATION

Refurbishment work provides an ideal opportunity to atone for the environmental recklessness of the industrial and post-industrial age. Small concentrated pockets of polluted soil are best removed altogether but lower-level more widespread pollution can be cleaned up by a variety of methods – physical, chemical, thermal and biological.

Biological methods of decontamination are often the most environmentally sustainable and best suited to renovation projects as they take longer to achieve the desired result than other methods. For new development, time is of the essence and there is usually insufficient time available to allow biological methods to work fully before the property is sold on.

Bioremediation techniques include adding a mixture of compost and minerals to the soil. This can 'fix' heavy metals within the soil so that plants, vegetables and trees may be grown

Oyster mushrooms.

safely on the site in the future. Preventing take-up of such substances into the food chain is technically known as breaking the pollutant-receptor pathway.[3] The action of composting can also break down some pollutants and the presence of compost in the soil introduces micro-organisms which can further break down certain chemicals.

Fungi have the capacity to break down a wide variety of substances including fuel oils and PCPs – biocides which were once widely used but are now banned. This technique is known as mycoremediation.

Phytoremediation involves growing plants specifically to deal with certain types of contaminants. This works either by the plants breaking down the pollutants into less harmful compounds or by taking the pollutants up into the part of the plant which is above ground. The plant can then be harvested (in some cases used for biofuel) and the contamination then removed from the residue rather than having to transport or lift and treat the soil. Willow and some species of rye, among other plants, are often used

Willow.

for this purpose. Phytoremediation is far cheaper than soil removal but potential for its success varies from site to site depending on the other conditions required by the relevant plants and their ability to withstand the toxins.

Soil chemistry is a specialist subject and professional advice should be sought. However, it is clearly more environmentally beneficial to clean soil than to dispose of it and bring in fresh soil, as transportation is avoided and the problem is eliminated rather than transferred to a landfill site, with all the associated risks of leaching and contamination in the future.

For further information see:

- Contaminated Land: Applications in Real Environments
- Contaminated Land Assessment & Remediation Research Centre
- The Environment Agency
- The Scottish Environment Protection Agency.

NOISE, DUST AND LIGHT POLLUTION

We tend to think of pollution as the presence of toxic substances in the ground, in the atmosphere, or in watercourses, but there are other forms of pollution that relate to buildings and construction work. You can't make an omelette without breaking a few eggs, but noise pollution can be managed and minimised. Dust arising from refurbishment work is easily carried from one property to another so measures to reduce dust plumes will minimise risks and nuisance both to the builders and to the neighbours.

For large construction schemes it is not uncommon to see the Considerate Constructors' Scheme logo on the site hoardings. This is a voluntary scheme designed to help contractors achieve and demonstrate good practice in relation to the environment, the workforce and the public. The aims are to be considerate, to protect the environment, to be good neighbours, to be clean, respectful, safe, environmentally conscious, responsible and accountable. Sounds sensible. Although domestic renovation jobs are at the wrong scale for this type of scheme, the basic principles can still be followed.

Light pollution is also a growing concern, as the view of the night sky from within our towns and cities is reduced or obscured by artificial light. The view of towns at night from nearby hills illustrates just how much energy is being used to light nothing in particular. On a smaller scale, permanently lit security lights and other outdoor space-lighting can cause nuisance to neighbours while often adding little to security or safety.

Dust control equipment in use.

10 EXTERIOR SPACE AND GARDENS

Photo: Chris Gibson, Natural England

In urban areas, gardens act as corridors for wildlife while creating pockets of eco-diversity in an otherwise sterile environment. By absorbing CO$_2$ and rainwater, gardens soften the environmental impact of city living while providing a place to relax or to take some exercise in the fresh air. This chapter examines the main issues that are important for the wider environment when thinking about how to renovate and improve exterior space.

Property renovators have a tendency to concentrate on the main dwelling and ignore the garden, or at best leave it right until the end, by which time the money has usually run out. Starting with the garden, on the other hand, allows neglected soils to recover and gives new plants and trees the chance to get established while the rest of the work is carried out.

PROTECTED SPECIES

Gardens which have been neglected for many years and left to grow wild can have a high ecological value and there may be legally protected species present. Bats may of course be using the building itself and particular care must be taken to avoid disturbing bat roosts. A neglected garden may have become home to slow worms, dormice, grass snakes, great crested newts, badgers and many other species which are protected by law so it may be necessary to carry out surveys before clearing what may appear to be waste land. Wherever possible it is best to maintain and work around existing features such as mature trees and hedges.

BIKE PARKING

Making provision for bike parking is also important when renovating a property. Over 60% of journeys made by car in the UK are under five miles. Short journeys to school or to the shops can usually be made by bike instead; congestion would be reduced and we would all get fitter by trading

four wheels for two as often as possible. However, roads and houses have been developed for decades with little thought given to public transport or bike use, so this is simply not possible for everyone.

To encourage bike use, safe and easily accessed bike storage is required. Direct access to a rear garden is best – so that muddy bikes do not have to be wheeled through the house. Most Victorian terraces have access to the rear, originally for coal deliveries and a shared entry gate adds extra security. Much semi-detached housing has side-alley access, which is also ideal for bikes. Many bike thefts from sheds are reported every year. If using a shed to store bikes it is wise to lock the bike to a secure fixing set in concrete and to have a good lock (not just a padlock) on the shed itself.

Where there is no accessible rear garden, bespoke secure bike storage boxes can be used.

Where a garage is planned, bike access is made easier by having a separate side door so that the main door does not have to be opened just for a bike journey. In garages which are wide enough to get past the car without damaging it, bikes can be stored by being hung from hooks or racks fixed to the wall or ceiling.

CLOTHES DRYING

Drying clothes in the garden saves money and energy. If there is not sufficient space to erect a clothesline, a rotary dryer (whirligig) will do the job just as well. Rotary dryers are easily removable when not in use, as a short length of pipe can be driven (or concreted) into the ground to act as a sleeve for the post.

Hard landscaping

The same principles apply to materials used in the garden as apply to any other construction materials, namely:

■ Use reclaimed or recycled products where possible
■ Source locally produced items
■ Avoid materials which can cause pollution.

The garden is a good place to reuse material which has been rejected from the fabric or interior of the house. Reclaimed materials also tone in much better with older properties – railway sleepers make ideal borders for raised beds, although for an organic garden an untreated sleeper would be best. The creosote in sleepers makes them unsuitable (in fact against EU law) for use in situations where there is a risk of frequent skin contact, such as tables or children's play areas.

Use of reclaimed materials in hard landscaping

SURFACING MATERIALS

Paving materials vary widely in terms of their cost, environmental impact and raw material. Concrete slabs are very effective but, as with all concrete products, they have a high embodied energy and may have travelled a long way before reaching the local merchant. If laid continuously and drained to the surface water system, slabs add considerably to the load on the drains, although this can be reduced by allowing gaps between the slabs and inserting low-growing plants so that water can drain through. Failure to insert plants will simply encourage weeds. Alternatively, a fine gravel can be used for the same purpose.

Cars can be parked on most paving materials as long as the sub-base is sound – it is certainly not necessary to concrete over the front garden to provide good hardstanding. Solid materials such as concrete and tarmac have a high environmental impact, add to the drainage problem and can also contribute towards the 'heat island' effect in cities, as they absorb excessive amounts of heat during the day. In extreme cases, impermeable landscaping materials have even been held responsible for subsidence as clay subsoils can shrink if they dry out, which is more likely if rainwater is prevented from entering the adjacent ground.

Blocks are more porous than slabs – clay blocks have a lower embodied energy than cementitious blocks and

Beech/Yew hedge: Above, winter; below, summer.

encourage a wider variety of lichens and small plants but they are expensive if purchased new and reclaimed paviors can be difficult to find.

Gravel is completely porous (unless laid on an impervious membrane) and has a low embodied energy – for more information on the importance of the porosity of hard landscaping materials see the section on 'Sustainable urban drainage systems' later in this chapter. If using gravel in a garden it may be necessary to lay it over a sheet of porous membrane to discourage weeds.

BOUNDARY PROTECTION

For security, longevity, cost and wildlife attraction, the most effective form of boundary protection is a hedge. In urban

Fencing can be divided into three main groups: post and rail (or wire); closeboard; post and panel.

environments, hedges can also be very effective at reducing traffic noise.

The main disadvantage with hedges is that they take a while to grow so they have fallen out of favour with a house-renovating public who require instant results. Hedges also take up more space than a fence, which may be an issue in small or narrow gardens; they do require some maintenance, although small clippings of most hedges provide good fuel for the compost heap.

To maintain privacy in all seasons, evergreen hedges are preferred, although it is possible to achieve excellent results by mixing deciduous and evergreen species to give year-round cover and changing colours through the seasons.

In just the same way that timber for structural use should be carefully selected, timber used in the garden should be certified as having come from a sustainable source (see the section on 'Sustainable timber use' in Chapter 2), and while treatment may be necessary this should be carefully selected to avoid introducing toxins into the outdoor environment. Local timber mills might not be certified by a major scheme but may be able to provide reassurance that their timber is sustainably harvested and that trees are being replanted. The embodied energy of locally produced timber will be much lower and choosing local goods helps to boost the regional economy.

Post and wire fencing can be used as an initial support for living fencing. Willow is a good example of a plant which does not take up much room but grows rapidly to form a visual screen. If land drains are present, care must be taken with the planting as willow roots can cause serious damage to drains; regular pruning will also be required.

Photo: www.westwaleswillows.co.uk

All softwood fence posts should be treated and, if they are set in concrete, their life can be extended significantly by good concreting techniques:

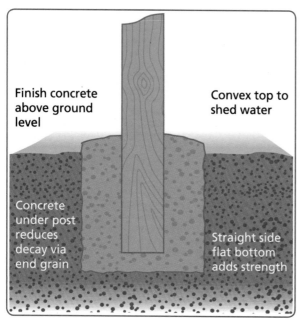

Finish concrete above ground level

Convex top to shed water

Concrete under post reduces decay via end grain

Straight side flat bottom adds strength

Closeboard fencing should also be treated to prolong its life and the end-grain capped to prevent excessive water intake and resultant decay. Cappings can be replaced easily every few years without having to disturb the rest of the fence.

Capping to protect end grain.

Post-and-panel fencing is usually the cheapest form of fencing and the fastest to erect. It does not last as long as any of the others mentioned as the softwood panels tend to rot or become damaged more quickly. The life of the fence can be extended by using a solid wooden gravel board at the base – firstly this will last longer than the fence panel when in contact with moisture and secondly the gravel board can be replaced in due course without having to disturb the fencing material above (although sometimes the panels will have slumped onto the gravel board).

Concrete gravel boards are also available, but they are a higher energy product and tend to outlast the rest of the fence (i.e. posts and panels) for which they are designed. They are perhaps best used where concrete posts have been used, as these normally last longer than wooden posts.

Panel fencing is often associated with larchlap or similar products, but many other types of panels are available, although they may take a little more effort to locate. The use of locally grown materials for panel fencing also adds local character to the garden, whereas larchlap is used throughout the country.

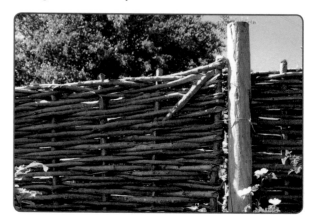

Sustainable urban drainage systems (SUDS)

The floods of 2007 caused an estimated £3Bn of damage. There is a dawning realisation that we have concreted over much of our urban environment and that most of the problems faced by our partly Victorian drainage system are due to the massively increased area which it is required to drain, and not simply to the increased frequency of heavy rainfall. Rainwater that used to soak into fields, gardens and lawns now lands on car parks, drives, roads, roofs and patios, from where it is channelled directly to the drainage system. Where rivers are used for drainage, the problem is gradually transferred downstream, with occasionally catastrophic results.

Photos: Hugh Hamner

Gravel surface

Ecoblock grid to stabilise grass or gravel.

Photo: Cooper Clarke Civils & Lintels

REGULATION CORNER – DRIVEWAYS

In October 2008 the permitted development rights for front gardens were changed in order to reduce the impact on the drainage system in terms of both flooding and pollution. Householders used to be able to pave front gardens without applying for planning permission but now this depends on what kind of surface is to be put down.

Planning permission is not required if the surface is permeable (porous) or if rainwater drains from the hardstanding directly into a lawn or border that is itself free-draining. Otherwise, driveways over 5sq m do now require planning permission, with its associated fees and requirements for scale plans.

Although these regulations only apply to front gardens, the same principles apply to back gardens if there is a risk that paved areas will discharge rainwater into the public drainage system.

Sustainable urban drainage systems (SUDS) is a relatively new science and at present it is largely directed towards new housing although there is no reason why many of the techniques which constitute SUDS should not be used in renovation – in other words, once people are aware of the issues they can avoid adding to the problem. In Scotland it is already a requirement for all new development to have a SUDS strategy in place and in England and Wales all new houses covered by the Code for Sustainable homes have to take into account and reduce the impact of surface water on the drainage system.

SUDS has three main aims:

1 To reduce or delay the discharge of rainwater into the drainage system
2 To enhance the quality of the water which is released into the drainage system
3 To improve the environment and provide habitats for wildlife.

In terms of quantity of discharge, the burden on the drainage infrastructure can be reduced by several different methods:

- Permeable surfaces
- Holding ponds
- Rainwater harvesting.

PERMEABLE SURFACES

Permeable surfaces allow water to permeate and soak through to the underground aquifers, replenishing the water table and reducing the burden on the drains. Just as important as the surface itself is the sub-base – this needs to be free-draining so that it can accept and dissipate rainwater. Permeable sub-base lacks the fine particles normally found in type 1 hardcore – so water can pass through the gaps around the larger stones.

The most common types of permeable surface are:

- Gravel
- Blocks
- Tarmac
- Grasscrete.

Some forms of block paving are more porous than others, mainly dependent on the size of gaps between the blocks. Ribbed blocks are specifically designed to allow the maximum amount of water to permeate through.

Not all sites are suitable for permeable surfacing – if the subsoil is impermeable the water will not drain away.

Free-draining blocks.

The SUDS 'triangle'

Conventional approach

Integrated approach

Quantity

Quality

Amenity

Quantity

Quality

Amenity

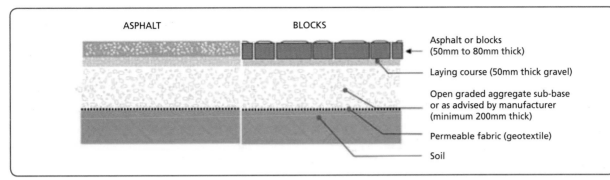

ASPHALT   BLOCKS

Asphalt or blocks
(50mm to 80mm thick)

Laying course (50mm thick gravel)

Open graded aggregate sub-base
or as advised by manufacturer
(minimum 200mm thick)

Permeable fabric (geotextile)

Soil

Image: Tarmac Dry

Alternatively, if the subsoil contains pollutants (for example in housing development on what was previously brownfield land), free-draining rainwater could transfer those pollutants elsewhere within the ecosystem. In some cases where there are clay soils present, a combination of methods can be used so that normal rainfall can soak through the permeable sub-base but heavy rainfall can be directed elsewhere.

Tarmac (asphalt) is normally thought of as being impermeable but porous systems are now available.

Another way of providing hardstanding without adding to the burden on drainage systems is to lay wheel tracks – cars can then be driven in without causing wheel ruts but any rainwater will simply drain off to surrounding grass or plants. Porous surfaces in general have the added advantage that ice is less likely to form in winter.

HOLDING PONDS

Ponds, drainage ditches (swales) and wetlands can all be used to store water so that it can be released gradually when the burden on the drainage system is reduced. This is known as attenuation. When rain falls on roofs or impermeable hard surfacing it is collected and then held in a pond or a series of ponds before being released into the drainage system in a controlled manner.

Attenuation pond. Doubles as play area.

Photo: David Michael

Holding pond for surface water drainage.

Pond fills up during heavy rainfall

Overflow pipe with restricted diameter

Photo: Blackdown Horticultural Consultants

Swale for collection and slow discharge of flood water.

HARVESTING WATER

Harvesting water for use in the garden is one of the cheapest and most effective ways of reducing both water demand and the burden on the drainage system. Of course once the water butt is full there is no effect on drainage if the overflow is connected to the original drain as often has to be the case.

Collecting water for garden use, WCs and washing machines are all covered in more detail in Chapter 7 on water efficiency.

GREEN ROOFS

Green roofs not only use rainwater to feed the plants in the vegetative top layer but also act to slow down the release of water into the drainage system, as the layer of soil and gravel that forms the bed for the plants can absorb a significant quantity of water (see the 'Roofing' section in Chapter 2).

WATER QUALITY

Rainwater often gathers pollutants such as oils, salts, litter or even sediments during its journey from the ground to the drainage system. Water quality is now a recognised concern for housing developments and SUDS techniques are increasingly used to clean the run-off from commercial property. An extreme example is the petrol interceptor tank commonly used on filling station forecourts, but reduced quantities of impurities can be dealt with by more natural techniques such as bioremediation. In general, SUDS techniques are most effective when used in combination, especially when the principal aim is to improve the quality of water discharge.

RECREATION AND WILDLIFE

Depending on topography, larger ponds can be created for existing developments as a shared community resource, acting as a holding pond for rainwater but also providing an amenity and a wildlife attraction. Native planting and careful design can therefore transform a potential flooding problem into an environmental asset.

For further information:
General info on SUDS:
http://environment-agency.gov.uk/business/ sectors/36998.aspx; www.ciria.org.uk/suds
Guidance on the permeable surfacing of front gardens – CLG/Environment Agency 2008

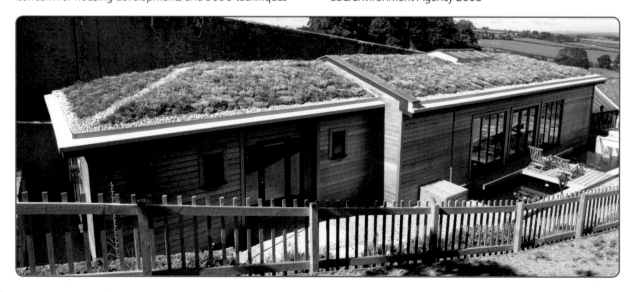

Eco-friendly gardening

Most gardeners prefer to work with nature rather than against it and are consequently eco-friendly by default. Gardening is a huge subject so this section will only focus on gardens insofar as they affect the wider environment.

ORGANIC GARDENING

The key to successful organic gardening is soil quality. If the soil is healthy and well drained with plenty of organic matter, plants will be healthier and less prone to disease. Disease-resistant varieties of many vegetables are available where soil quality is poor but the best thing to do in such cases is to improve the soil. The main strategies for gardening without chemicals might be summarised as follows:

- Enrich the soil with manure or compost rather than chemical fertilisers
- Grow green manures to protect and improve the soil
- Use companion and sacrificial planting to ward off pests from vegetables
- Encourage natural predators by providing suitable food and habitats
- Use barriers to stop pests attacking young and tender plants
- Prune and dispose of diseased plants or parts of plants
- Pick off and dispose of slugs, snails and other pests (best done at night)
- Rotate crops, even in small vegetable gardens
- Choose species appropriate to the soil and other conditions
- Hoe, mulch and dig to control weeds, even perennials
- Protect plants from stress by good husbandry.

By using these strategies it is possible to create an environment in which plants can be grown successfully

'Digging in' the compost.

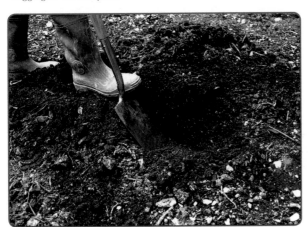

without damaging or polluting the soil or the wider environment.

AVOIDANCE OF CHEMICALS

Chemicals are easily transported through the action of wind and rain, so may end up affecting areas some distance from their intended location or – worse – in neighbouring gardens. Pesticides have a tendency to affect a much wider variety of creatures than their intended victims – the widespread decline in butterflies and moths is in great part due to the indiscriminate use of pesticides.

Some otherwise organic gardeners are prepared to countenance the use of glyphosate to kill perennial weeds such as couch grass, dock, thistle, bindweed and ground elder. However, Friends of the Earth have carried out a study of this chemical. For further information on this subject visit **www.foe.co.uk/resource/reports/impacts_glyphosate.pdf**.

For further information on all aspects of organic gardening visit 'Garden Organic', at **www.gardenorganic.org.uk**.

PEAT

Peat is produced over thousand of years as dead plants build up rather than decay due to acidic waterlogged conditions. In addition to their importance as a historical record, peat bogs are a unique habitat and several rare plants depend on them for their survival.

Forestry and agriculture have already accounted for much of our peatland but commercial extraction of peat for nurseries and gardens is now the major threat to the little peatland which remains. An incredible 94% of lowland raised peat bogs in the UK has been lost. Large-scale harvesting of peat for horticultural purposes only commenced in the 1950s as the result of a successful marketing campaign by peat producers. The harvesting

Photo: K Denham

method used causes destruction of the bog, as it is deep drained and the plant layer is stripped off.

Reducing peat consumption can be achieved not only by using more traditional alternatives such as compost or leaf mould but also by selecting plants grown in peat-free materials. The Government's Biodiversity Action Plan set a target of 90% reduction in peat use by 2010. Peat has been cut for fuel for centuries but hand-cutting of peat does allow for partial recovery of the bog and may be sustainable on a small scale in the future.

For further information visit **www. peatlandsni.gov.uk** and **www. wildlifetrust.org.uk/facts/peat.htm.**

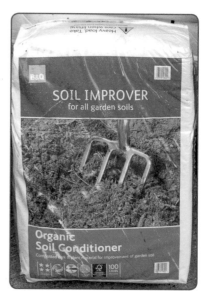

GROWING VEGETABLES AND FRUIT

Fruit, vegetables and herbs grown organically in the garden are cheap and any produce grown at home has zero 'food miles'. In addition, the pleasure of growing and eating your own food is impossible to describe.

Even small gardens can yield surprising amounts of produce but, for people with no gardens who would like to grow food, there are plenty of allotments available in many towns in the UK – local councils usually have a register of allotment areas and contact details for each. If there are no allotments and sufficient people register an interest, the local authority is obliged to provide land under the 1908 Allotment Act (as amended).

For people who have no garden or nearby allotment, another option is Landshare, launched through River Cottage in 2009. This national service brings together people who have spare land with those who would like to grow something on it. By inputting location details in www.landshare.net you can find growers, land and even helpers in your area.

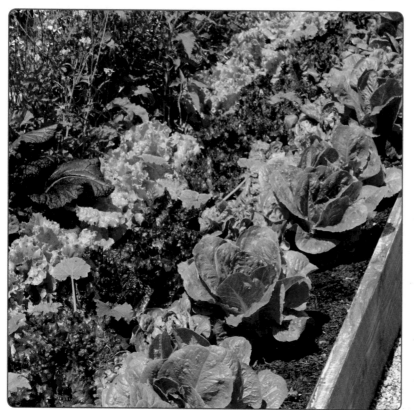

INVASIVE NON-NATIVE SPECIES

The cultivation of non-native plants is in a sense what ornamental gardening is all about and non-native plants can enhance any garden. However, a minority of non-native species have escaped from the garden and are causing considerable environmental damage and becoming a threat to a number of native plants.

In addition to the plants listed in the revised Schedule 9, several others are causing widespread problems. Spanish Bluebells are invading woodland and cross-breeding with our native bluebells, causing them to lose their distinctive characteristics. Botanists have also warned that the 'Tree of Heaven' (Ailanthus altissima) may become a serious problem, as it spreads rapidly and prevents other species from germinating and establishing in its vicinity by leaking toxins into the ground.

COMPOSTING

Composting turns a problem into an asset. If there is sufficient space in the garden for a good compost heap, garden waste (and some household waste) can be broken down into soil-enriching organic matter, all without the trouble and expense of removing waste and importing compost. The keys to good composting are to have a good mix of soft and woody materials and to have sufficient size (around 1m^3) to make the heap work properly. Temperatures in a well-designed compost heap can reach 70°C and, in general, the warmer the heap, the faster will be the microbial action that breaks down the organic matter.

Turning the heap speeds up the process by introducing air and helps to ensure that material which might otherwise be left at the edges of the heap is also composted.

■ *Compost these*

Dead leaves
Lawn mowings
Soft hedge clippings
Shredded paper (not magazine paper)
Old bedding plants
Uncooked vegetable peelings and trimmings
Tea and tea bags, coffee and filters
Eggshells
Annual weeds
Pond weed
Cotton and wool.

■ *Don't compost these*

Food scraps
Meat or bones
Diseased plant material (unless the heap is hot)
Soil pests
Any weeds with seed heads
Perennial weeds
Dog or cat faeces and litter
Synthetic material
Cardboard
Nappies.

REGULATION CORNER

Schedule 9 of the Countryside and Wildlife Act 1981 lists plants which cannot be planted or caused to grow in the wild – the Schedule was updated in 2010 and is now much longer, including a variety of additions such as Himalayan Balsam and Rhododendron Ponticum which have increasingly become a nuisance in recent years.

In 2008 the Invasive non-native species strategy for Great Britain was launched. This is intended to provide a framework for a coordinated approach to the management of problem plants and animals. The strategy is focused around three main aims:

■ Prevention
■ Detection/Surveillance
■ Control/Eradication.

The website has a reporting facility to track non-native species and provides detailed information on species and how to identify them. Information sheets on over 60 species are available to download from this site:
   https://secure.fera.defra.gov.uk/ nonnativespecies/home/index.cfm

The Environment Agency also provides detailed information on managing invasive non-native plants that proliferate on or near fresh water. The main aim is to prevent the public from introducing or spreading these plants, and to identify and eradicate them where they take hold. The 7 listed are:

■ Japanese knotweed
■ Giant Hogweed
■ Himalayan Balsam
■ Australian Swamp Stonecrop
■ Parrot's Feather
■ Floating Pennywort
■ Creeping Water Primrose.

In Scotland, the Wildlife and Natural Environment (Scotland) Bill (2011) lays down regulations for dealing with plants that grow 'outwith their native range'. The definition of plants that are covered by this legislation will be determined by subsequent 'species control orders'. (This legislation also applies to animals which could become invasive.)

Shredders

Woody material such as thicker prunings and stems of vegetables may need shredding first before adding to the heap. These materials will break down eventually but may need several passes through the composting process. It is a nuisance to have to pick out uncomposted material each time so shredding is the most efficient option. A shredder is a good example of a resource which is best shared between several households, as it would otherwise only be used for a few hours each year. Sharing a resource such as this enables a larger and more robust machine to be purchased at a reduced cost to everyone.

Moisture content

Composting needs some moisture to get started but too much moisture will stop the process so there is a balance to be struck between the two. Generally there is enough moisture in the materials which have been assembled but when building a heap after a prolonged dry spell it may be necessary to add a little water. To avoid the heap getting too wet, covering it with a scrap of carpet or a tarpaulin will prevent it from absorbing too much rainwater.

For further information visit **www.recyclenow.com/home_composting/index.html**; call the WRAP (Waste & Resources Action Programme) composting helpline on 0845 600 0323 or see the Composting Association at **www.compost.org.uk** or call 0870 1603270.

Community composting

There are a number of advantages to organising composting on a community basis – for example, an individual garden might not produce the right kind of mix of constituents to build a successful heap. By pooling resources (and also expertise) there is a much better chance of getting a good result. There may also be social benefits to be gained from getting small groups of people to work together towards a shared goal.

To find out how to set up a composting club in your area or for further information visit **www.communitycompost.org**.

Finished compost.

Encouraging wildlife

By planting a variety of perennials, shrubs and trees in the garden, wildlife will be encouraged to visit or to make a home there. These plants do not have to be native, it is more important to provide a good structure with as many layers of vegetation at different heights as possible. In larger gardens, leaving an area wild or uncut will encourage a wide variety of helpful creatures. Hedges are particularly welcome as they provide nesting opportunities for birds and shelter for voles, hedgehogs and many useful insects.

Bees are the gardener's best friend, as they perform a vital role by pollinating plants – yours and your neighbours'. Around 25% of native bee species are now thought to be endangered. There are many plants which are rich in nectar and pollen and bees are best attracted

to gardens where they have flowers to visit for as much of the year as possible. Mason bees can be encouraged by providing nesting cylinders which can be bought or made simply from bamboo canes and attached to a tree or a solid garden structure.

Butterflies and moths will be attracted by a range of plants, especially those which are rich in nectar. Herbs and flowers planted in sunny positions are best at encouraging these welcome visitors and some species will come to particular plants. It is equally important to provide plants which caterpillars like to feed on. At all costs avoid the use of pesticides. A healthy population of moths can also bring bats to the garden to feed on them (six of the 16 species of bat in the UK are endangered or rare).

Birds will visit if food (and water) is provided – cats and dogs permitting – and will repay the gesture in many ways, including pest control. Thrushes, for example, feed on slugs and snails. If there is space, plant a tree in the garden – birds will be grateful for the perch and might even make a nest there one day. If a suitable tree already exists, a nesting box can be erected (taking care not to damage the tree) to encourage small birds to nest. For houses or flats with little or no garden, nesting opportunities for swifts can be provided by holes in the structure of the house itself or by fixing boxes to the wall. Swift nesting bricks can even be inserted into walls. For further information visit **www.rspb.org.uk/gardens.**

Photo: Chris Gibson, Natural England

Photo: Jacob Jayne & Shwegler

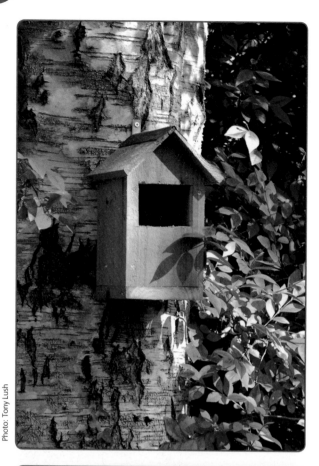

Photo: Tony Lush

Ladybirds and lacewings (and their larvae) devour aphids, so they can be used as a natural form of pest control and reduce reliance on chemical methods. They can be attracted to the garden by planting pollen-rich plants such as angelica, dill, parsley, caraway, catnip, lemon balm and thyme. They can also be imported as larvae from specialist suppliers. Hoverflies are also beneficial and are attracted to open-structured plants of the daisy family.

Photo: Dr. Roger Key, Natural England

Photo: Tony Lush

Insect Hibernacula.

Hedgehogs can eat up to half their bodyweight in slugs, snails and caterpillars every day so they are a very welcome garden resident. They can be encouraged by putting out food during periods of shortage (cat or dog food in jelly is recommended) and piles of brush or leaves make ideal places for hedgehogs to hibernate. Shrews and voles need to eat through the winter so they can be helped by making protected feeding areas for them near to the base of hedges, where they prefer to live for safety.

For further information visit Natural England (English Nature) at **www.naturalengland.org.uk** and see 'Nature in the Garden' or visit **www.plantpress.com/wildlife/home.php**; to find lists of plants that attract each of the groups of wildlife mentioned above visit **www.englishplants.co.uk**; for further information on conserving wildflowers, fungi and lichens visit **www.plantlife.org.uk/uk/index-uk.html**; and for further information on wildlife and habitats in general contact your local wildlife trust.

Building a compost heap

There are plenty of purpose-made compost heaps on the market, but if you would like to build one out of recycled materials, here's how.

TOOLS REQUIRED
- Spade
- Wire cutters
- Spirit Level
- Hammer

1 Find 4 pallets from a local building yard or other commercial enterprise. Pallets should be at least 1m square in order for the heap to generate sufficient heat to work properly. It's much easier to build the heap if pallets are of the same size.

2 Identify a suitable area for the compost heap. If this is on a slope then you'll need to level the ground first with a spade. It's not necessary to put anything on the bottom of the heap – leaving it open makes it easier for tiger worms to find it and accelerate the composting process.

3 Ensure that the sides are level – this will make it much easier to attach the back and front sections.

4 Set 2 pallets at right angles to each other. Pallets generally have more timber on one face than the other, so have the side with the most timber facing inwards.

5 Connect these two pallets together with strong wire. This can also be achieved with screws or bolts but it requires a little more work.

6 Repeat the process to form the other side of the heap.

7 Composting does require oxygen to work properly. However, if your material is small pieces and you're worried about it falling through the sides of the heap, chicken wire can be attached to the inside of the pallets. Measure the rear of the heap and add the two sides to work out the total length of mesh required.

8 Measure the full length of the three sides and mark the roll of wire mesh.

9 Cut the mesh with tin snips or electrical wire cutters.

10 Fix the mesh to the inside of the pallets using galvanised staples.

11 Construct a removable front for the heap. This can be done using a fourth pallet. Being able to

remove the front section makes it easier to dig out the heap at the end of the process. More sophisticated versions use planks which are dropped into slots at the front of the side pallets.

12 Fill the heap (see main text section for guidance on what can and can't be composted) and cover to keep the majority of the rain off. An old piece of carpet can be used, or a sheet of polythene as long as it's weighted down. Sit back, relax, and let nature do the rest.

13 For the really efficient composter, it's easy to add a feeder heap and a finished storage heap either side of the main heap, simply by adding more pallets. A feeder heap is useful as it helps to achieve a good mix of rich and woody materials ready for the main cooking heap. A finished storage heap may not be required if your compost goes straight back onto the garden as soon as it's ready.

GLOSSARY

Accumulator – Device used to store the heat produced by a wood burning stove and release it in a controlled manner.

Acid rain – Rain or other precipitation which has been contaminated with sulphur and nitrogen compounds in the atmosphere, largely released from the combustion of fossil fuels, leading to a weak acidity which can have a significant cumulative effect on living organisms and on building materials such as limestone.

Air conditioning – Changing the quality of internal air to the desired levels of temperature, humidity and purity.

Back boiler – Device fitted to the rear of a solid fuel stove which heats water for space heating or domestic use.

Ballast – Material used to hold down or add weight.

Batt – Semi-rigid form of insulation material that will not slump in vertical applications.

Binder – Any substance that adheres material together or, when added to loose aggregate, forms a solid mass when activated.

Biodegradable – Able to be decomposed by biological agents such as micro-organisms.

Biodiesel – Oil for heating or other combustion consisting of mono-alkyl esters of long chain fatty acids produced from processed plant matter such as soybeans. Raw vegetable oil must first have glycerin removed to be termed biodiesel.

Biogas – Gas (often largely methane) generated by the bacteriological degradation of biological material in the absence of oxygen (anaerobic digestion).

Biomass – Fuel derived from non-fossilised organic material. (Also 'biofuel', 'bioenergy'.)

Blinding – Layer of fine aggregate (usually sand) laid over coarse aggregate to provide a smooth surface.

Blockwork – Sections of walls constructed from cementitious blocks.

Breather membrane – Membrane which is porous to air and water vapour but impervious to water.

Breathing wall – Form of wall construction that allows air and water vapour to pass through the structure, primarily from inside to outside.

Car club – Arrangement by which a group of people own or lease a vehicle or series of vehicles in common, thereby sharing the fixed costs and making more efficient use of resources and space.

Carbon cycle – The fundamental chemistry of all living material on earth. The main transmission compound is CO_2 (Carbon Dioxide) which is emitted (through respiration and burning) and then absorbed in oceans, or is chemically changed, for example via photosynthesis.

Carbon neutral – Any process or material which takes up as much CO_2 as is released over its life cycle; fuel which is grown and burnt and re-grown may be said to be 'carbon-neutral'.

Carcassing – Manufacturer's term for the main body of kitchen units, excluding doors and worktops.

Carcinogen – Substance which causes cancer.

Casement – Inner section of window carrying the glass, hinged on one edge and designed to open inwards or outwards.

Cavity wall – Modern form of construction whereby two leaves or skins of brickwork or blockwork are built with a gap between them, and the two leaves are connected together with wall ties. More recently the cavity has been widened to accept insulation during the construction process but a gap is still maintained.

Cellulose – Carbohydrate forming the chief component in cell walls of plants and trees. Wood pulp is almost pure cellulose.

Cement – Binder made from clay and calcined limestone.

Cladding – Timber used to provide a rain screen on the outside of a building.

Closeboard – Form of fencing where vertical overlapping feather-edged boards are fixed to horizontal bearers.

Combined heat and power – Plant which has the capacity to generate electricity while the heat produced is used for space heating

Communication pipe – The section of a water pipe running from the mains supply in the street to the property boundary. It is the responsibility of the supply company.

Concrete – Solid mass formed by combining aggregate of differing sizes with a binder such as cement.

Condensing boiler – A boiler that recovers and uses some of the heat present in the flue gases, causing water vapour in those gases to condense.

Counterweight – Attached to the other end of a sash cord, a counterweight is designed to balance a sliding sash window and make it easier to open and to keep in position. Rarely seen.

Creosote – Formed in chimneys and flues when wood is incompletely combusted. Fine particulates in the smoke condense to form creosote, which is flammable. Creosote may be dry and flaky or tarry and wet in appearance.

Cylinder – Vessel for storing hot water or for heating water.

Damp-proof membrane – Impervious layer of polythene or bitumen laid under, over or within a concrete ground floor slab to prevent rising damp.

Dead leg – Length of pipe through which water must pass from boiler or cylinder to taps (or the amount of water which must pass) before the water at the tap becomes hot.

Decrement delay – The time taken for changes in external temperature to affect internal temperature, passing through the building structure.

Dew-point temperature – The temperature at which condensation forms, given the humidity level. If the temperature is relatively warm on one side of a wall and below the dew-point temperature on the other, there is a risk that the moisture-laden air will reach the 'dew-point temperature' within the wall and liquid water will form and be deposited at this point.

Dichroic lamp – see *Halogen lamp*. In this context dichroic means the property of reflecting different colours of light when viewed from different angles.

Dry lining – The use of plasterboard, sometimes insulated, to form the finished inner surface of a wall. plasterboard may be fixed to battens or glued directly to the wall.

Dry rot – *Serpula lacrymans*, fungus that attacks and destroys timber in the presence of moisture, especially in unventilated situations. Dry rot can also spread through masonry, although it does not attack it directly. It has several forms or stages, ranging from a white cotton-like sheet appearing on affected surfaces, to dark strands (hyphae) through which it travels, and yellow fruiting bodies that turn red as spores are released.

Dual flush – Mechanism on WCs which allows the user to choose the flush volume.

Ecology – The study of organisms in terms of their relationships with other organisms and with their local environment.

Economy 7 – Electricity pricing structure whereby different prices are charged according to the time of day the electricity is drawn from the grid. The timing of the cheaper tariff normally starts at 12:00 midnight and ends at 8:00am.

Floating floor – A timber or laminate flooring surface that is not mechanically fixed (such as glued or nailed) to the subfloor in any way.

Floor slab – The concrete slab that is commonly poured directly on the ground to form the ground floor construction of a property.

Fossil fuel – Fuel derived from the remains of prehistoric plants and animals that did not decay into carbon dioxide due to anaerobic conditions. Once buried, exposure to heat and pressure within the earth's crust produced coal, oil and gas, the main 'fossil fuels'.

Gravel board – Concrete board placed horizontally at the base of a fence to prevent timber fencing from coming into contact with damp ground and suffering decay.

Grid connection – Where embedded renewable energy generating technology, such as PV or a wind turbine, is connected to the mains electricity supply.

Halogen lamp – A lamp which consists of a tungsten filament in a sealed chamber containing a halogen gas such as iodine or bromine.

Hardcore – Aggregate of relatively large size used as the base for roads or concrete.

Hardwood – Timber obtained from broad-leaved, deciduous flower-bearing trees. The term does not strictly indicate the hardness of the timber, although in general hardwoods are much harder than softwoods.

Heat exchanger – Device designed to transfer heat from one substance to another such as air-to-air, air-to-water, water-to-water etc, without mingling the two.

Heat island – Effect noticed in cities when the sun's warmth is absorbed by the dense masonry of buildings and roads, then radiated back out, leading to warmer temperatures than in the surrounding areas. The energy burnt in cities adds to this effect.

Heat pump – Pump that drives a circuit capable of transferring heat from one body to another. A heat pump may provide cooling or heating, depending upon the configuration of the pump within the vapour compression cycle.

Heat recovery – The extraction of heat from air or water that is expelled from a building and the reuse of this heat within the building.

Heavy metal – Metal with relatively high density (atomic weight). Mercury, cadmium and lead are the most widespread heavy metals with potential toxicity to humans.

Hemp – Plant grown for a wide variety of purposes, including fibres for paper and cloth.

I-beam – In cross-section, an I-beam has wide top and bottom sections and a narrow separating section, like a capital letter 'I'.

Import/Export meter – Meter which measures the net electricity generated from micro-renewables such as PV or wind turbines and also the incoming energy received from the grid.

Joinery – Generic term for windows, doors and other timber items assembled and substantially finished prior to fixing.

K-glass – In a double-glazed k-glass unit, the surface of the inner pane of glass which faces into the air gap is coated with a microscopically thin film that reduces its emissivity. The heat absorbed by this glass from within the property is inhibited from radiating across the air gap, improving the insulative value of the glass.

Landfill – Disposal of waste by means of transportation to and burying in low-lying areas of land.

Light-emitting diode – Solid state light source that emits light or invisible infrared radiation when electricity is passed through it.

Light pollution – Glow from multiple light sources in towns and cities that alters the visual landscape at night and prevents the night sky from being fully visible. Can be reflected back to earth in cloudy conditions, leading to a coloured glow.

Lime – Calcium hydroxide (slaked lime) is either dried to a powder or preserved wet as lime putty. Used extensively in the building industry as a binder in mortars and renders.

Lintel – Horizontal bearing member, usually formed from timber, stone or steel, that accepts the loads above a doorway or window and transfers them to the supporting structure either side of the opening.

Masonry – Anything made principally from stone, brick, sand and gravel.

Mechanical ventilation – Fan-driven ventilation, whether individual room fans or a whole-house system.

Membrane – See *Breather membrane*, *Damp-proof membrane* and *Vapour control layer*.

Mortar – Combination of fine aggregate (such as sand) with a binder (lime or cement) to form thin adhesive joints between masonry elements such as bricks and blocks.

Net metering – see *Import/Export meter*.

Neutraliser – Device introduced into a heating system where more than one boiler is present to ensure that one boiler, when in operation, does not supply another boiler with hot water when it is not in operation.

Passive infrared – Sensor which operates by detecting the heat given off by a body that passes through its 'field of vision'. When motion is detected, a message is relayed to the control panel.

Passive ventilation – Ventilation drawn through a building by a combination of the stack effect and wind pressure, assisted by natural leakage or purpose-designed ventilators.

Payback period – The time it takes for an investment in any form of resource-saving device to pay back in the form of reduced bills, with allowance for the effect of interest rates.

Phenolic foam – Type of cellular plastic insulation.

Pigment – Substance used to give colour to another substance (paint, plaster etc).

Plasterboard – Rigid gypsum board faced with paper, primarily used to cover walls and ceilings prior to a skim finish.

Pollutant-receptor pathway – Means by which contaminants in the ground or air are collected, concentrated and transferred into the food chain or other vegetation.

Polyisocyanurate –Type of cellular plastic insulation.

Potable – Fit to drink.

Purlin – Major roof member running horizontally between walls or major trusses, used to support rafters mid-span.

Rafter – Sloping roof member running from apex to eave or valley.

Reclaim – To use an item (especially a building material) again in the same function or a different one, without reprocessing.

Recycle – To gather the waste at the end of life of a material (empty glass bottles, for example), reprocess it, and produce a new product from the resulting raw material (such as insulation).

Render – Sand and cement/lime mix applied externally to walls of buildings, primarily to protect them from the weather.

Renewable – In this context energy that can be reproduced by the same method, such as wind, solar or biomass, in contrast to fossil fuels.

Resistance (in the context of insulation) – The thermal resistance of a given thickness of a material is its ability to prevent heat from passing through. Measured in $m^2 K/W$.

Resistivity (in the context of insulation) – The thermal resistivity of a material is the ability of that material to prevent heat transfer. Measured in $m^2 K/W$.

Resource depletion – The gradual consumption of the earth's raw materials and sources of energy.

Reveal – The side and top sections of an opening in a wall where a window or door is inserted.

Riser – The vertical section of a staircase between each tread.

Road miles – The distance that a building material has to travel from mining or harvesting through processing and ultimate delivery to the merchant or place of use.

Sash box – Hollow section of a sash window frame that contains a counterweight to assist the operation of vertical sliding windows.

Screed – Smooth finish coat on top of a solid floor slab, usually comprising sand and cement.

Segregation – Keeping waste separate by type, so that recycling becomes easier.

Service pipe – The section of a water pipe that runs from the water main to the stopcock serving a building. See *Supply pipe* and *Communication pipe*.

Sick building syndrome – Generic term used to describe the cumulative effects of poor ventilation, inadequate daylight levels and toxic building materials, leading to noticeable effects on the health of the occupants.

Siphon – The key part of the flush mechanism within a cistern; a bent tube whereby water may be drawn off over a higher point to a lower level.

Smart Meter – A meter capable of two-way communication with the supplier and linked to an in-home display unit.

Softwood – Timber produced from trees bearing needles or cones, generally evergreen.

Solar gain – The heat from the sun that is able to enter a building, primarily through windows where the resistance is lowest.

Solvent – A liquid that is capable of dissolving another substance.

Stud – Vertical member of a timber wall.

Supply pipe – The section of a water pipe that runs

from the property boundary to the stopcock serving a building.

Suspended floor – Floor normally constructed from timber and spanning from wall to wall with an air gap below, rather than resting on the ground.

Sustainable – Being able to meet present needs without compromising the ability of future generations to meet their needs.

Swale – A shallow linear depression in the ground, used for storing and dispersing rainwater.

Thermal break – An element of low conductivity placed within material of higher conductivity in order to reduce heat transfer.

Thermal bridge – A conductive material that bypasses an insulation system.

Thermal mass – Dense material within the insulated shell of a building, capable of accepting and storing significant amounts of heat.

Thermal resistance – See *Resistance*.

Thermostat – Temperature-sensitive device that sends a signal to the control switch on a heating or cooling system when it reaches a specific level.

Timber frame – Type of building in which the primary vertical loads are borne by a timber construction.

Toluene – Aromatic hydrocarbon widely used as a solvent. It is readily absorbed by contact, ingestion or inhalation and considered to be a toxin.

Transmission loss – Energy lost during the transmission of electricity, mainly due to heat production as a result of resistance in the transmission wire.

Turbine – Device to create rotary mechanical power from a stream of air or fluid.

Two-way metering – See *Import/Export meter*.

Useful heat – Heat produced by electrical appliances designed for other purposes, but which contributes towards the thermal comfort of the occupants.

Vapour compression cycle – Process whereby a substance changes state from a liquid to a gas and back again, absorbing and releasing heat energy as it passes around the loop.

Vapour control layer – Sheet material that does not allow water vapour to pass from the inside of a building into the wall and roof structure. 1,000 gauge polythene is often used for this purpose.

Virgin aggregate – Sand or gravel freshly mined, as opposed to recycled aggregate.

Woodchip – Logs or sawmill offcuts which have been processed down to a small size to make them suitable for use as fuel, horse bedding, path surfacing, etc.

Woodworm – Wood-boring larvae of a number of beetles including Common Furniture Beetle, House Longhorn Beetle, and Deathwatch Beetle.

Xylene – Aromatic hydrocarbon widely used as a solvent. It is readily absorbed by contact, ingestion or inhalation and is considered to be a toxin.

Abbreviations

BFRC	British Fenestration Rating Council
BRE	Building Research Establishment
CCA	Copper chromated arsenic
CFC	Chlorofluorocarbon
CFL	Compact fluorescent lamp
CHP	Combined heat and power
CO_2	Carbon dioxide
CoP	Coefficient of performance
CSA	Canadian Standards Association
DIY	Do-it-yourself
DPM	Damp-proof membrane
EA	Environment Agency
EC	European Community
ELV	End-of-life vehicles
ESCO	Energy Services Company
EST	Energy Saving Trust
FENSA	Fenestration Self-Assessment Scheme
FiT	Feed-in Tariff
FoE	Friends of the Earth
FSC	Forestry Stewardship Council
GJ	Gigajoules
GSHP	Ground source heat pump
GWP	Global warming potential
HCFC	Hydrochlorofluorocarbon
HETAS	Heating Equipment Testing and Approval Scheme
IARC	International Agency for Research on Cancer
kW	Kilowatts
kWh	Kilowatt-hours
kWp	Kilowatt peak
LCA	Life cycle analysis
LEC	Levy Exemption Certificate
LED	Light-emitting diode
LPG	Liquefied petroleum gas
LSOH	Low smoke zero halogen
MDF	Medium density fibreboard
MTCC	Malaysian Timber Certification Council
NOABL	Numerical objective analysis of boundary layer
ODP	Ozone depleting potential
OSB	Oriented strand board
PEFC	Program for the Endorsement of Forest Certification
PIR	Passive infrared
PVC	Poly vinyl chloride
PVC-u	Unplasticised PVC
PV	Photovoltaic
RHI	Renewable Heat Incentive
RoHS	Restriction of hazardous substances
SFI	Sustainable Forestry Initiative
SPAB	Society for the Protection of Ancient Buildings
SUDS	Sustainable Urban Drainage System
TRV	Thermostatic radiator valve
uPVC	Unplasticised PVC
WEEE	Waste electrical and electronic equipment
WHO	World Health Organisation

REFERENCES

Chapter 2

(1) Lime Technology Ltd.
(2) Rainforest action network via www.savetherainforest.org
(3) www.seattle.gov/environment/TierTablesFriendlyFormat.xls
(4) IARC press release 2004.
(5) Wood Panel Industries Federation.
(6) AECB.
(7) West Sussex, North Somerset.
(8) Paul Hymers *Converting to an eco-friendly home*,
(9) National Green Specification (2006).

Chapter 3

(1) Department of Energy and Climate Change 3219 energy Act 2011.
(2) Energy Saving Trust GPG 155.
(3) Table A1: Approved Document L1B: 'Conservation of Fuel and Power in Existing Dwellings'.
(4) Energy Saving Trust CE184, page 26 table 9.
(5) Energy Saving Trust GPG155, page 8, and Energy Saving Trust CE184, page 17.
(6) Research into the Thermal Performance of Traditional Windows: Timber Sash Windows, Prepared for English Heritage by Dr Paul Baker, Glasgow Caledonian University (2009).
(7) *Window of opportunity: The environmental and economic benefits of specifying timber window frames*, Christian Thompson, WWF-UK (2005).
(8) Energy Saving Trust GPG268: 'Energy efficient ventilation in dwellings – a guide for specifiers'.
(9) 'Detoxification of Formaldehyde by the spider plant and by soybean suspension cultures', M. Giese, U. Bauer-Doranth, C. Langebartels, and H. Sandermann, Jr, April 1994, GSF-Forschungszentrum fur Umwelt und Gesundheit GmbH, Institut fur Biochemische Pflanzenpathologie, D-85764 Oberschleissheim, Germany.

Chapter 4

(1) Association of Electricity Producers.
(2) 'Getting warmer: a field trial of heat pumps'.

Chapter 5

(1) Market Transformation Programme BNW18: EC Energy Labelling of Domestic Tumble Dryers.
(2) Energy Saving Trust.

Chapter 6

(1) Feed-in Tariffs Scheme: Summary of Responses to the Fast-Track Consultation and Government Response DECC 2011.
(2) Environmental Impacts of Crystalline Silicon Photovoltaic Module Production – Erik A. Alsema et al 2006.
(3) Location location location: Energy Saving Trust 2009.

Chapter 7

(1) OFWAT Security of supply, leakage and water efficiency 2005-06 report.
(2) Environment Agency Website.

Chapter 9

(1) POST.
(2) Naturegrid.
(3) 'How to Remediate Heavy Metal Contaminated Sites with Amended Composts' by René van Herwijnen, Vishnu Priya Gadepalle, Tony R. Hutchings, Abir Al-Tabbaa, Andy J. Moffat, Mike L. Johns and Sabeha K. Ouki1.

INDEX

Author: Nigel Griffiths

Project Manager: Louise McIntyre

Copy Editor: Ian Heath

Design/layout: James Robertson

Illustrations: Rob Loxston,
                         Matthew Marke &
                         Dominic Stickland

Architect's drawings: Alan Coles

Index: Peter Nicholson